Josiah Parsons Cooke

The Credentials of Science the Warrant of Faith

Josiah Parsons Cooke

The Credentials of Science the Warrant of Faith

ISBN/EAN: 9783337035822

Printed in Europe, USA, Canada, Australia, Japan

Cover: Foto ©Lupo / pixelio.de

More available books at **www.hansebooks.com**

THE

CREDENTIALS OF SCIENCE

THE WARRANT OF FAITH.

BY

JOSIAH PARSONS COOKE, LL.D.,

ERVING PROFESSOR OF CHEMISTRY AND MINERALOGY IN
HARVARD UNIVERSITY.

NEW YORK:
ROBERT CARTER AND BROTHERS,
530 BROADWAY.
1888.

IN MEMORIAM

Roswell Dwight Hitchcock.

———◆———

"QUI DOCTI FUERINT FULGEBUNT QUASI SPLENDOR FIRMAMENTI;

ET QUI AD JUSTITIAM ERUDIUNT MULTOS, QUASI

STELLÆ IN PERPETUAS ÆTERNITATES."

THE ELY FOUNDATION.

THIS series of Lectures was delivered, by appointment, as one of the course on the foundation established in the Union Theological Seminary by Mr. ZEBULON STILES ELY, of New York, in the following terms: —

"The undersigned gives the sum of ten thousand dollars to the Union Theological Seminary of the city of New York, to found a Lectureship in the same, the title of which shall be 'THE ELIAS P. ELY LECTURES ON THE EVIDENCES OF CHRISTIANITY.'

"The course of Lectures given on this foundation is to comprise any topics that serve to establish the proposition that Christianity is a religion from God, or that it is the perfect and final form of religion for man.

"Among the subjects discussed may be, —

"The Nature and Need of a Revelation;

"The Character and Influence of Christ and his Apostles;

"The Authenticity and Credibility of the Scriptures, Miracles, and Prophecy;

"The Diffusion and Benefits of Christianity; and

"The Philosophy of Religion in its Relation to the Christian System.

"Upon one or more of such subjects a course of ten public Lectures shall be given at least once in two or three years. The appointment of the Lecturer is to be by the concurrent action of the directors and faculty of said Seminary and the undersigned; and it shall ordinarily be made two years in advance.

"The interest of the fund is to be devoted to the payment of the Lecturers, and the publication of the Lectures within a year after the delivery of the same. The copyright of the volumes thus published is to be vested in the Seminary.

"In case it should seem more advisable, the directors have it at their discretion at times to use the proceeds of this fund in providing special courses of lectures or instruction, in place of the aforesaid public lectures, for the students of the Seminary, on the above-named subjects.

"Should there at any time be a surplus of the fund, the directors are authorized to employ it in the way of prizes for dissertations by students of the Seminary, or of prizes for essays thereon, open to public competition.

"ZEBULON STILES ELY.

" NEW YORK, May 8th, 1865."

PREFACE.

THE lectures now published were first prepared at the invitation of the UNION THEOLOGICAL SEMINARY of NEW YORK CITY, and delivered in the Adams Chapel of the Seminary during the early spring of 1887, the course of eight lectures closing on Easter Eve. The material was subsequently considerably amplified, and delivered as a course of twelve lectures before the Lowell Institute of Boston, closing on Christmas Eve of the same year. The lectures have been printed as thus extended, although in some cases the limitations of a lecture-hour compelled a division of subjects, which are here united under the same heading, thus reducing the number of chapters in the book to ten. The motive of the work is sufficiently indicated by its title, and requires no further introduction.

CAMBRIDGE, March 31, 1888.

CONTENTS.

Lecture		Page
I.	The Argument of Natural Theology	1
II.	Preparing the Way	29
III.	The Induction of Newton	59
IV.	Deduction	93
V.	Examples of Scientific Investigation	127
VI.	Laws of Nature	158
VII.	Determinate and Indeterminate Laws	184
VIII.	Theories or Systems of Science	209
IX.	Predominant Principles of Scientific Thought	260
X.	The Systems Compared. — Religion and Science	289

THE CREDENTIALS OF SCIENCE

THE WARRANT OF FAITH

LECTURE I.

THE ARGUMENT OF NATURAL THEOLOGY.

NATURAL Religion is as old as man's consciousness of dependence, and Natural Theology is coeval with literature. Its fundamental arguments were urged by the Greek and Roman philosophers, and the illustrations of the subject by Galen have scarcely been equalled in modern times. During the last two centuries works on natural theology have formed a conspicuous feature in English literature, — in consequence chiefly of several pious foundations which have provided for the discussion of the subject at stated intervals. These works have as a rule been written in a popular style, and have dealt with illustrations of old arguments rather than with the arguments themselves. They have served an excellent purpose by keeping before the popular mind the ever accumulating mass of evidence of skill and of plan which nature offers, and by exhibiting the religious aspects of scientific facts and theories. Unfortunately they have often been open to criticism, and too frequently have justified the contempt into which teleology has so generally fallen.

A recent writer, in his "Critique of Design Arguments,"[1] has done an excellent work, not only by fixing attention on the arguments, but also by furnishing a carefully prepared synopsis of all the important writings bearing on natural theology from the earliest times. But while freely admitting the justice of this writer's criticism in many respects, even when we ourselves have fallen under the ban, we cannot concur with him either in his general estimate of design arguments, or in the essential character of the distinction which he seeks to draw between the argument from general plan and the so-called argument from design. This last phrase has become one of the universal terms of our language, and it is not to be supposed that acute Scotch logicians like Dugald Stewart and Reid overlooked the obvious begging of the question which a precise definition of the words would involve. There has been undoubtedly as frequent misuse of language in essays on natural theology as in similar popular expositions; but much of this has resulted from the necessities of the case.

In popular discourse language cannot be used with the precision of mathematical terms, and often a hypercritical spirit defeats the main object of the teacher. Singular as it is, the more a man knows, the more difficult it becomes to present a subject in language that can be easily comprehended. The teacher

[1] Critique of Design Arguments, by L. E. Hicks. New York. Charles Scribner's Sons, 1883.

is hampered by his knowledge of the limitations to the general propositions he enunciates, and he is forced to avail himself of all the latitude which the most liberal interpretation of language will allow. No one who has not had the experience knows how difficult it often is to reconcile exact accuracy with that concise statement which is one of the essential conditions of effective teaching; and the intended purport of rhetorical writing can always be misrepresented by the quotation of isolated passages.

When an able theologian writes, "Design supposes a designer," it is reasonable to infer that he does not intend to involve his readers in the logical absurdity of an identical proposition, but simply intends to declare the undoubted fact, that a multitude of relations in nature suggest to the mind of man an intelligent author.

The confusion implied in this and in similar phraseology arises from an attempt to gauge such reasoning by the rules of deductive logic. Man has not risen to knowledge of Divine things by deduction but by induction. These things always have been, and always will continue to be to the logical Greeks of every age foolishness, and so long as the theologian cherishes the conceit that the Godhead can be demonstrated, he cannot hope to escape from the web of logical fallacies which his argument must involve.

The knowledge of God has come to man through nature precisely in the same way as the generalizations of science, and is subject to the same limitations and carries the same conviction as all general truths. Man knows God by the same means and through the same sources that he knows the principles of gravitation, heat, and electricity. In each case an assumed energy acting through special channels under definite laws is the best explanation he can form of a certain class of phenomena. So also the assumption of an Intelligent Will, with power to create and power to sustain, is the commonly received explanation which man has formed of the origin and continuance of this universe in which he dwells.

The fundamental principles of science may be said to be suggestions of nature confirmed by experience. When once conceived, we can often deduce from a general principle, mathematically or otherwise, a host of inferences which observation substantiates. This indeed is the normal way by which our knowledge of nature is enlarged; and such deductions, verified by experience, furnish the strongest confirmation of the truth of the principle with which we started. But the principle itself was no deduction, it was a suggestion of nature; and this is all we know of its origin. We may seek to study the conditions and circumstances under which such suggestions have come into the minds of the favored men of the race, but we get no nearer to the source.

Among essential conditions we at once recognize a familiar acquaintance with nature, and a powerful but well regulated imagination. We also readily trace the influence of analogies, and even of accidental associations. We easily see anthropomorphic elements in such conceptions; but all these things are merely accessories to a mental process of which the discoverer himself can give no clear account, as the trivial stories of swinging lamps and falling apples so plainly show. It is a mental faculty which, though in its highest manifestation only known to a few highly gifted men, is in some small measure within the experience of every student of nature. To such students the method seems perfectly natural, even when they may not be able to discover its elements. Many philosophers, like Bacon, have attempted to analyze the method, and have named it "induction;" but few of those who are in the habit of using the method would recognize the mechanism that has been described. The so-called induction resembles inspiration, and the loftiest inspiration seems to be only the same faculty of mind more highly developed.

As are the fundamental principles of science, so is the conception of God a suggestion of nature confirmed by experience. It is an induction which commands belief, not a deduction which compels consent. This difference between inductive and deductive truth does not depend upon the degree of certitude, but on the completeness of knowledge. The highest truths can be known only in part, and it is such truths that are reached only by induction. Thus alone can men "rise on stepping-stones of their dead selves to higher things." Moreover, of such truths certitude of conviction comes only with experience. Christ said "If ye do my will ye shall know of the doctrine" and the principle thus announced applies to all inductive truths.

It is only beliefs thus attested which command the enthusiasm of men. For such beliefs alone will men sacrifice their lives. The deductions of Geometry are great truths fully comprehended; but how inconceivable, a martyr to the theorem of Pythagoras! And there never would have been a martyr to religious beliefs, if these verities could have been reached by deduction, — in a word, could have been demonstrated.

Regard now the fundamental truth of natural religion as an induction, comprehended only in part, but having all the certitude which the experience of the ages has given, and your natural theology becomes a system which is not only consistent throughout, but which harmonizes with all knowledge. Attempt, however, to claim for this truth deductive demonstration, and you at once involve your system in contradictions, and miss the very certitude you are seeking to secure.

More than twenty-five years ago the writer delivered a course of lectures at Brooklyn, on the Graham Foundation, in which the position just defined was distinctly taken. These lectures were subsequently published, and the book is well known under the title of " Religion and Chemistry, or Proofs of God's Plan in the Constitution of the Atmosphere." The lectures were written for a popular audience, and therefore in a rhetorical form, and it would be easy to misrepresent the argument by a quotation of isolated passages; but no one who actually reads the book can mistake either the intentions of the writer or the spirit of his work. No one could have been more dissatisfied with the work than the author himself, and for this reason he suffered the book to remain out of print for many years; and when after repeated requests from clerical friends the work was revised for the recent edition, the expository and rhetorical form was retained simply because in the judgment of these friends the usefulness of the book depended in no small measure on its popular style. Thus called upon to review what was written at a time when enthusiasm might be expected to somewhat blind logic, the writer could find nothing in the tenor or spirit of the work that he desired to change; and the general argument appears to him still, as it did at first, unanswerable.

Now, however, that I am invited to address the members of this influential theological seminary on the same general subject, I feel that the best service I can render is to present the same argument in a more methodical and compact form, — a form in which its strength will better appear, and its weakness, if any, will be more conspicuously exposed. With no desire to magnify my office, I cannot but feel that the subject under discussion is one of great importance to theological students. It is the ground on which the conflict between science and theology has always been fought. Whatever may have been the incidental advantages, no one can question that the conflict itself is a great evil. Is it, indeed, necessary that the promulgation of every important doctrine of science should be followed by a partial eclipse of faith, like that through which so many minds have recently been passing? Brought as I have been into sympathy with the advocates on both sides, I believe I am in a position to form an impartial judgment; and while fully recognizing the evil spirit on the other side, I feel constrained to express the opinion that the clergy are largely responsible for the bad effects of the controversy. Remember that science is paramount in its own sphere, that its methods are legitimate, and its only object is truth; and be assured that if any one of its devotees is irregular in his methods, or false to his profession, his own associates will be the first to criticise and condemn his errors. Moreover, the doctrines of science are held with great jealousy; and, although the evils of partisanship are as great in scientific controversies as elsewhere, the doctrines themselves will stand or fall solely on their own merit in the end. Once attested they cease to be safe subjects for the uninitiated to discuss, and much less, proper objects to anathematize. I can assure you that there have been times when the obligation which the church enjoins to hear sermons has been a painful duty to one who holds the truth in reverence, and desires also to reverence the defenders of the "faith once delivered to the saints." I cannot but believe that if the clergy understood more fully the true relations of scientific doctrines, and saw clearly that the fundamental postulate of theology rests on the same basis, they would be more patient with the inevitable friction which attends the progress of truth as well as the coming of the kingdom.

In discussing the broad subject of natural theology the limitations of my own studies must necessarily constrain me to limit myself to those arguments which may be drawn from the facts of external nature; and this I shall do without in the least undervaluing the purely ontological arguments based on the equally definite facts of consciousness. But let it also be clearly understood that I shall regard as a part of the phenomena of nature the undoubted historical facts of Christianity, as well as the clearly established facts connected with other religions; and in my opinion the evidences of natural theology are most incomplete when these all-important phenomena are left out of view. Of course such facts will be here considered in their objective, and not in their subjective aspect.

By considering the development of the conception of God in the mind of man, I think we can gain some insight into the nature of the mental process by which the conception is reached, and in the same way that by the study of embryology we gain a better knowledge of animal structure. There can be no question that there are certain uniform stages in the order of this development, both in the history of the race and in the education of each individual man. This very uniformity under such diverse conditions plainly shows that the conception is not the accident of circumstances, but the normal product of the human mind under its environment. We do not call it intuitive, because we do not care to raise the question that the word intuition suggests, — a question with which we have no immediate concern. But whether the result of intuition or of inspiration, or, more probably, of both of these ideal functions of the mind, acting, as we have said before, under its environments, the conception is unquestionably as spontaneous as it is real.

In discussing the development of the fundamental conceptions of all religions, it is not necessary for us to enter upon any abstruse questions of ethnology, archæology, or philology, although all this learning might be brought to bear on the subject. The general conclusions with which alone we shall have to deal, are so patent that they will be accepted by every one, and this circumstance alone shows how fundamental are the phenomena we are considering.

When the child first becomes conscious of his free will he finds that will opposed by other wills like his own, and we all know what an essential condition of education is the conflict which results. In our short-sightedness how greatly do we regret this conflict, how earnestly seek to avoid it, and how often do we shun the responsibility it involves; and yet how fully do we recognize that no strength of character, no force of will, no power of intellect, no assurance of faith, can be gained except by conflict; how often only after repeated disasters are these virtues secured, and how forcibly does some of the most beautiful imagery of our language illustrate this truth.

As to every child, so with freedom of the will there must have come at some first time to primeval man the conception of an opposing will; and the warfare then began through which the race has been educated. Admit that this conflict is but a continuation of the struggle for existence which began with life, yet now certainly the struggle involves for the first time conscious personality, and the mysterious knowledge of good and evil, so inseparably associated with that freedom which makes us responsible beings.

Through the conflicts of his will man acquired his first conception of power, the earliest measure of his own strength. In his fellow-men he at once recognized powers commensurate with his own, to which he was frequently forced to yield, but which he could often overcome; and with such powers he from the first associated personality. But it required only a short experience with nature to force upon him the knowledge that he was under the control of powers vastly superior to those of men, which he could not withstand, and by which his fellows were frequently overwhelmed, — powers so mighty and so hidden that he quailed and trembled before them. As he knew power only as an attribute of personality, he ascribed the powers of nature to mighty and exalted personages capable of such vast effects; and hence came man's first conception of God. The God thus conceived was merely the God of might, the God who rules in the tempest and directs the thunderbolts, the God who rejoices in war and carnage. Moreover, these powers did not seem to be wielded by a single person. Man was still far from the conception of a Jehovah; but as he was opposed by many persons so his fancy filled the heavens with a host of warring gods.

It is not our purpose to sketch the numberless fanciful forms which under different associations the early conception assumed. We desire only to emphasize the fact that the earliest conception of God was that of a God of Might, and that this conception came to the savage as an obvious suggestion of nature. It was an induction from observed facts; and simple and obvious as the induction was, the mental process by which it was reached differed in degree only, not in kind, from the inductions of modern science.

Such inductions do not of course bring with them their credentials; but in so far as they embody truth, they become accredited through experience, and chiefly in two ways: first, by their universality, that is, by coming to many persons independently, thus showing that they are in harmony with the constitution of the human mind; and secondly, by their permanency in retaining their hold on men, indicating that they have stood the test to which they have been exposed, and by which they have been tried.

The primitive inductions of men must necessarily be very partial truths, and the grain of truth is constantly so incrusted with error that it is with difficulty discovered; but I feel persuaded that beliefs which are long held in reverence by men owe their power to this grain of truth, however small.

A most striking feature of inductions, by which they are plainly distinguished from deductions, is to be found in that inductions are progressive, and become clarified with experience. A deduction is demonstrative, and if the premises are correct, the conclusion naturally follows. There is no question as to degree, no room for doubt except as regards the premises of the argument. An induction, however, may have every possible degree of certitude, from an unverified conjecture to a law of nature confirmed by experience. Moreover, in the progress of knowledge it has been constantly the case that the conjecture has appeared as a law only after a slow clarifying process. As the dregs have settled from the intellectual medium, the truth has been seen in ever clearer outlines; its essential features have become evident, while the grosser aspects of the original crude conception have disappeared. Such has been the uniform history of the great generalizations of science, and through such a clarifying process are most, if not all, of them even now passing. Possibly in a very few cases the truth even now appears in all its simplicity; but there can be no question that in the case of most of the fundamental principles of modern science of which we feel so proud, and which have been such valuable guides in the study of nature, the truths they embody are still only seen as in a glass darkly. It has been the privilege of a few gifted minds to see the truth of the inductions they have made generally recognized during their life on earth, but as a rule so many minds have concurred in developing these general truths that they must be regarded as the product of the age, rather than as the gift of any one man to the knowledge of the world.

These features of scientific generalizations are strikingly characteristic of the fundamental religious conception, which is also, as we have claimed, an induction from observed facts. As first seen through the mists of barbarism, God was a Moloch, or a Thor, or at best a Jupiter; but as in proportion to his mental growth man's spiritual vision became clearer, the image became ever more definite, more beautiful, and more lovely. It is not our purpose to trace the connection between the thousands of fantastic shapes which the first crude shadowy form assumed, in the history of different peoples, but we must mark four important stages of the conception, that are associated with different phases of the argument of natural theology.

It was a very important, although doubtless a very early advance in the progress of our race, when men first invented weapons and tools, in order to apply their brute strength more effectively, or direct it to more useful ends. By the use of tools primeval man was most markedly distinguished from all the animals with which he was associated, including the highest anthropoids, from some of whose progenitors man is supposed to have descended.

No one has claimed that even the rudest tools were ever made by anthropoids, however close their resemblance to man; and the appearance of stone implements in the strata marks the introduction of man upon the earth with remarkable sharpness. There seems to be here a most striking break of continuity, which the doctrine of gradual evolution has not hitherto explained. The bones which we invariably find with these rude tools are those of well developed men, oftentimes with skulls at least as capacious as our own.

However the evolutionists may explain these noteworthy facts, there can be no question that tools, even in their most primitive form, are proofs of a degree of intelligence which did not appear on earth until, outwardly at least, man had become essentially the same creature that he is to-day. In proportion as man has risen in the scale of intelligence he has displayed an ever increasing ingenuity in the invention of tools; and the printing-press, the power-loom, the steam-engine, the electric telegraph, are the tools of our civilization, as the flint arrow-heads and stone axes were those of primeval man.

Obviously, all tools or other implements are evidences of intelligence. If now we inquire on what basis this evidence rests, I think it will be found to depend on the fitness of these implements for an intelligent use. We use the word "implements" here in the broadest sense, for any utensils, even ornaments, wrought for a specific use; and it is the fitness of such implements for an intelligent use which constitutes the evidence of intelligence that such objects as are collected in an archæological museum afford. It may be that the archæologist cannot determine the use of certain objects, but even such objects bear marks of having been wrought with tools, whose intelligent use is known, and must therefore be classed with them. In the last analysis intelligent use is the fundamental evidence on which our conclusion as regards the intelligence of the agency which fashioned the implements depends; and the fitness of the implements for such use, or even the traces of tools having such fitness, are a secondary but still a conclusive evidence of intelligence; because such fitness, or traces, distinctly point out the intelligent use for which the implements were made. It is not the marks of the inscription which are the fundamental evidence of the intelligence that an inscription always suggests, but the thought which these marks have often concealed. Before the Assyrian characters could be read it was not seriously doubted that they were the writings of men, because they bore a close resemblance to such writings. But evidently if the arrow-head characters had proved to be simply the effect of natural causes, like the crystal outlines on a slab of graphic granite, such markings would be no longer any evidence of intelligence. On the other hand, if they had proved to be simple ornamentations they would still be evidences of intelligence; and, even if it had only appeared that they had been cut or moulded with tools, however rude, they would likewise be evidences of intelligence through the intelligent use of the tools employed.

In discussing this question we cannot be too careful constantly to bear in mind that it is the intelligent use of tools which is the evidence of intelligence; and that the fitness of the tools is also a proof of intelligence only so far as it clearly indicates an intelligent use. It is not necessary in this connection to distinguish the fabrication of a tool from its use; for the fabrication implies the use, and also the use of other tools, from the most complex down to the simplest tools furnished by nature, — a bamboo from the thicket, a stalk of flax from the field, or a sharp stone from the brook. It may often be that a tool will be found better adapted for some other use than for the one for which it was originally made, when its use in the new relation will be just as much an evidence of intelligence as its first use.

Every one has heard the story of Timothy Dexter, who, in his absurd, and probably not very truthful, personal narrative, says he made a successful venture by sending a cargo of warming-pans to the West Indies, where they were found to be admirably fitted for the purpose of straining sugar. Evidently the use of the pan for straining sugar was as much an evidence of intelligence as its use as a warming-pan; but the fitness of the tool for either purpose was of value as evidence only so far as it indicated an intelligent use. The warming-pan, however admirably adapted for the purpose, was not designed for straining sugar; and the illustration, whether authentic or not, plainly shows that in human relations fitness proves design, that is, intelligence, only so far as it indicates intelligent use. In the relations of an infinite being who knows all the ends from the beginning it is doubtless otherwise; but this we cannot assume in our argument from design, and the failure to make the distinction we have drawn has often exposed this argument to undeserved contempt.

Another anecdote illustrating the same distinction has the advantage of being certainly true. A West India planter sent to his overseer from New York a number of wheelbarrows, by whose use he expected to economize labor on his plantation. They were duly received, and the overseer wrote that they had been found to be very useful; but what was the planter's surprise on returning home, to see the negroes, after shovelling in the earth, lift the barrows on to their heads and march off with the load in their old accustomed way. One can easily see that, compared with the wicker basket previously used, the wheelbarrows, even thus handled, might prove a saving of labor, and can recognize a low intelligence in the negroes who accommodated the new tool to their old habits. But if they ever thought at all, those negroes must have been puzzled by the wheel, and it must have presented to them a problem of very much the same kind that the much discussed rudimentary organs offer to the modern teleologist. Certainly, the wheelbarrow was not designed to be carried on the head, and the neglected wheel was the constant witness of this fact; but the ultimate evidence of intelligence in the wheelbarrow was not in its fitness for one use or for the other, but in the use itself which the fitness indicated. The fitness is important solely as testifying to the intelligent use.

Our early ancestors, however, were not troubled by the analysis of any such distinctions as those to which we resort, to justify their usually correct conclusions, however much they may have erred in special cases. They associated an intelligent personality directly with fitness, wherever found. As nature offers numberless examples of fitness vastly more wonderful than that displayed by any human tools, they ascribed all such relations in the scheme of nature to the wise designs of the gods whom they already recognized as wielding the powers of the world. From the brain of Jupiter came Minerva with her loom, and Vulcan with his forge; and from such beginnings the argument from design has been handed down to our day. And so closely have men always associated fitness with personal intelligence that in all languages the words expressing these relations have acquired such a coloring that when we use them in connection with teleological arguments we appear to beg the question in the simple statement of the case. Such words as "design," "contrivance," and "adaptation," all imply a personal agent; and in looking for a word which would express simply the external relation from which the inference of personal agency is drawn we could find no other than the one which we have so continually used, namely, fitness. Largely in consequence of the misuse of terms the argument from design has in recent years fallen into such disfavor that the very word, "teleology," carries with it a suggestion of opprobrium; and yet the argument is intrenched as strongly as ever behind defences which have always been assaulted in vain; but let us be sure that we fully know where the strength of our position lies.

It is not true that fitness in nature in any limited relations is satisfactory evidence of design, and the easy "reductio ad absurdùm" with which such an assumption is readily met has done not a little to bring teleology into contempt. As has been shown, this assumption is not true even in human relations. With the tools of men it is not their fitness for certain uses but the intelligent use which is the real evidence of an intelligent mind; and far less in nature can we claim to know the purposes of the Original; and if we attempt to enforce our argument by the plea that there can be no use which Omniscience could not have foreseen, as before intimated we directly assume the very point we are attempting to prove. Nevertheless the premises of our argument are unquestioned; and these are the relations of fitness in nature, wonderful beyond language to express, intricate beyond thought to unravel, sublime beyond imagination to conceive, useful beyond words to admire. Now men have been able to discover but one satisfactory explanation of these relations, namely, that they are the outcome of an intelligence like their own, only of an immeasurably higher order, — in a word, that they were created by the Jehovah of the Bible. We must not claim that we have here logical proof, for we cannot have any such demonstration. But we have something which is far better than all logical proof, something which, while it carries conviction, inflames our imagination, and appeals to our faith. We have what we technically call an induction. But it is an induction of the highest order, with material so ample and experience so extended as to leave no room for reasonable doubt.

In claiming for an induction the validity of a deductive demonstration, we compromise the whole strength of our logical position; and hence many writers on natural theology, even though they may not have attempted to analyze the argument from design, have discussed the examples of fitness in nature as illustrations of an admitted principle, and not as proofs of an intelligent author. In the book before referred to, we ourselves have most distinctly and emphatically maintained this attitude towards the subject. It must be remembered, moreover, that on this view and for the argument's sake such discussions are perfectly legitimate; for the conviction which an induction produces depends chiefly on the extent of the field which it grasps; and when we study this great induction of natural theology how wonderfully do we find that it has borne the tests both of universality and of experience. Not only is it an induction which omits no known fact, but it is an induction of all people, in all ages, and under all conditions. How unmoved also has it borne the test of experience. Every attempt has been made to set it aside by showing how this universe might have issued without an intelligent Creator, — from the time of the "fortuitous concourse of atoms" of Lucretius to the "struggle for life" of Darwin. But although by stimulating thought and inciting deeper study these attempts have profoundly modified and enlarged man's earlier crude conceptions of the Divine methods, they have always resulted at last in impressing the great mass of thinking men with a deeper conviction of His being, with a grander conception of His power, and with a more profound reverence for His skill, who is the Alpha and Omega of all knowledge, the Beginning and End of all life.

Beauty is simply that harmony of proportions and qualities which results from the most complete fitness of all the parts in a perfect whole; and in the education of mankind the worship of skill naturally grew into the worship of beauty, or rather of that material perfection which is manifested in beauty. Early in the history of civilization the culture of beauty reached its highest development in ancient Greece; and then appeared another phase of the argument of natural theology, which, for the sake of distinguishing the stages in the development of the subject, we may call the argument from beauty, although it does not differ essentially from the argument from design. As before, the argument is solely an induction. We have for the premises the infinite beauty of nature, and for the induction the inference that all this beauty must have issued from a Personal Being vastly more susceptible than any human nature to the harmonies of form, of color, and of sound.

This argument, although not recognized as such, has a singular attraction to a well marked class in modern society, who, having revolted from the prevailing creeds, seek satisfaction for their minds and hearts in the contemplation of all that is most perfect in art; and this argument strongly appeals to a vivid imagination and a cultivated taste. These worshippers of the beautiful hold in highest honor the products of Greek art which have come down to us, and often even look back with regret to that old civilization as the highest stage ever reached in the intellectual development of man. But Greek beauty was simply a material beauty, and the God which the Greek apprehended was simply a perfect sensuous being, capable of realizing in his person and his creation the most perfect harmonies, but also revelling in the sensuality with which, before Christianity, material beauty was always associated. Lifted into a more spiritual sphere, and protected by the safeguards of Christian morality, the modern devotees of art may disassociate material beauty from such gross accompaniments; but who that has known human nature in its lower moods can for a moment question that the vilest orgies would again become rife if the religious convictions by which alone our Christian civilization is maintained were undermined?

As the Greek passed under the Roman sway, so did the supremacy of beauty yield to the supremacy of law; and this was a natural and an intellectual progress. Beauty, as we have seen, is the harmony of relations which perfect fitness produces; but law is the prevailing principle which underlies that harmony, and without which no harmony can be maintained. In the ancient world Greece appeared as the representative of beauty, and Rome succeeded as the expositor of law. In the fluctuations of nature the material forms of beauty are transient, and unless constantly reproduced under the operations of permanent laws can have no lasting influence. In Greece the productiveness of art soon ceased, through failure of the authority of law to restrain her civil dissensions, and the power of beauty to mould men lay dormant until Christianity had wrought its work, and the genius of beauty became wedded to the spirit of religion. On the other hand, the fundamental principles of law are eternal, and Rome, through her civil law, has never ceased to rule the world.

It was a very long step in the progress of mankind from the promulgation of the civil law of Rome to the recognition of the laws of nature, — from Justinian to Newton; and since the discovery of the law of gravitation so slowly has this conception pervaded the popular mind that not until our own day have even cultivated men fully realized that their race has been educated under a reign of law, which embraces the universe, and which began with time, — a system of laws of which the best of human codes offers only a feeble type.

The study of natural laws has brought fresh evidence to the support of the conclusions of natural theology, and evidence of the most impressive kind. These laws are at once so grand and yet so simple, so high and yet so near, so universal and yet so particular, so far reaching and yet so present, so invariable and yet so beneficent, that while they tax to the utmost his intellectual power, they are calculated to impress the mind of the student with awe, with reverence, and with trust. Newton has described the impression which the discovery of the law of gravitation made on him, and many of the great masters of science join to his their united testimony that the study of the laws of nature has wrought the most profound conviction of the presence of an overruling Mind. The devout student of science finds it difficult to conceive how it could be otherwise, and simply wonders at the perversion of the intellectual vision to which the heaviness of the flesh or the subtleties of the brain may sometimes lead.

The phase of the argument of natural theology which is based on the laws of nature, we have called in another place the argument from general plan; although, like the argument from beauty, it is not essentially different from the argument from design. The writer to whom we have before referred regards the argument from general plan as the only legitimate form of the argument from design, and urges that while we cannot prove that fitness may not have resulted from natural selection, or from some other undefined principle of nature, order must always be a product of intelligence. But, obviously, — as long ago

Spinoza so powerfully argued, — order, or law, may be merely a subjective attitude or posture of our own minds towards external nature; and the words "law," "order," "plan," imply personal intelligence as plainly as do the words "design," "contrivance" and "adaptation" before discussed. To say that law implies a lawgiver is just as much a begging of the question as to say that design implies a designer. The truth simply is that this last phase of the argument of natural theology, like all the other phases, is an induction, and not a necessary deduction. Of this induction the premises are the invariable relations of natural phenomena; and the inference is that these fixed relations must have been determined by a Supreme Intelligence, who ordained the order and law of which the universe is the expression. Christian students are most firmly persuaded that this conclusion is the only reasonable or intelligible explanation of the facts, and the wider our knowledge becomes, the more fully is their conviction confirmed. But it is easy to cavil, — that the observed constancy of relations may have been caused by some undefinable potency of material things (the law of philotaxis, for example, resulting from a tendency in the leaves of a plant to expose the most surface to the sun), and then the whole matter is summed up with the scoffing remark of Voltaire, " The heavens only declare the glory of the astronomers," who see their own intelligence reflected in the circling orbs. If we would protect our sacred cause from such sneers, we must be careful to establish it in truth, and not claim for it a sanction which it does not, and never can possess.

We have now passed in rapid review four phases of the argument of natural theology, corresponding to four stages in human development, — namely, the argument from might, the argument from design, the argument from beauty, and the argument from general plan. Corresponding to the recognition in nature of energy, fitness, beauty, and order, we have the inferences that might, skill, perfection, and law are the attributes of an Intelligence which created and sustains the whole. Here the scheme of natural theology ordinarily ends; but, as it seems to us, the culminating phase of the argument, corresponding to the highest phase of human development, still remains to be stated.

The doctrines of Christianity as a system of revealed religion do not of course come under our consideration; but the facts of Christianity as historical verities are as much subjects of natural theology as any other natural phenomena. The movements of history are phenomena of nature as well as the movements of the planets; and considering the admitted facts of our holy religion from this point of view, what a broad basis for induction do they furnish! Indeed, the basis is so ample that we may at once waive everything that any sceptic will question. We may admit that all the miraculous features of the narrative are myths, and that the Bible has no more authority than the plays of Shakspeare, or any other book that portrays character. Still, after all concessions, there remains the character of Jesus, the revelation of perfect holiness, the exemplar of the noblest self-sacrifice, the manifestation of the purest love.

Admit that the same traits have in some degree appeared in the founders of other religions, and even in classical literature, as they have in thousands of humble Christian lives ever since. Still, there remains the wonderful fact that this one character has transformed the world, and led to incomparably the highest and the purest civilization which the race has known. From these premises there never has been but one inference which has satisfied the mass of mankind who have come to the full knowledge of the facts,—the conclusion of that great apostle who, himself overpowered by the force of the evidence, declared that " God was in Christ reconciling the world unto himself."

Here as in every other previous phase of our argument we have simply an induction; not a demonstration, but an induction which has produced conviction in a multitude which no man can number; which has satisfied the deepest yearnings of humanity; which has given superhuman courage to martyrs, and sustained the unwavering devotion of saints. It is an induction, moreover, which has always stood the test of experience under every circumstance of life; and among its confessors have been all sorts and conditions of men, from the humblest intellect to the most gifted genius. It is never outgrown, but its power increases as men grow in wisdom and in virtue. It is an induction which opens ever fresh fields of spiritual knowlege, and directs in the way of truth. In a word, as it is the noblest induction that man has ever grasped, it is also the greatest power in the world.

We thus lay hold of the last phase of the argument of natural theology; and this we may call the argument from love. At the same time we reach the highest stage in the development of man's conception of God. How gradual but how majestic has been the progress in the education of mankind from the first! How large the result! In nature man found Energy, Fitness, Beauty, Order, and Sacrifice; and through these he has been led to recognize Might, Skill, Perfection, Law, and Love, in a Supreme Intelligence. The argument, however its materials may differ, is in spirit one throughout all its varied phases; and the one point we would impress is that this argument is an induction. To show the validity of the argument by comparing the inductions of natural theology with the inductions of science will be the object of these lectures.

LECTURE II.

PREPARING THE WAY.

IN the first lecture, when drawing the distinction between inductive cognition and deductive demonstration, we used the word "induction" in the familiar sense in which it is usually employed among physicists, to include the numerous phases of the experimental method of discovering general truths, without overlooking the fact that the logicians have generally given to the same term a more precise and definite meaning. In its Greek form the word "induction" is as old as Aristotle, who gives a formal analysis of this mode of reasoning, which is not more obscure than a similar philosophical analysis of so complex a mental process might be at the present day.

Certainly the great Stagirite had grasped the essential distinction between induction and deduction when he wrote: "Induction makes clear only, and does not prove." And although he confuses his modern reader when he discusses induction as a proof which may be formulated in a syllogism, he elsewhere clearly recognizes this mode of reasoning as a kind of inference through which we arrive at general principles. A more precise definition of the mental part of the process could not now be given.

Bacon, who is regarded by English scholars as the father of the inductive method, held a more mechanical view of the subject. In nature general truths are constantly obscured through the complexity of the data furnished by experience; and Bacon proposed to sift them out, as it were, by a perfectly definite method of exclusion or elimination. We seek the cause of a certain class of effects; say, for example, of motion in circular orbits. Bacon would make a critical comparison of all cases in which the effect is produced until by exclusion of one after another of the various circumstances he is able to detect some phenomenon constantly present when the effect is present, and varying in degree with the effect, and without which the effect is never produced; when this phenomenon — if one lived long enough to distinguish it — must be a cause of the effect in question. Obviously, an exhaustive elimination of conditions is rarely possible; and this Bacon recognizes, and gives rules for procedure in various cases and recommends various aids to induction, — " admincula " as he calls them, — by which the process may be greatly expedited.

Bacon's method was the normal outcome of his metaphysics, — that is, of his *à priori* conception of nature and of natural processes, — and as the conception was very partial the method was necessarily, even in theory, equally limited. Practically no great originator in science ever followed Bacon's rules, or any other rules; although under the circumscribed conditions of ordinary experimental work every physical investigator naturally resorts to a method of elimination in seeking the cause of any accidental disturbance, such as a leak in his apparatus, or a break in his electrical connections.

It is a singular fact that Bacon, who is usually regarded among English-speaking people as the champion who freed the human mind from servitude to *à priori* dogmas, should himself have been so greatly influenced by his metaphysics. Bacon constantly set induction in opposition to deduction, and regarded syllogism as of service only for the communication of knowledge. But, obviously, wherever the universal can be connected with the particular the process of thought can be expressed in a syllogism; and if Bacon could have succeeded in realizing his metaphysical conception he would have also succeeded in placing induction on the same basis as deduction, and rendered the method equally demonstrative.

It is also a current opinion that Bacon was the first to make the results of observation and experiment essential factors in scientific reasoning. But this, again, is only partially true. Aristotle constantly appealed to the facts of nature in support of his conclusions, and there are at least hints in his writings of experimental methods; and in classical writings of a later date we have abundant evidence of accurate, discriminating, and intelligent observations. As compared with Aristotle, the greater influence of Bacon on the advancement of knowledge is not to be found so much in the superiority of his methods as in the larger knowledge of nature and the clearer scientific conceptions among the men whom he influenced; and it is safe to say that if the "Novum Organum" had been given to the world a few centuries earlier it would have led to no greater results than those produced by the far older "Organon" which it superseded.

One influence of Bacon's great genius has been to spread very widely the narrow meaning which he appropriated for the word "induction." Indeed, according to a common popular misapprehension, Bacon invented the word, as well as the mechanical method which it is often used to indicate. But, as has been intimated, this word, or its equivalent in different languages, has been in constant use from the time of Aristotle; and was employed by the Stagirite with a far more comprehensive and deeper meaning than was ever conceived by King James's at once great and contemptible chancellor. We now use the term in a far broader sense than ever before; but so far as the preliminary mental act is concerned, our conception of the process of induction does not differ materially from that of Aristotle. Its essential features are, first, the conception or guess; secondly, the verification of this conception by experiment and observation. The verification may be direct, or through some more or less remote deduction; and if the appeal to nature shows that the first conception must be rejected, the experience will probably suggest some modification which will be tested in like manner in its turn, until the truth in more or less completeness is reached.

This system of observation and experiment, continued during a long period of time, has given to the modern world a far more intimate acquaintance with natural phenomena than the ancients possessed; and it is to this, and not to superior philosophy, that our great success in the advancement of knowledge is to be attributed.

You pronounce with confidence on the probability of a friend's action in a given case in measure as you are acquainted with his principles and inclinations. In a very similar way the investigator who is acquainted with nature and her processes is likely to make inferences, which will be confirmed by experience in just the proportion that his knowledge is wider and more exact. The ancients were often as ingenious and as profound in their conceptions as modern philosophers, and their anticipations of knowledge surprise us. But as their conceptions remained unverified, they laid no sure foundations on which they could build. Because wild and scattered, all their ingenuity was misdirected and unavailing. The value of a man's guess depended on his reputation; and questions of fact were settled on authority. Thus it came to pass that Aristotle's unverified conjectures, through the sheer force of his intellectual pre-eminence, misled the world for two thousand years.

Besides his more intimate acquaintance with nature, the modern student is constantly acquiring improved methods of testing his inferences; and such instruments as the telescope, the microscope, the polariscope, the spectroscope, the thermometer, the galvanometer, and the telephone have not only immensely widened his field of observation, but also vastly increased his power of experimenting; so that his progress in knowledge has been so constantly and so rapidly accelerated that more has been gained during the lifetime of men still living than during all human history before.

As our object in these lectures is to show that the inductions of natural theology are as legitimate as the inductions of physical science, it is essential that we should first describe the characteristics of scientific inductions, in the broad sense with which we use this term; and since, as we have endeavored to show, it is impossible to define this mode of reasoning by any concise formula, we shall best attain our object by studying a few striking examples, — selecting for examination great discoveries whose history is well known, and of which the important steps can readily be traced. Let us begin, however, with a brief description of some of the speculations of the old Greek philosophers, in order that by comparison we may more fully appreciate the value of our modern inductive methods.

It will be remembered that the Father of History, when seeking to explain the cause of the annual inundations of the Nile, — after giving his reasons with a truly scientific spirit (if sometimes with insufficient knowledge) for rejecting the hypotheses which had been proposed to him, — proceeds to argue that the effect is caused by the sun, which unequally draws the water from the sources of the stream at different seasons of the year; and that the overflow takes place when the sun has gone north, and draws less powerfully on the Libyan fountains, which then pour out their full supply.

Assuming the sufficiency of the alleged cause, the explanation of Herodotus is still confused; but what, as it seems to me, he distinctly implies is this: The Nile is unique among rivers, first, because it flows from the south to the north, across the region twice traversed by the sun in the course of the seasons; and secondly, because, having no tributaries, it is not affected by the rains along its banks. Hence the alternations of its floods must depend on its sources alone; and the sun-god must produce the greatest possible difference of effect on these springs when at the extreme limits of his annual journey.

Were the cause adequate this explanation certainly would not be unphilosophical; but all turns on this one point. Herodotus does not appear to have had any doubts about the adequacy of the sun's agency, or to have made any attempts to estimate the magnitude of the effect which could thus be produced. His whole theory was expressed by the phrase, "he (the sun) draws the water to him," — a form of words which has been used to describe a certain familiar appearance in the heavens from that day until this. In using this expression — with which his readers at once associated the optical phenomenon just referred to, and which they connected in an obscure way with the evaporation of water — Herodotus felt that he was giving a triumphant explanation; and this example shows in a marked way the reason of the unsoundness of the Greek philosophy when applied to the study of nature. The old Greeks had as vivid imaginations, and were as acute reasoners as ourselves; they were also in many cases diligent and careful observers. But they mistook abstract conceptions for realities; and having given names to these forms of thought, they sought to advance knowledge by analyzing the words and the thoughts suggested, instead of studying the facts which the words signify.

This vicious method of Greek philosophy is well described by Whewell in his " History of the Inductive Sciences: " "As soon as they had introduced into their philosophy any abstract and general conceptions, they proceeded to scrutinize these by the internal light of the mind alone, without any longer looking abroad into the world of sense. They took for granted that philosophy must result from the relations of those notions which are involved in the common use of language, and they proceeded to seek their philosophical doctrines by studying such notions. They ought to have reformed and fixed their usual conceptions by observation; they only analyzed and expanded them by reflection. They ought to have sought by trial, among the notions which passed through their minds, some one which admitted of exact application to facts; they selected arbitrarily, and consequently erroneously, the notions according to which facts should be assembled and arranged. They ought to have collected clear fundamental ideas from the world of things by inductive acts of thought; they only derived results by deduction from one or other of their familiar conceptions."

But although the false method, thus so clearly described, was especially characteristic of the ancient philosophy, it is a vice from which the modern world has by no means wholly escaped. How often do the controversies of the present day turn on purely verbal distinctions. How imperiously, and yet often how insensibly, are our thoughts ruled by the mysterious mechanism of language. How conscious is the effort to force language to express our exact and deliberate thought, and to prevent our thought from being moulded by language. Of course to a very large extent the influence of language is legitimate. Language is the medium of thought, and cannot be separated from it. Exact thought is not practicable without language, and the very effort to clothe thought in words awakens thought. Moreover, the general terms in language represent stages of intellectual progress. They form a scaffolding, as it were, by which the mind mounts to ever higher levels from which it gains a more general and wider prospect. But it is one thing to use language, and another thing to be a slave to it. Some men are slaves to language all their lives, and from such a slavery the ancient philosophy was not liberated until modern times.

Man was made in the image of his Maker; or, to express the same truth in the phraseology of a recent philosophy, has developed into harmony with his environment; and, undoubtedly for this reason, those acute thinkers of ancient time in their unverified conceptions not unfrequently anticipated the results of modern science. So it was with Herodotus; and, although he attached no definite meaning to it, his explanation of the annual overflow of the Nile was in the main correct. The sun is indeed the cause; and the great pump which the sun maintains in ceaseless action not only supplies the Nile, but also all the rivers of the globe. Moreover, such is the peculiar equatorial position of the basin of drainage of this remarkable river that the evaporation from this area greatly diminishes as the sun moves north of the equator, when naturally an increased amount of water flows down the only other outlet.

By the Greek philosophers the contrasts emphasized by language were regarded as fundamental distinctions in nature, or first principles, which they made the basis of discussion, and from which they sought to deduce general truths. Aristotle enumerates ten such principles, as based by the Pythagoreans on the contrasts of number: limited and unlimited, odd and even, one and many, right and left, male and female, rest and motion, straight and curved, light and darkness, good and evil, square and oblong; and from oppositions of this kind Aristotle himself deduced the doctrine of the four elements.

"We seek," he says,[1] "the principles of sensible things, — that is, of tangible bodies. We must take, therefore, not all the contrarieties of quality, but those only which have reference to the touch. Thus black and white, sweet and bitter, do not differ as

---

[1] As translated from De Gen. et Corrupt.: Whewell's History of the Inductive Sciences, vol. i. page 49, edition of 1847; and the translations from Aristotle which follow are quoted from the same standard work.

tangible qualities, and therefore must be rejected from our consideration. Now the contrarieties of quality which refer to the touch are these: hot, cold; dry, wet; heavy, light; hard, soft; unctuous, meagre; rough, smooth; dense, rare." Then, after rejecting all but the first four of these, either because they are not active and passive qualities, or because they are combinations of the four first, and concluding for these reasons that the four retained must be elements, he proceeds: —

" Now in four things there are six combinations of two; but the combinations of two opposites, as hot and cold, must be rejected. We have therefore four elementary combinations which agree with the four apparently elementary bodies; fire is hot and dry; air is hot and wet (for steam is air); water is cold and wet; earth is cold and dry."

In a similar way by considering light as opposite to heavy Aristotle came to regard levity as a quality of a body, and distinguished bodies as absolutely heavy or absolutely light. " Former writers " he says, "have considered heavy and light relatively only, — taking cases where both things have weight, but one is lighter than the other; and they imagined that in this way they defined what was absolutely heavy and light." Fire and air, according to Aristotle, were absolutely light, with fire the lighter of the two. Hence it followed " that each of the four elements tends to its own place, — fire being the highest, air the next, water the next, and earth the lowest." In another place he writes: " heavy and light are, as it were, the embers or sparks of motion ;" and he considered that the tendency of light bodies to rise, like the tendency of heavy bodies to fall, was an inherent quality.

It is obvious that all this fallacious reasoning had a purely verbal origin; and that the great error consisted in inferring that there must be an opposition of material qualities corresponding to verbal distinctions. Since light was opposite to heavy, the conclusion was drawn that levity, like weight, must be a quality of matter; and it was nearly two thousand years before men found out that levity, or buoyancy,— as we now call the upward tendency of timber in the sea, or of flame and other forms of heated vapors in the atmosphere,— the phenomena out of which the Stagirite made so much,— was simply an effect of the weight of a surrounding fluid; and we retain in our language the term specific gravity— originally opposed to specific levity — as a constant reminder of the persistency of error. Moreover, it is a striking illustration of the spirit with which the ancient philosophy was cultivated, that this error prevailed in spite of the fact that Archimedes discovered and correctly enunciated the simple principle of buoyancy, — a discovery rendered most notable by its connection with the testing of King Hiero's crown.

We must also briefly notice Aristotle's absurd conclusions in regard to motion; since they were generally received even down to the period of the great astronomical inductions which we are next to consider, and without some knowledge of them we cannot comprehend the intellectual conditions under which the great astronomers of the sixteenth and seventeenth centuries studied and labored. Motion, according to the Stagirite, was simply the effect of the inherent tendency of the body. In consequence of their nature, light bodies move upwards and heavy bodies downwards; and, as was fully recognized, such motions acquire an ever increasing velocity. Since, then, acceleration was the characteristic of the motion of a body obeying its natural tendency, such motions were regarded as natural. On the other hand, when a ball is rolled along the ground the motion rapidly diminishes, and finally ceases, because the ball is forced against its inherent disposition; and hence, on the principle of oppositions, such retarded motions were distinguished as violent.

This explanation, if it may be so called, of the motions of bodies remained almost unquestioned to the time of Galileo; and the results of his experiments were gravely questioned because they were inconsistent with the Aristotelian dogmas. But the climax of these unbridled dynamical speculations remains yet to be stated, and will form the turning-point in this discourse.

In his book "On the Heavens" Aristotle wrote: "The simple elements must have simple motions; and thus fire and air have their natural motions upward, and water and earth have their natural motions downward. But besides these motions there is motion in a circle, which is unnatural to these elements, but which is a more perfect motion than the other, because a circle is a perfect line, and a straight line is not; and there must be something to which this motion is natural. From this it is evident that there is some essence of body different from those of the four elements, more divine than those and superior to them. If things which move in a circle move contrary to nature, it is marvellous, or rather absurd, that this, the unnatural motion, should alone be continuous and eternal; for unnatural motions decay speedily. And so from all this we must collect that besides the four elements which we have here and about us, there is another removed far off, and the more excellent in proportion as it is more distant from us." This fifth element was called the "quinta essentia" by Latin writers; and the word "quintessence" in our own language frequently brings to mind this singular conception, which, although so absurd to us, held for ages a wonderful control over the human mind.

Having thus shown how vain and foolish are the imaginations of men unless directed and controlled by experience, we turn next with satisfaction to a far more glorious record, and shall attempt to illustrate by a conspicuous example how this same noble and powerful imagination of man becomes like a divine inspiration if only he approaches nature with meekness, and strives to learn what she alone can teach. It is the disposition of the mind and the fulness of knowledge, more than method, more than skill, more than ingenuity, more than intellect, which makes the difference between foolish speculation and pregnant conception.

The change from the ancient philosopher to the modern investigator is as great as the difference between the sophist and the scholar, between self-assertion and self-devotion, between conceit and humility, between pretension and worship. This change of attitude of the students of nature since the revival of learning is often ascribed to the influence of Bacon. But great thinker as Bacon was, he did not lead the change, and knew little of its true spirit. To explain such a wide-spread intellectual movement we must look to a more potent cause than the influence of any man, however great; and, as it seems to me, this great revolution can be directly traced to the influence of Christianity, and to the spirit of humility and self-devotion which its Founder sanctified and rendered glorious.

The Law of Universal Gravitation, says Dr. Whewell, the historian of the inductive sciences [1] "is indisputably and incomparably the greatest scientific discovery ever made, whether we look at the advance which it involved, the extent of the truth disclosed, or the fundamental and satisfactory nature of this truth." And although it may be doubted whether this discovery was an intellectual achievement any greater than many others which have been made since, there can be no question that not one of these, however brilliant, has had so great and lasting an effect in the advancement of learning. Selecting, therefore, the law of gravitation as a most conspicuous example of a scientific induction, let us endeavor to follow, as far as is possible, the several steps by which the great result was achieved, in order that we may thus gain a clearer conception of the mental process, called induction, which we are seeking to illustrate.

[1] Whewell's History of the Inductive Sciences, vol. ii. p. 187.

In order to understand what Newton accomplished, it is essential that by studying the state of knowledge at his time we should put ourselves in some measure in his position when, at the age of twenty-three, he received the degree of Bachelor of Arts at the University of Cambridge. Thorough mathematical student of great ability that he was, we must suppose him versed in all the astronomical learning of the day; but at the same time he must have been more or less hampered and prejudiced by the forms and doctrines in which he had been educated, — limitations from which only men of genius are able to escape. On the other hand we must remember that besides the astronomical works which had been actually published and were then common property, Newton also had the advantage of a large amount of floating discussion, which did not ripen into definite results until a later day, but which made Newton's grasp of the great ideas involved in his discovery a more natural and less transcendent effort than it would otherwise appear.

Such historical relations as we would establish are, however, very difficult to secure; for even if we can fully realize the conditions of actual knowledge in Newton's time we cannot appreciate those influences of education, surroundings, and other circumstances which so greatly modify the intellectual atmosphere in which men live and work, and by which facts and opinions are always more or less colored. Hence, it is impossible for any one at the present day, even after long continued study and investigation, to stand where Newton stood in his opening manhood, and

THE ALMAGEST. 45

view the field of knowledge as he saw it; and for me it is only practicable to sketch the situation in rudest outlines.

The knowledge of astronomical facts acquired by the ancients was very extensive. From the time of the Chaldean shepherds there were always numerous and assiduous observers of celestial phenomena. Indeed, among eastern nations the heavenly hosts were so universally objects of worship, and the conjunctions of the planets were supposed to be so intimately connected with men's lives that astronomical occurrences received an attention which no other phenomena of nature secured. As early as 150 B. C. Hipparchus constructed a system of astronomy which even now commands our admiration. We have a very full exposition of this system by Ptolemy, who lived under the Emperor Hadrian two hundred and fifty years later, and whose work has been preserved for us by the Arab astronomers under the title of "The Almagest." Ptolemy added but little to the theory of Hipparchus, but he did a great deal to extend and verify it. "The Almagest" is a monument to his learning, accuracy, judgment, and skill; and is by far the most important contribution to scientific knowledge which we have received from the ancient world.

When we remember that the observations of the ancients were made with no aids, or with only the rudest tools, the knowledge of celestial phenomena which had been acquired at the time of Hipparchus appears wonderful. The fixity of the stars had been established. The brighter stars had not only been grouped in constellations and mapped, but their relative positions had been determined, by alignments, with such accuracy that the observations are of value at the present day. The paths of the planets and of the moon — and what is still more remarkable, the course of the sun through the constellations — had been followed, and the varying rapidity of their motions in different parts of their sinuous, and often involuted, courses recorded. Numerous cycles had been discovered which enabled the astronomers to regulate the calendar, predict eclipses, and foretell other astronomical conjunctions. Some of these cycles, like the cycle of Meton, — which is still used for calculating the time of Easter, and in which the Golden Number is the number of the current year, — are so extended that their discovery implies the maintenance of observations and the preservation of the records through long periods of time. In addition to all this the great circles of the celestial sphere had been marked out, the equinoctial and solstitial points had been fixed, and Hipparchus himself had discovered the precession of the equinoxes. Lastly, the spherical form of the earth had been recognized, and some approach had been made to a knowledge of its dimensions.

The circumstance that the vault of the sky forms a sort of natural map on which the paths of the planets and of the moon can be directly traced by the unaided eye, and that of the sun readily inferred from what was called the "heliacal" rising and setting of known stars, in connection with the religious importance attached to the subject, was undoubtedly the reason that the ancients acquired an acquaintance with astronomical facts so far beyond their general knowledge of natural phenomena; and it is not to the credit of our modern education that the learned men of those early times had a better acquaintance with the changing appearances of the spangled dome of heaven than any of our scholars at the present day, except those who especially devote themselves to astronomical studies. It is certainly a matter of great regret that our methods of education should not invite our children to observe what is going on around and above them. With the help of diagrams and orreries they learn from more or less popular text-books the outlines of the modern system of astronomy, and perhaps gain some conception of the immensity of space ; but they remain ignorant of the appearances which the skies unroll every clear night before their eyes.

When looking from my summer home towards an uninterrupted eastern horizon I have often heard intelligent people express surprise that the full-orbed moon which rose from the waves the previous night should rise behind the hills the next; and although this may be an unusual experience, I question whether many of the graduates of our colleges have a clear conception of the singular involutes which the planets would be seen to follow if each left a shining track in its wake; and certainly still fewer have any idea of the very tortuous course of the moon in her successive lunations, until after a long period she retraces very nearly the same course again. But these are the very phenomena out of which our system of astronomy was constructed; and if we would understand what the great astronomers did we must first become acquainted with the appearances whose coils they unwound and whose complexity they unravelled.

During the long night of the dark ages which succeeded the fall of the Roman Empire, the records of ancient astronomy were preserved at Bagdad, at Cairo, and at Cordova, those centres of Moslem culture. With the revival of learning in the Christian world, soon after the capture of Cordova by Ferdinand the Third, of Castile, in 1236, astronomy became a favorite subject of study throughout Europe, and in this study the " Almagest " of Ptolemy was the great authority; and two centuries and a half later, just at the dawn of the Reformation, when Ferdinand and Isabella were raising the united standards of Aragon and Castile on the last stronghold of the Moors in Spain, where Columbus was present seeking from their Catholic Majesties commission and supplies for his first memorable voyage, there was at the University of Cracow in Poland a young student, named Nicholas Copernicus, who was soon to become the greatest master of the astronomical knowledge of his age. After finishing his course at Cracow, Copernicus studied astronomy first at Bologna, then at Padua, and afterwards at Rome; but having gained the highest honors at these great seats of mediæval scholarship, and the reputation of being the most learned man of his time, at the age of thirty he retired to the little town of Frauenburg in eastern Prussia, where he spent the remaining forty years of his life as a tender and devoted pastor of a rude and ignorant flock. To Frauenburg Copernicus had carried a grand conception, and in his simple lodgings, still shown in the neighboring hamlet of Allenstein, that conception was matured.

The astronomy of which Copernicus was so great a master was the science constructed by Hipparchus and illustrated by Ptolemy, and which had remained essentially unaltered for more than a thousand years. The chief merit of existing treatises was the wealth of facts, and the records of conscientious observations which they contained; and Copernicus was as familiar with the dubious ways of the celestial wanderers as is a shepherd with the by-paths of his straying lambs. His knowledge, moreover, was not mere erudition; but the facts were ever present with him, and the paths of the heavenly bodies were engraved as clearly on the crystal sphere of his imagination as if on the firmament they were marked with a shining thread among the stars.

But all this real knowledge came to Copernicus in the guise of a system which, although based on assumption, was consecrated by authority and tradition, and held by the learned world with the same reverence with which it still honors the models of classical literature. As the earth was regarded as the centre of the universe, and the circle as the most perfect of figures, the astronomers assumed that the heavenly bodies must move around this globe in circular orbits. But as the involutions of the planetary paths were obviously inconsistent with this simple assumption, Hipparchus sought to explain the anomaly by what has ever since been known as the system of epicycles. The planets were assumed to move in circular paths around an immaterial point, which was itself moving in a circle around the earth; just as if the planets were fastened to the rim of a vast wheel, revolving in a plane passing through the earth, while the wheel was rolling round the crystal sphere which formed the celestial vault. Perhaps the wheels of the chariot of the Sun in the Greek mythology suggested the idea; and absurd as it seems to us, it was not inconsistent with the philosophy of motion taught by Aristotle, and universally held even at the time of Copernicus. In its more abstract form the conception had indeed an element of truth, and has been preserved by modern astronomy in the devices of mathematical analysis for computing a planet's apparent place. That such a device would give a general explanation of the stationary and retrograde phases in the planetary motions is obvious. But to the Ptolemaic school the conception was of far greater value than this. By carefully collating and plotting observations, they were enabled to determine the periods of revolution both in the epicycle and in the cycle, and thus they calculated tables predicting the planets' positions; which, although vastly inferior both in accuracy and reach to similar tables in our nautical almanacs, were wonderful achievements for the time, and tended to give great confidence in the theory on which the calculations were based.

To rude observation the motions of the sun and moon are far more regular than those of the planets; and Hipparchus was able to explain the anomalies, so far as they were known to him, by a theory of eccentrics which placed the earth, not at the centre of the circles around which these great luminaries moved, but at another point some distance from the centre, called the equant. As before, the conception was perfectly definite, and received a quantitative expression. The position of the earth with regard to the centre of motion was determined, the points of apogee and perigee in the heavens were marked out, and from these data Hipparchus calculated tables of the sun and moon. In the time of Ptolemy, when the inequalities of the motions of all the heavenly bodies were better known, it became necessary to add epicycle to eccentric in order to reconcile the observations; and the result was a most complex system, which is graphically described by Milton: —

> " . . . how gird the sphere
> With centric and eccentric scribbled o'er —
> Cycle in epicycle, orb in orb ! "

This was the system in which Copernicus was educated, and by whose traditions and methods he must have been more or less bound. It would be very easy to misrepresent this system, and thus to undervalue the work of Copernicus, by showing how absurd and childish were the theories he overthrew. In many of the materialistic aspects in which it was presented by classical writers, with its mechanism of crystalline spheres, it does seem as if the Ptolemaic system must have appeared to thinking men even then incredible and monstrous; and one sympathizes with the King of Castile, who, when the system was explained to him, is said to have remarked that, "if God had consulted him at the Creation, the universe would have been made on a better and simpler plan."

But when regarded abstractly, as the resolution of unequal motions of the heavenly bodies into two or more equable circular motions, it was not only a legitimate scientific method, but is closely analogous to the empirical methods followed at the present day to connect a series of observations in any department of physical science when, as is usually the case, the dynamical causes are unknown; and, as before intimated, is essentially the same method which is followed by the modern astronomer when he resolves unequal motions into a series of terms or expressions of partial motions involving the trigonometric values of circular arcs.

This point, which has been so well made by Whewell, should be strongly emphasized. The dynamical law which governs the motions of the heavenly bodies was wholly unknown until discovered by Newton; and as a system of calculation the theory of Hipparchus was not only good, but, as Whewell adds, "no better has yet been discovered;" and the maze of epicycles is simply the complexity which the calculations of apparent place in astronomy always present. Moreover it appears very plainly from the writings of Ptolemy that his school regarded the whole machinery of epicycles and eccentrics as imaginary, and used them simply as devices for the graphical representation of apparent motions. As such they are true expressions, and the best that have been yet devised. Indeed more than one half of our modern physics rests on no better basis today. We have learned, however, to dissociate our partial generalizations from the material symbols in which they find expression, and are content to use these aids as guides so long as they lead us aright, and to wait until advancing knowledge shall give to them a wider and a fuller significance. The tendency among the ancients was the very reverse of this. They sought to materialize everything, as their mythology so plainly shows. But at the same time we have the best of evidence, as in the works of Ptolemy, that their more gifted minds rose superior to this spirit, and were able to discern the true ideal under the conventional dress of the symbols they habitually employed; and it may be questioned whether the "crystalline spheres" by which in the imagery of their poets the complex motions of the heavens were maintained are one whit more absurd than the "luminiferous ether," without substance but with indefinite elasticity, with which modern science has filled the inter-planetary spaces. .

If we would appreciate what Copernicus achieved we must remember that he was educated in the system whose striking features we have been attempting to sketch, — a system which had all the authority of tradition, all the charm of antiquity, all the attractions of learning, and beneath its conventional symbols all the sanctions of sound philosophy and all the spirit of true science.

We are familiar with the outlines of the Copernican system, and I trust are now prepared to see clearly just what this great master contributed to the world's real knowledge, just how far his keen intellectual vision was able to penetrate the darkness of the then unknown. It can be stated in a few words; for the offering which any man, however great, can bring to the altar of truth, though relatively it may be large, is always absolutely very small.

Amidst the complexities of the apparent, Copernicus discovered the simplicity of the real. He saw law under inequalities, regularity under variation, order under confusion; and having gained a glimpse of the true structure of the solar system, he showed, by a careful comparison of the theory with observations, that the facts of nature harmonized with this conception. The large knowledge, the grand conception, the scrupulous confirmation, — these were the essential and inseparable stages of this grand discovery.

Popular writers on astronomy often lay great stress on the statement that a heliocentric hypothesis was a favorite tenet among the disciples of Pythagoras, and therefore not original with Copernicus. But if they cite this well-known fact in disparagement of the work of the great father of modern astronomy, they must wholly misconceive the character of a scientific induction. Those speculative philosophers of antiquity did not place the sun in the centre of the solar system on any basis of facts, but merely as an idle fancy by which they sought to pay honor to the sun-god. How utterly different with the system of Copernicus! This was not only an inference from the largest knowledge of facts which the best scholar of his age could gain, but was also an inference verified by observation, and by the most exact measurements which could then be made. Unverified hypotheses are accounted of no value in exact science, and in the opinion of competent judges no such anticipations in the least detract from the merit of a real discovery.

It is not the least among the noble qualities of this hero of science that throughout all his work he displayed such deep humility of spirit and such profound reverence for truth. His system must have been matured soon after he settled at Frauenburg, if not before. It was a vision of his youth over which he thought and worked for forty years before he told it to the world. He did not hasten like a young knight to slay the dragon which had guarded so long the opening of the pathway to the great treasure. He did not at once enter the lists against the defenders of old dogmas, because they were antiquated and seemed to him erroneous. Truth was sacred; but so was just authority, so was noble learning, so were old institutions. And truth could wait; and truth did wait, fresh and unimpaired, long, long years. In those lonely lodgings at Allenstein amidst the humblest pastoral and charitable duties, he questioned night after night that vision of his youth, multiplying observations and repeating calculations, until the truth grew upon him with such conviction that he could no longer be silent; and then he declared it, in spite of interest, in spite of opposition, in spite of contumely, in spite of persecution.

In the long record of illustrious men who have devoted their lives to the advancement of knowledge for truth's sake alone, I know of no incident more impressive, more truly sublime, than that which is narrated of the death of Copernicus. The forty years of patient labor in confirmation of the early vision had passed. The book had been written, and under great opposition had been printed at Nuremberg. The last revisions had been made; but the author, worn out at seventy years with labor and anxiety, lay dying without any token of the travail of his soul. Indeed reports have come that bigotry has succeeded in stopping the publication for which his life has been spent, and all hope has fled, — when at the last moment a special messenger arrives, and places in the hands of Copernicus the long expected volume fresh from the press. The dying man is just able to return a sign of recognition, and whisper the final prayer, " NUNC DIMITTIS SERVUM TUUM, DOMINE, SECUNDUM VERBUM TUUM, IN PACE! "

Were study always conducted in the spirit in which that book was written, the harmony of all real knowledge would become clearly manifest. In the dedication of the work " DE REVOLUTIONIBUS ORBIUM COELESTIUM " to Pope Paulus III., Copernicus expressly states that he has kept his book by him for four times the nine years recommended by Horace; and remarks that " the study of a philosopher is to seek out truth in all things so far as is permitted by God to human reason."

The Copernican system was not at once generally accepted. Long cherished doctrines with their prescriptive rights are not so readily set aside; nor is it well that they should be. But the system did very soon receive from astronomers that form of recognition which would most have pleased its author. In 1551 Reinhold published tables, or " ephemerides," as they are usually called, based on the principles of Copernicus, whose verified predictions tended greatly to strengthen his theory; and the demonstration was complete when in 1610 Galileo's new telescope revealed to sight, in the system of Jupiter's satellites, a model on a small scale of the solar system according to the views of Copernicus, and not long after showed that Venus had phases like the moon, thus making visibly manifest the planet's relation to the sun; so that in less than a century after the death of its author, in spite of prejudice and in spite of theological rancor, the heliocentric theory was almost everywhere received by learned men as an established doctrine of astronomical science. It is a striking illustration, however, of the conservatism of philosophical thought that Lord Bacon, who lived until 1628, long after the decisive discoveries of Galileo, never gave his assent to the Copernican doctrine, and even Descartes, who lived until 1650, gave to it at most only an implied recognition, rejecting the form while he adopted the substance.

We can readily account for the position of Descartes, who had a theory of his own which seemed to him to include all that Copernicus had discovered; but we cannot but be surprised that Bacon was so blind. It is one thing, however, to think and write learnedly about induction, and another thing to make discoveries. Bacon was a metaphysician, not a physicist, much less an astronomer. He had not the familiarity with nature by which alone an insight into her methods and processes can be gained. He could not therefore comprehend the vision of Copernicus, and it seemed to him a dream. To his introspective mind the order and finish of the Ptolemaic system had a great charm; and he was bound hand and foot by traditions while protesting against them. Should we have been wiser? And may not his experience lead us not only to honor more highly the great man whose character I have sought to portray, but also to appreciate more fully, and value more highly, that wonderful power by which he accomplished such great results?

LECTURE III.

THE INDUCTION OF NEWTON.

DURING the fifty years that followed the death of Copernicus, preparations were being made for another great advance in the theory of astronomy. These preparations consisted chiefly in the extension of observations, the calculation of tables, the improvement of methods,—all resulting in the collection of fuller and more accurate data in regard to the motions of the heavenly bodies. A very skilful observer appeared, the accuracy of whose measurements exceeded anything that had yet been obtained. Copernicus had declared to a pupil, who was disturbed about single minutes, that "if he could be sure to ten minutes of space, he should be as much delighted as Pythagoras was when he discovered the property of the right-angled triangle;" but it was claimed for Tycho Brahe that an error of eight minutes in his observations was impossible.

In the last year of his life at Prague Tycho received into his observatory, as an assistant, a young man named Johann Kepler, who with these eight minutes, to use his own boastful words, was able to reconstruct the whole of astronomy. There could not be a greater contrast than that between Copernicus and Kepler, — the one, the ideal philosopher; the other, a veritable astronomical Don Quixote, turning what he must have known to have been a dishonest penny by astrology in his youth, and in his mature manhood discussing like a Lothario the qualifications of eleven different damsels to become his second wife. There never was a wilder imagination than that of Kepler, and he gave it full rein. The wisest of men have doubtless at times idle fancies; but then they have the wisdom to keep their folly to themselves, or at least to their homes. Kepler, on the other hand, seems to have had no sense of decorum. He not only entertains and cherishes the most absurd speculations, but he publishes them all to the world; so that his voluminous works are a most singular medley of sound thoughts and unmitigated nonsense. But beneath all this there is the true scientific spirit. He submits his ridiculous conceptions to the test of experience, and rejects them at once if they do not stand the trial. He displays without reserve all the inner processes of his thoughts, exaggerating his follies, and parading his conceits like an actor; and this makes his works a curious study of the inductive method of reasoning; for among all these wild guesses he discovered three great truths, which have ever since been known as Kepler's Laws, and which will render his name honored so long as astronomy is studied.

Copernicus had divined the great central feature of the solar system, but he was trammelled to the last by the Aristotelian dogmas in regard to the nature of motion, and assumed throughout that the heavenly bodies must maintain an equable circular motion in their orbits; and in order to explain the obvious anomalies which remained, even on his heliocentric theory, he was obliged to retain the system of eccentrics and epicycles of the Ptolemaic school, although very greatly reduced in proportions. This was a manifest blemish on the Copernican system; but these devices were evidently regarded by Copernicus as temporary modes of representing the irregularities, for the purposes of computation. And it must be remembered that in physical science apparent irregularities are inseparable from observation and experiment; and that the most conspicuous feature of modern astronomy is the discussion of just such seeming discrepancies, only of course of a much lower order of magnitude. In reducing the magnitude of the anomalies Copernicus recognized that he was approaching a true theory; and in the study of nature this is all any man is permitted to do. The inmost shrine cannot be entered; and Copernicus did not feel the necessity of reconciling his empirical methods with modern dynamics.

Kepler had no better knowledge than Copernicus of the laws of motion,— although he was a younger man by seven years than Galileo, and the experiments of the Pisan professor on falling bodies, and his sarcastic attacks on the notions of the Aristotelians, had been published long before the famous laws of planetary motion were discovered. Kepler not only held to the dynamical conceptions of Aristotle, but put them into the most grotesque guise, likening the planets to huge animals rushing through the skies.

He was not, however, hampered by deference to dogmas of any kind. He had no more respect for a circle than for any other curve; and since an oval, like a circle, returns upon itself, and would thus obviously satisfy one fundamental condition of a planet's orbit, he inquired, with the aid of careful plottings and computations, how far observations of positions in the case of the planet Mars could be satisfied on the assumption of an oval orbit.

In the first place he found that by considering the plane of the planet's orbit with reference to the sun alone, a position could be given to this plane from which the planet had none of the librations which both Ptolemy and Copernicus had attributed to it. Copernicus, influenced evidently by his Ptolemaic education, had assumed that the orbits of the planets must have some connection with the plane in which the earth moved; and this simple step of Kepler's at once freed the heliocentric theory from the machinery of epicycles with which Copernicus had left it encumbered.

But the eccentrics remained, for they were facts of nature; and it was then apparent that the planet did not have an equable motion in its orbit, as had been until then assumed; so that with the epicycles the old dogma of equable circular motions was banished forever from astronomy. Thus freed from a blinding prejudice, Kepler was soon able to take a great step forward. In studying the conditions which on the new theory regulated the changing velocity of the planet's motion in different parts of its orbit, he discovered what has since been known as Kepler's

"Second Law," that the areas described, or swept, by the line drawn from the planet to the sun are always equal in equal times, or are proportional to the durations of the motion. The "First Law," that the orbits of the planets are true ellipses, of small eccentricity, with the sun at one of the foci, was not reached until some time after the "Second Law," and the step between the two was a very long one for Kepler. He tried all sorts of hypotheses of circular and oval orbits before he hit on what would seem to us the most obvious conception of all; and the detailed history of his struggles with this problem occupies thirty-nine chapters of his work "De Stella Martis." The "Third Law," that the squares of the periodic times of the planets are proportional to the cubes of the solar distances, had in Kepler's mind no logical connection with the first two, but was the one valuable result of the extravagant and often preposterous speculations which he narrates at great length in his book on "The Harmonies of the Universe."

There is a great deal in Kepler's character which might naturally impair that respect for the scientific investigator which the graces of Copernicus have done so much to establish. It seems inscrutable that such a "krank," as Kepler appears in a large part of what he wrote, should have accomplished such great results; and it would be natural to judge the work by the man. But this was not the first case in which "God hath chosen the foolish things of the world to confound the wise;" and it is possible that just such a man was required to break up the superstitions which the dogmas of Aristotle had become. And however weak in some of the relations of life, Kepler united all the conditions of successful induction. He had a very large knowledge of astronomical facts, and was familiar with all their limitations. He had an exuberant imagination, and great fertility of invention. He was loyal to nature, and never harbored his errors when once refuted. As Whewell very justly says, "Kepler certainly was remarkable for the labor which he gave to such self-refutations, and for the candor and copiousness with which he narrated them; his works are in this way extremely curious and amusing, and are a very instructive exhibition of the mental process of discovery."

To illustrate the characteristic features of the inductive method here referred to is the chief object of these lectures; and I trust that the story of Kepler has made prominent three essential conditions of success: first, a large knowledge of facts, based on an intimate acquaintance with the phenomena of nature; secondly, a fertile imagination, ready to suggest the possible relations of these facts; thirdly, a conscientious scientific spirit, which submits every hypothesis to the test of observation or experiment.

The laws of Kepler were purely formal; that is, they were expressions of facts or relations for which no explanation was given, or could be given at that time. It was a fact that the planets moved in elliptical orbits; it was a fact that the radius vector swept over equal areas in equal times; it was a fact that the squares of the periodic times were proportional to the cubes of the sun's mean distance; and the circumstance that these facts were learned by inference, and not by direct observation, does not alter their relation to the scheme of knowledge. They are in no respect efficient causes. They are simply facts and nothing more, and to Kepler they were wholly disconnected facts; and this distinction between a formal or phenomenal law, which merely expresses a general fact of nature, and a dynamical law, which gives the mode of action of an efficient cause, corresponds to a most important step in the progress of science. We can distinguish three stages in this progress: first, the phenomenal stage, in which only isolated facts are observed and recorded; secondly, the formal stage, in which facts of general relationship are discovered; thirdly, the dynamical stage, in which the relations are traced to some efficient cause. Astronomy was raised to its second stage by Hipparchus, to its third stage by Newton. Until the end of the seventeenth century it was still in the formal stage, and the discoveries of Kepler did not alter its position, although they prepared the way for the great advance which was soon to follow. According to Kepler's loftiest conceptions the planets moved in the manner which he had discovered simply because it was their nature so to move. But a far more gifted seer was soon to come, who should show that the laws of Kepler were the necessary and very partial results of the action of a force which controlled the universe.

If after his work was done Kepler had been told that in less than a century the laws he had discovered would be shown to be merely phases of the action of universal gravitation, there can be little doubt that he would have regarded the prophecy as grandiloquent nonsense. Kepler associated no clear conception with the word "force," and did not recognize a force of gravitation. By Kepler, and by all scholars before him, as well as by many after him, the word "force" was used to denote any manifestation of energy, which might vary widely not only in its nature but also in its mode of action. There were forces innumerable, each with its own special virtue and mode of action. It was obvious then as now that muscular force would produce motion, and that a moving body would exert force; but there were no clear conceptions of the relation of motion to force. A stone fell to the ground, not because it was pulled by a force which we now call gravity, but because it was the tendency of heavy bodies to move downward, through a virtue residing in the body itself, not in the earth. It must have been known to Kepler that while he was at work on the theory of Mars an Italian named Galileo, with whom subsequently he maintained a friendly correspondence, had been making some curious experiments on swinging pendulums and falling bodies, which were subversive of all the old mechanical notions; but he did not dream that they had any bearing on his studies. Yet Galileo was doing for mechanics almost precisely what Kepler was doing for astronomy, and the labors of both men were the necessary prelude to the induction of Newton. In order that we may the better understand the bearing of this new and converging line of investigation it may be well for me to review very briefly the fundamental conceptions of the modern theory as to the relations of motion and force.

We know nothing more about the origin of force than our fathers, but we have a very clear idea about the uniformity of its manifestation. Force, however produced, always manifests itself either as a pull or a push, and no matter what may be the circumstances, this pull or push varies only in strength. The force may be produced by muscular action; it may be due to electrical excitation; it may be an effect of magnetism; it may be caused by heat; it may be gravity; but in all these cases the ultimate effect is a pull or a push. We do not, of course, by this analysis, remove in the least degree the mystery which still surrounds the origin of force; we know nothing more about the nature of gravity than we knew before: but we do know that gravity acts as a pull of definite strength; and we have made a great advance towards clear thinking when we have been able to banish from our minds all the indefinite and mysterious accessories with which the term has been associated, and whenever the word "force" is used, to think only of a pull or a push between two definite bodies. So also with motion. It would be easy to bewilder the imagination by attempting to combine the various motions of which every object on the surface of the earth must simultaneously partake; or confuse the mind by discussing whether independent motion in space is conceivable. But in physics we deal only with relative motions. We do not recognize absolute rest or motion. An object is at rest or in motion solely with reference to some other object.

A body, therefore, may be at the same time at rest in relation to one object and in motion in regard to another. If two bodies are moving with relation to each other it is wholly arbitrary which is regarded as at rest and which in motion. It is not necessary to dwell on illustrations of these points, which the moving trains on our railroads so frequently bring to mind. Rest and motion in mechanics are, therefore, simply relative states, and should only be considered from this point of view. Never think of motion as an attribute of a body, but only as change of place with reference to some other body. If the old Greeks could have realized this simple conception the progress of astronomy would have been hastened by at least a thousand years.

It will now be seen to be an obvious phase of the fundamental conception, that the same body may partake of several motions at once, and that each of these motions will be entirely independent of the others, and uninfluenced by them; so that the resulting path and final goal will be simply the combined effect of all. This conclusion, if not at once obvious, will appear if it is remembered that according to the fundamental conception of motion, a body assumed to be at rest in relation to several other bodies assumed to be in motion is in the same condition towards each one as if these assumed states were reversed; and hence, that its relations to the several bodies must be as independent in one state as in the other. Thus arise all the familiar principles of the composition and resolution of motions, which, however complex in some of their applications, are very simple in theory.

As with motion, so also in regard to direction, we have only relative knowledge. It is useless to inquire whether we could form any idea of direction independently of the objects around us; and it was merely their limited acquaintance with the dimensions of the universe which led the Greeks to speculate about absolute directions. Upward and downward have reference solely to the earth; and directions can be known only in relation to the positions or features of material bodies. Practically, we refer both direction and motion to the earth, with its fixed axis and constant time of rotation, and with well marked features on its surface; and we come to associate our ideas of motion and direction solely with this standard. But we should bear in mind that this standard, though natural, is arbitrary,—that other standards might be used, and are used in astronomy. When in analytical geometry or crystallography we refer directions and positions to a set of arbitrary lines called axes, we merely do for our problems what nature has done for our every-day life, by placing us on a globe with definite outlines which set bounds to our habitation, and fixed limits on which our thoughts may rest. To the young student of mathematics all this system of co-ordinates, with the arbitrary transformations, seems very artificial; but they are essential conditions of clear thought; and it was the want of the very conception which they embody which made the method of Euclid so limited in its applications.

Few works that have come down to us so strikingly illustrate the fertility, acuteness, and versatility of the Greek mind as the "Geometry of Euclid;" and it remains to our time one of the chief tools in education. As a training in intellectual gymnastics it is an admirable study, but as a means of investigating nature it is practically useless; and the defect of the Greek geometry, like the defect of the Greek mechanics, arose from seeking the fundamental conceptions, not in the observation of nature, but in the accidents of thought, — although, from the nature of the subject, the first defect was, of the two, far the less serious in its consequences. This defect appears conspicuously in Euclid's treatment of the straight line, which is defined as the shortest distance between two points; leaving out of account the fundamental characteristic, that of definite direction. The Greeks were, with reason, very proud of their geometry; but the science could not measure the earth, as its name denotes, much less the heavens, until it was re-established by Descartes on the basis of accurate conceptions of direction. Even at the present day, since most of us have derived our knowledge of geometry either directly or indirectly from Euclid, it is not unimportant to insist that direction, like motion, is a fundamental condition or state, inseparable from material existence, whose relations we must accept as facts of observation, and not merely as modes of consciousness.

With the fundamental conceptions clearly established, see how very simple all the relations of force to motion at once become; and how intelligible, in the light of our familiar experience. If a body is at rest with reference to another it can be set in motion only by the application of force, — that is, by what is the equivalent of a pull or a push between the two; if it is in motion it can only be brought to rest in the same way; and to start a body when at rest, or to stop it when moving, are, mechanically, equivalent operations.

When a constant force acts on a body in the direction of its motion, the velocity of the motion must be constantly accelerated, because the effect of the pull at any instant must be added to the previous condition. Remembering that the pull or push at each instant simply adds its effect to the previous state, it will be seen that the laws of accelerated or retarded motions — including the laws of falling bodies — follow at once from the fundamental principles; and that acceleration or retardation are indications of the action of some force; and that the amount of acceleration or retardation is the measure of that force. If a body is acted on by two or more forces at once, each produces its effect independently of the others, and the final result is found by simply combining the several effects.

Evidently, very complex problems may arise under the conditions last named. One of the simplest is when a bomb-shell is thrown from a mortar. The exploding gunpowder gives to the ball a tremendous push in a given direction, and were it not for the pull of the earth and the resistance of the air, — which last we here leave out of the account, — the ball, with reference to the gun, would move on forever and with a uniform velocity; but the moment it starts from the gun it begins to fall to the earth, and falls the same number of feet in a given time that a stone, or any other object, would fall if dropped from an elevation. The actual path is a combination of the two motions, and would be a parabola were it not for the resistance just referred to. Another and somewhat similar problem assumes great importance from its astronomical relations. A body is moving with reference to another, and much more massive, object, which for distinction we will call the central body, — not directly to or from it, but on a line which leaves the central body on one side at a greater or less distance. On this moving mass the central body exerts a constant pull. What will be the effect? This will depend on the strength of the pull; but, in general, the path assumed by the moving body will be that of one of the conic sections, drawn round the central body as the nearer focus, and in a plane containing both this centre of force and the original path. If the force were comparatively feeble the body would describe the arc of an hyperbola, and fly off on a new course in the direction of the asymptote to this curve; but if the force were beyond certain limits the path would be a circle or an ellipse returning on itself; and we should then have the counterpart of the motions of the planets.

In this connection it is to no immediate purpose to inquire what was the cause of the primitive motion, unless as a matter of curious speculation about world-building; for the motion was a primitive state, just as much as the chemical elements or any other fundamental conditions. The solution of the problem of central forces, as it has been called, is independent of such considerations, and is complete without them.

With our present conceptions of force and motion it seems perfectly simple, and as given in our college text-books it can be followed by any scholar with a moderate knowledge of mathematics; but only two hundred years ago it taxed the best minds of an age remarkable for the powerful intellects it produced.

From the primary conceptions of direction, motion, and force, it would be very easy to develop all the fundamental principles of mechanics, — to show that when a pull or a push acts between two bodies both must partake equally in the effect, or in other words that action and reaction must be equal and opposite, — to make evident that the mass of the bodies, as measured by their weight, is a most important factor in the result, and that the velocity imparted by a force of constant strength, other things being equal, must be proportional to the amount of material on which the force acts, — to point out the distinction between tension, or pressure, and work, or between momentum and *vis viva*, a distinction which, although now so familiar, was during the eighteenth century the subject of a long and warm controversy among the most eminent mathematicians of Europe. But these points have only an indirect bearing on my present argument; and I will close this summary of essential preliminaries with the statement of the three laws of motion as given by Newton in his " Principia." First Law: Every body continues in a state of rest, or of uniform motion in a straight line, unless acted on by some external force. Second Law: Change of motion is proportional to the force impressed, and is in the line in which the force acts. Third Law:

To every action there is always opposed an equal reaction.

Although at the present day the relations of force to motion might be summarized to advantage in more general terms, yet these formulas show a perfectly clear conception, on the part of Newton, of the true relations, and indicate a wonderful advance in clearness of thought on this subject between the publication of Kepler's work "De Stella Martis" in 1608, and that of the "Principia" in 1686. This is not the place to follow in detail the history of this progress; but we will touch on one or two points, of which the summary we have just given will enable you to see the bearings.

Galileo — who was born in 1564, and became a teacher at the University of Pisa in 1589 — laid the foundations of modern mechanics; and chiefly by the remarkable series of experiments which he made at Pisa during the three years (1589-91). In general terms it may be stated that Galileo discovered, and verified by experiment as formal laws, most of the fundamental principles of dynamics. He taught that all matter has weight, and that gravity and levity are only relative terms. He pointed out the relations of the centre of gravity, and insisted that weight was a constant force, pulling all bodies towards the centre of the earth. He maintained that motion was the result of force, and clearly enunciated the laws of falling bodies, — illustrating the theory by experiments from the "Leaning Tower of Pisa" which have become memorable in the history of science. He clearly distinguished between uniform and accelerated motion. He showed that motion caused by a single force is always in a straight line, — that is, in a definite direction; but that under the influence of several forces a body may move in as many directions at once, simultaneously and independently. He established the principle of the composition of forces, and gave the true theory of projectiles. He distinctly recognized, at least by implication, the principles of action and reaction, and even of virtual velocities. His works are full of ingenious demonstrations of mechanical theorems, both theoretical and experimental; and he was versatile as an experimenter as he was sound as a reasoner. But still, his results were for the most part formal, and not co-ordinated under general principles. Unquestionably, the principles of Newton's three laws of motion may be regarded as implied in the whole tenor of Galileo's experiments and computations, but they are nowhere definitely formulated in his writings, — although in the review of the principles of mechanics which he published near the close of his life he shows much more distinct conceptions of the nature and relations of force and motion than he did in his earlier work. This book, entitled " Dialoghi delle Nuove Scienze," and printed by the Elzevirs at Leyden in 1638, gained universal admiration, and drew wide attention to the subject. Like a well-known book, " Heat as a Mode of Motion," which has done a similar work in our own day, this last and best of the publications of the great Florentine familiarized men's minds with the interdependence of force and motion, which up to this time had been only a disputed doctrine known to a few scholars. The works of Galileo were among the most important means of education for the future Newton, and through them this noble father of mechanical science, as well as great discoverer in astronomy, was in fact one of the chief teachers of his far greater successor.

In estimating the ability of Galileo and the merit of his labors, we must remember that, like Copernicus, he had to contend with the prejudices among all scholars in favor of the dogmas of Aristotle; which at the time were not only a belief but a religion. Still, we cannot but regret that so much of the energy of this great originator was wasted in fruitless disputations with the upholders of the old doctrines, whom he followed with such pertinacity and bitterness that they became his violent enemies. In this, however, he was but taking the course to which his dispositions and abilities inclined him; for Galileo had a most remarkable power both as an expositor and as a writer. He was what we should call a most successful popular lecturer; and when, driven by the old schoolmen from Pisa, he accepted a professorship at Padua, a hall holding two thousand persons was provided to receive the vast audiences which thronged to his lectures.

It was his controversial spirit, rendered especially irritating by the great influence of his powerful utterance, which led to the collision of Galileo with the Papal authorities. At heart he was a good Catholic and a faithful son of the Church. He had many friends among the most influential of the clergy; and there can be no question that he would have been left to teach as he pleased, and even been honored for his innovations, if only he had avoided theological issues, instead of rushing into them. There was no need of forcing that greatly irritated lion caged at the Vatican to show its claws. Neither truth nor honor required it; and though we may not think that a scholar can honorably hold an equivocal position in regard to facts of demonstration, yet the distinction between " ex hypothesi " and " ex animo " was one which he avowedly accepted. And when he violated his pledges, and again revived the old issues, we cannot wonder that his conduct provoked censure; and it may be questioned whether he was treated any more harshly than is many a man at the present day, for a much less departure from prescribed creeds.

In the next generation after Galileo the theory of mechanics became much more clearly developed, and chiefly by his pupils or by those whom he directly influenced. Of this generation, although only surviving Galileo eight years, was Descartes, one of the most powerful minds which the world has ever produced. Descartes, however, was a metaphysician rather than a physicist; a better reasoner than observer; a better mathematician than experimentalist. He never fully entered into the spirit of the inductive method, or made any far-reaching induction,—although he spent much time in experimental work, especially in physiology, and made some notable discoveries in physics, particularly the cause of the rainbow. His theory of vortices, received with great applause at the time as a mode of explaining the motions of the heavenly bodies, and in its essential features revived of late in connection with molecular physics, plainly shows that Descartes had not a clear appreciation of the fundamental conceptions of mechanics. Nevertheless his enunciation — for little less can it be called — of the principle of the conservation of energy is an anticipation of one of the very latest results of science, than which none more remarkable can be found in the whole history of speculative thought; and this prevision will appear still more wonderful when it is remembered that it involved the assumption of molecular motion, with the plain suggestion that heat may be a manifestation of the internal motions of material bodies. Nevertheless, apart from his metaphysical writings, the great contribution that Descartes made to the world's progress was his geometry, to which we have before referred, and whose leading principle we have pointed out. Descartes not only gave a new life to this oldest of the sciences, but he endowed it with a power of interpretation which has done more than all other agencies combined to extend our knowledge of the heavenly bodies.

Into a world thus prepared for a great revelation of knowledge was born, Christmas day, 1642, at the close of the very year in which Galileo died, the child who was to render illustrious his father's homely name of Isaac Newton.

It is always highly interesting to study the career of a man who has fulfilled an important mission, — to attempt to discover inherited tendencies; to trace the influences by which his mind was moulded; to notice early indications of peculiar power, even if remarkable only because they seem prophetic; to mark the guidings of opportunities, if not the leadings of Providence; to discriminate between native genius and acquired talent; to see force of intellect and of will rising superior to circumstances; or, what is often most singular, to find in the limitations of mental endowments a more potent influence than natural abilities in leading the specialist apart from the beaten track; to realize what were the conditions under which the great leader worked, and what were the materials at his command; and finally, to learn how small, after all, were the single steps by which he attained success.

Unfortunately, we have only the most meagre outlines of the early life of Newton. He does not seem to have been a precocious child; and the tales of early mechanical skill are only such as are told of many a boy who has become only an ordinary man. Even at college — to which he appears to have been sent on an after-thought, like the weakly son of a New England farmer — there is no evidence that he gained great distinction; so that when, in 1667, at the age of twenty-five, two years after he received the Bachelor's degree, he was appointed Fellow of Trinity College, Cambridge (his own college), we are surprised to find him in possession of a power of mathematical analysis far in advance of the best mathematicians of his day. He himself tells us that while an undergraduate he studied the Geometry of Descartes, which he had some difficulty in mastering; and already by his method of fluxions he had vastly extended the grasp of the new Cartesian instrument of research.

HIS SYSTEM OF FLUXIONS.

As is well known, "Fluxions" was the name given by Newton to the Infinitesimal, or, as it is now more frequently called, the Differential and Integral Calculus; and the advance made by the introduction of this new method into geometry was incomparably greater than any step which had hitherto been taken. It was, moreover, peculiarly an intellectual achievement; and, although some advance had previously been made in the mathematical treatment of the infinitesimal quantities of geometry, especially by Fermat and also by Barrow, Newton's predecessor in the Lucasian chair of mathematics at Cambridge, yet the improvement made by Newton was very great. That this improvement should have been made by an undergraduate was wonderful; and we find it difficult to explain why it did not at once win admiration, and was not widely proclaimed and highly honored, except on the assumption that though far in advance of his instructors, Newton's abilities and attainments were limited to special lines, which did not at the time find favor among the university authorities.

The method of fluxions, although from this early period constantly used by Newton in his own work, and doubtless taught by him as Professor of Mathematics, — an office which he filled at Cambridge from 1669 to 1701, — was not fully described in print until 1691, and then not by himself; although the principle of the method was given in a geometrical form in the "Principia" four years earlier. It thus came to pass that in publication Newton was anticipated by Leibnitz, who, in the "Acta Eruditorum," Leipsic,

1684, described essentially the same method, though under a different name and with a different notation. In England Leibnitz was accused of borrowing his first conceptions from hints in letters of Newton, and no little bitterness on both sides was the result. But in the discussion which arose, while Newton's priority was established beyond a question, the originality of Leibnitz was also made equally clear; and it is the notation and forms of Leibnitz, and not those of Newton, which have been retained in science.

We do not know how early Newton applied his new calculus to the solution of the so-called problem of central forces. Since the principles of the composition of forces had been established by Galileo it had become evident that the path of a planet might be, as we have already pointed out, the resultant of a primary motion of translation, modified by some power constantly pulling the body towards the centre of motion; and the question was, what would be the form of the orbit under such conditions. Attention had been drawn to this problem in many quarters, but the resources even of the geometry of Descartes were not adequate to a complete solution. One conclusion, however, quite plainly followed from the third law of Kepler,—although the complete demonstration even of this point was first given by Newton, —and this conclusion was that if such a central force as had been assumed existed, it must diminish as the square of the distance from the sun; otherwise the squares of the periodic times of the different planets would not be proportional to the cubes of the distances, as Kepler had found them to be.

As early as January, 1684, the problem of central forces was discussed by three eminent English mathematicians, Sir Christopher Wren, Halley, and Hooke; but the discussion leading to no definite result, Halley, in August of the same year, went to Cambridge, to consult Newton on the subject; and without mentioning that a discussion had been held, "went straight to the point, and asked what would be the curve described by a planet round the sun, on the assumption that the sun's force diminished as the square of the distance." Newton replied promptly, "An ellipse;" and on being questioned by Halley as to the reason for his answer, he replied, "Why, I have calculated it." That the calculation had been made some time previously is evident from the further circumstance, we learn through Halley, that Newton could not at once put his hand upon his former work; but he soon afterwards reproduced it, and in November sent Halley a copy of the result. Soon after, Halley again visits Cambridge to confer with Newton about the same problem, and these conferences led to the preparation of the " Principia," which was published under the auspices of the Royal Society, at Halley's own charge, two years later. The demonstration of the law of gravitation first appeared in the " Principia;" and it is a most noteworthy fact—which marks a most striking difference between the scientific activity of those days and the investigations of our time—that so important a result, which in all its essential features must have been reached at least ten years before, should have been kept so long by the author to himself, and even by him so far forgotten that he could not at once reproduce one of the chief steps in his reasoning.

The problem of central forces as solved by Newton involved, as we have seen, two distinct questions. In the first place, it was necessary to determine the rate according to which the central force varied with the distance; and Newton had shown that it followed from the third law of Kepler that the force must diminish with the square of the distance; but in this he had been to some extent anticipated. In the second place, assuming a force thus varying, it was required to find what would be the character of the orbit of a body revolving round the centre of force under its control. Newton was the first to answer this last question correctly, and he had shown, not only that the orbit would be an ellipse as the first law of Kepler required, but also that, as the second law required, the radius vector must describe equal areas in equal times.

These results, however, had been deductions drawn from established principles of mechanics by the aid of the new calculus. No one thus far had suspected the nature of this central force; and by most scholars of the period it would have been thought degrading to astronomy to associate the mechanism of the heavens with the mechanics of the earth. The two subjects were never thought of in the same connections. There were, it is true, the deductions just referred to, by which it appeared that the planets might be sustained in their motions round the sun by the action of a constant central force controlling their primary motions. There were also the undoubted facts of mechanics, that weight was the effect of a direct pull or force exerted by the earth on all bodies, and that the strength of this pull was directly proportional to the amount of material on which it acted. As yet, however, these two classes of facts, so closely associated in our own minds, belonged to wholly distinct categories of thought, and were no more associated than we connect the fluctuations of the market with the motions of the moon. Indeed that there was any intimate relation between force and motion was then a very modern conception.

The idea, that, after all, this sublime, inscrutable, central force of astronomy was simple commonplace gravity seems suddenly to have flashed into the mind of Newton. We all know the anecdote of the falling apple. The authority for the story is Voltaire, who narrates it in a somewhat popular account of Newton's work, which he wrote for French readers soon after his return from England in 1729. He gives as his authority Catharine Barton, a favorite niece of Newton. She married Conduit, a Fellow of the Royal Society and one of her uncle's intimate friends, with whom also Voltaire was intimate during his well known residence in London from 1726 to 1729; and it was during this time, in 1727, that Newton died. The story has been discredited by Sir David Brewster in his "Life of Newton;" but, as must be admitted, it is as authentic as such a personal reminiscence could well be; and it is certain that tradition marked the tree near his mother's house at Woolthorpe in Lincolnshire as that from which the apple fell, till 1820, when owing to decay it was cut down, and the wood carefully preserved. Tradition also fixes the date as 1666, soon after Newton's graduation from Trinity, when he was passing several months at his old home on account of the fear of the plague at Cambridge.

Why may not the force which pulls the apple pull the moon? We are left in no doubt whatever in regard to the general tenor of Newton's thoughts, either in the garden at Woolthorpe or elsewhere; for we are told the story by Pemberton in the preface to his "View of Newton's Philosophy," and he had it from Newton himself. If the power of gravity, Newton thought, is not sensibly diminished at the greatest heights to which we can rise from the earth's surface, neither at the tops of the loftiest buildings nor even on the summits of the highest mountains, why may it not extend much further than is usually thought? Why not as high as the moon? If so, her motion must be influenced by it; perhaps she is retained in her orbit thereby.

This was the simple thought suggested, and it was this which constituted the greatest induction ever made in physical science. The moon is only distant from us some sixty times the earth's radius, and why should not the immense pull of the earth on all matter near itself be felt at that distance? Of course if this is the force which holds the moon and the planets to their orbits it must, as can be proved by Kepler's third law, diminish with the square of the distance from the centre of motion. From the well known relations of the centre of gravity, the pull of the earth on all bodies near its surface, as well as its pull on distant bodies, may be regarded as proceeding from its centre of figure. Hence the force of the pull at the moon must be as much less than the pull at the earth's surface as the square of sixty-one is greater than the square of unity, that is, 3721 times less. But as the earth's pull is proportional to the quantity of matter on which it acts, so that all bodies great or small fall towards the earth with the same rapidly increasing velocity, — the moon just as fast and no faster than a stone under the same conditions, — we ought to expect that the moon, at its distance, would fall 3721 times more slowly than a stone near the surface. Now such a stone falls 16 feet the first second, and would fall if it had a chance 57,600 feet the first minute; so that the moon should fall about fifteen and a half feet during the first minute of time. But how much does the moon fall? This is the next question which Newton asked; and it is by no means so easily answered as the one we have just solved so readily.

If the moon and planets have the compound motion which Newton assigned to them, they are in the paradoxical condition of beginning to fall at every moment of time towards their primaries; always beginning to fall but never falling. Should the earth's pull at any instant suddenly cease the moon would at once resume its primary motion of translation, starting off on a tangent with the uniform velocity which it had at that moment in its orbit. If now we construct in imagination an arc of the moon's orbit described around a centre representing the earth, with a tangent starting off at the point where the earth's pull is assumed to stop; and from this point of contact measure off the distance on the arc over which the moon actually moves in one minute; and finally through the extremity of the arc thus found draw from the centre a radius, and extend the line until it intersects the tangent, — then this intersection will be the point which the moon would have reached in one minute had it started off on the tangent as assumed; and the portion of the radius between the tangent and the arc will represent the distance through which the moon actually falls to the earth during this same minute of time. Knowing the radius of the orbit and the angle subtended by the arc at the centre, and assuming — as we may — that such a small arc is practically circular, it would be the simplest of trigonometrical problems to calculate the distance in question. In Newton's time, however, the calculation involved many uncertain elements, which he showed great judgment in selecting and skill in combining. But the first result was unsatisfactory, for it appeared that the fall was only thirteen feet, instead of fifteen and one half feet as the theory required.

Most men would have regarded this as at least a sufficient approximation to induce them to continue the investigation; and no circumstance indicates more plainly the balance of Newton's mind and the dispassionateness of his temperament than that he regarded the result as disproof, and at once dismissed the theory from his thoughts.

In a few years, however, the cause of this failure to verify the theory was fully explained. The calculation which Newton had made involved a knowledge of the moon's distance in feet, while the astronomical determination of this distance depended on trigonometrical measurements of which the earth's radius was the base; and only gave the information that the distance was about sixty-one times this radius. To reduce the result to feet, it was necessary to know the length of the earth's radius in feet, and here was the difficulty. We cannot of course measure the radius directly, but we can measure an arc of a meridian circle on the earth's surface, and from the length of an arc of known extent—say five degrees—calculate the length of the radius. This is what Newton had done, assuming, according to the received estimate at the time, that one degree on the meridian measured sixty miles. In 1671, however, a new measurement of an arc of a meridian, between Amiens and Malvoisine in France, was made by the astronomer Picard, which showed that the received length of a degree was greatly in error; and that instead of being sixty it was sixty-nine English statute miles of 5280 feet each. When this result became accredited in England, Newton revised the calculation which had so long been laid aside; and the result was an agreement with theory so exact as to leave no longer any doubt in his mind of the truth of his early conception. As the story is told by Robinson, "He went home, took out his old papers, and resumed his calculations. As they drew to a close he was so much agitated that he was obliged to desire a friend to finish them."

This in outline is the history of the greatest scientific induction which man has ever made. In drawing the sketch, I have given prominence to those features which from my point of view seemed most essential, and have doubtless passed unnoticed facts and relations which others might deem more important. But the interaction of mind on mind, which scientific progress involves, is usually very complex; and, in the absence of detailed information, there is room for great differences of opinion. It is much to be regretted that we have not fuller knowledge, especially in regard to the sequence in which the various elements of the problem were presented to Newton's mind; but he, unlike his predecessor Kepler, was very reticent, and did not display all the processes of his thoughts.

We might, with Whewell, classify the general results of Newton's work under five different propositions, which undoubtedly came before him at one time or another as separate problems: first, that the strength of the pull of the sun on different planets diminishes with the square of the distance; secondly, that a force so acting would cause the planet to move in elliptical orbits, in accordance with the first and second laws of Kepler; thirdly, that the earth so acts on the moon, and that this force is identical with gravity; fourthly, that this force is universal, causing an attraction between all bodies under all conditions; fifthly, that the strength of the force increases in the same proportion as the combined weights of the attracting bodies, and may be regarded as the sum of the actions of the various particles or units of mass of which they consist.

Such a classification is useful, as a summary of

what has been — in great measure — already stated, as pointing out the separate elements of the problem, and as showing how great the work really was. But all these propositions except the third, were deductions from known principles; and the identity of the central force with gravity being granted, the rest necessarily followed. Not that we would in the least degree depreciate the skill with which these deductions were worked out. On the contrary, as with every investigation, this was Newton's real work; "hic labor, hoc opus est;" and it has always won, and ever will claim the admiration of the world. But it was the great induction, and not these deductions which we are endeavoring to illustrate. The induction was to a large extent — if not wholly — a spontaneous action of the mind; but it is by just such action that the level of knowledge is raised. After any great induction it always requires time — it may be long time — to work up to the new level. It was so after Hipparchus; it was so after Copernicus; it was so after Kepler; and astronomy has not yet reached the level which Newton set. The deductions may require greater intellectual skill, as they necessarily involve incomparably greater labor; but they do not raise the level. As in building, it requires little work to raise the scaffolding, but then comes the long and arduous toil of the builders to prepare the walls on which to mount still higher.

If gravity reaches to the tops of the highest mountains, why not as high as the moon? This was the fundamental conception which led to the great result. Seeing how apparently trivial and accidental was the thought which bound together the universe in its all embracing grasp, some may imagine that the individual merit of the conception was inconsiderable. But they must remember that the thought would have been barren without the knowledge to make it pregnant, or without the labor to make it real. Others, like Hooke and Cassini, did claim to have had the thought as well as Newton; but their thought was barren, and the world has paid no regard to their claims. Again, some may think that, given the knowledge and the intellectual power, the thought came without observation, and that to God and not to man belongs all the glory. If by this is meant that the thought came as an inspiration to a mind prepared to receive it, I should agree to the proposition;

> "For merit lives from man to man,
> And not from man, O Lord, to Thee."

And I myself believe that just as to the intellectually strong and teachable there come revelations of larger knowledge about material things, so to the spiritually minded and open-hearted there comes in a similar way a deeper insight into the spiritual life; and it is because I believe these material relations to be a type of the spiritual, and to have the same, though no more certain sanctions, and it is because I hope, through a more intimate knowledge of the facts, to aid in reconciling the two orders of truth, that I have dwelt so long on this instructive history.

The character of Newton was entirely in harmony with his lofty career. It was marked by sedateness of demeanor; soberness of conversation; sobriety of conduct; persistency in effort; devotion of will; humility of disposition; reverence of mind, and absorption in thought. He never would admit there was any difference between himself and other men; and when asked how he made his discoveries, replied, " I keep the subject of my inquiry constantly before me, and wait till the first dawning opens gradually, by little and little, into a full and clear light." It is into minds in such a frame that the light shines; and by waiting on the Eternal Purpose the revelations of great truths come.

LECTURE IV.

DEDUCTION.

IN my last lecture I said that a new induction raises the level of human knowledge; and this figurative expression very exactly indicates the new relations which are thus introduced into the world of thought. There is not simply an addition to knowledge, but the old knowledge is seen in a new light. Facts previously disconnected are found to be united by common bonds. Phenomena which appeared mysterious and fortuitous now appear regular and natural. Principles which were supposed to be fundamental are found to be dependent. Partial and formal laws are merged in more universal and simpler modes of action. Order and harmony prevail where before was only confusion and discord.

But to show what are the results of the new principle that has been introduced, to trace all its connections, to develop the consequences, both near and remote, to test by observation or experiment, the deductions in every detail, and to follow out the lines of investigation thus opened, requires a great amount of thought and labor, and the more in proportion as the previous induction is broader and more commanding. In this way the general standard of knowledge is brought up to the new level, and the foundations are laid on which to rise to a still more commanding position. It is work of this sort which almost exclusively occupies the time and taxes the energies of the great body of scientific investigators; and in the economy of nature many thousand workers are ready to carry out the conceptions of one great master.

The great originator is highly favored among men, but let it not be inferred that the part of his fellow-workers is less honorable, or their labor less difficult, or less necessary. Not only is it that

> "All are architects of Fate,
> Building on these walls of time,"

but it is also true that some of the greatest intellectual achievements have consisted wholly in following out well-established principles to their necessary consequences. Newton's great induction commands our highest admiration, but so do equally the deductions which Laplace and Lagrange and Gauss severally drew from Newton's all-embracing law. No work of science can be compared with the "Principia" in the effect produced on the progress of knowledge; but it may be questioned whether it shows as great intellectual power as the "Mécanique Celeste."

The mathematical sciences give us the most characteristic examples of the deductive method, and mathematics is the most important tool in such processes of thought. The necessity of such aid arises from the limited power of the human mind in combining details, in following sequences, in remembering successive steps, and in general in concentrating thought. The various forms of calculus help the reasoning powers very much in the same way that the microscope, the telescope, or the telephone, aid the eye or the ear in observing natural phenomena.

This fact we recognize in the simplest forms of mathematical calculation. The Arabic numerals, with the so-called decimal system of arithmetic, enable any one readily to obtain results which, without their aid, would be attainable only by a mathematical genius; and if we analyze the mental processes of the remarkable calculators who from time to time appear, we find that their wonderful ability depends chiefly on a vividness of memory and imagination, which enables them to keep before their minds, and thus combine, a great number of partial results. Each of these by itself might have been obtained mentally by the average man; but he finds it necessary to aid his memory by noting down every step of his calculation on slate or paper.

Men with such a knack at figures are also able to combine results by quick methods which are out of the reach of ordinary computers; while the common rules of decimal arithmetic are adapted to the average mind, and give just the aid which will enable it to reach most rapidly and accurately, the required result.

It may be well here to set right a common misapprehension, that the rules of arithmetic have some special relation to the number ten. Since Nature gave man ten fingers or digits, which make a very simple but efficient calculating engine, he instinctively, at a very early period, distinguished and gave names to ten corresponding numerals, also frequently called digits; but it was not until man had tried various clumsy expedients of combining these digits to express larger numbers, that some good genius, supposed to have been an Arabian, devised our simple method of expressing numerical values. The arithmetical rules are the outcome of this method, and would work just as well with any other number of digits as with ten. Eight digits would have given us a simpler arithmetic, and twelve digits, in many respects, a more convenient one. Such, however, is the force of habit and the conservatism of education that a change now would probably be impracticable; but we cannot but regret that our early parents did not omit the thumbs in the first count. Eight units can be evenly divided three times, ten units but once; and this power of successive subdivision is of paramount importance in commercial transactions, as the experience in France with decimal weights and measures plainly shows.[1]

[1] The truth of this statement, although really so simple, seems so inconsistent with our familiar habits and ordinary experience, that some further illustrations of it may be desired. In our system of enumeration we use in addition to the zero mark separate signs for the first nine digits, and express all higher numbers by an ingenious method of combining these signs, or figures, as the signs are called. The system consists in writing the figures in a definite order on a horizontal line, and assigning to the digits a value increasing by powers of ten as we proceed from right to left. The figure in the first or units' place stands for single digits; the figure in the second or tens' place stands for ten times the number indicated by the

The French system of weights and measures is constantly advocated on account of its decimal subdivision, but these are a positive disadvantage. The one valuable feature of the French system is the simple relation which it establishes between measures and weights, and it would doubtless be a great gain if such a system were adopted by all nations; but it would be a still greater gain if we could get rid of

sign; the figure in the third or hundreds' place for ten times ten, or one hundred times, the number indicated; that in the fourth or thousandths' place for ten times ten times ten, or one thousand times, the number expressed; and so on. The expression 63,597, for example, signifies six ten thousand, added to three thousand, added to five hundred, added to nine tens, added to seven; and we are so familiar with this method of enumeration that we are apt to forget how artificial it is, and how much we are indebted to the ingenious men of Arabia, or elsewhere in the East, who invented the system.

The efficiency of this system, and the validity of the rules which arise under it, depend not on any peculiar virtue in the number ten, but simply on the mode of combining the figures to express values. As above said, there was no reason for selecting the number ten more weighty than the authority of the ten of fingers and the ten of toes; and any other number might have been taken as the basis of the system equally well. For example, we might use eight as the basis of the system, and assign to the digits, arranged as before, values increasing by powers of eight. We should then discard two of our figures, 8 and 9, and omit the corresponding names in counting, thus:—

| 0 | 1 | 2 | 3 | 4 | 5 | 6 | 7 | 8 | 9 | 10 | &c. | Decimals. |
| 0 | 1 | 2 | 3 | 4 | 5 | 6 | 7 | 10 | 11 | 12 | &c. | Octuples. |

We might use the same names and figures for all the numbers up to seven; but we should be obliged to give a wholly different significance to all compound numbers, while assigning to them two of our digits, and establish our system of arithmetic on an octonary instead of a decimal basis.

the names we use for the corresponding compounds (not the corresponding numbers) on the decimal system. Thus ten (10) in the octuples would have the same value as eight (8) in the decimals; twenty in the octuples the same value as sixteen in the decimals; one hundred in the octuples the same value as eight times eight, or sixty-four, in the decimals, &c. How completely the introduction of a new system would destroy our association with numbers will be evident from the following multiplication table on the octonary system: —

MULTIPLICATION TABLE.

Octonary System.

1	2	3	4	5	6	7	10
2	4	6	10	12	14	16	20
3	6	11	14	17	22	25	30
4	10	14	20	24	30	34	40
5	12	17	24	31	36	43	50
6	14	22	30	36	44	52	60
7	16	25	34	43	52	61	70
10	20	30	40	50	60	70	100

Obviously, it would be impracticable for us who learned to cipher by the decimal system to change our habits of thought, and acquire a second nature under which twice four would suggest involuntarily ten, or four times six thirty, with corresponding changes in all processes of simple addition and subtraction. Think of the confusion of bank clerks and other lightning calculators if six and seven became fifteen, or three from ten five! Nevertheless, apart from the force of habit the transition would be a very simple one. The fundamental operations of arithmetic would not be essentially altered thereby; and to those educated in it the octuple system would appear as natural as the one we so familiarly employ. A single example will make this point clear.

Let us assume that we have two numbers 234 and 345 written on the octuple system to multiply together. We proceed

OCTUPLE SYSTEM. 99

Although this digression has no immediate bearing on our subject, it shows how conventional our system

exactly as we should on the decimal system only using the new multiplication table, and making the corresponding additions, thus : —

```
    234           156
    345           229
   ————          ————
   1414          1404
   1160           312
    724           312
  ———————       ————
  105,614       35,724
```

We read the two numbers two hundred and thirty-four and three hundred and forty-five, and the product one hundred and five thousand six hundred and fourteen just as we should on the decimal system. But on the octuple system the same numbers express wholly different values. These values, however, can be readily reduced to the decimal basis, if we remember that on this basis the value of the successive places in the octuple enumeration increase by powers of eight. Hence, the value of 234 in octuples would be found in decimals thus : —

```
   Octuples.            Decimals.
   200 = 2 × 8 × 8  =   128
    30 = 3 × 8      =    24
     4 =            =     4
   ———                 ————
   234                  156
```

So also the value of 345 in octuples would be found : —

```
   300 = 3 × 8 × 8  =   192
    40 = 4 × 8      =    32
     5 =            =     5
   ———                 ————
   345                  229
```

The product of 156 by 229 decimals has already been found above to be 35,724, and we can now prove that the ordinary rule of multiplication applies to octuples as well as to decimals, by of arithmetic really is, and what an efficient aid it is in our mental processes.

As we go forward in the study of mathematical subjects the more necessary does the aid furnished by mathematical symbols become, and we very soon reach a point where even the most gifted intellect cannot dispense with their arbitrary forms. They enable the mind to combine conditions and see relations which otherwise it could not possibly grasp. Hence it is that every great improvement in mathematical methods has always been followed by a great extension in our knowledge of material relations; new deductions from old principles have become possible, and thus knowledge has been broadened and the way made ready for larger inductions.

showing that this product is the exact equivalent of the octuple product 105,614 also before obtained by following the regular arithmetical rule, of course using the octuple multiplication table and the corresponding octuple additions as before described.

Octuples.		Decimals.
$100000 = 1 \times 8 \times 8 \times 8 \times 8 \times 8$	$=$	32768
$5000 = 5 \times 8 \times 8 \times 8$	$=$	2560
$600 = 6 \times 8 \times 8$	$=$	384
$10 = 1 \times 8$	$=$	8
$4 =$	$=$	4
$105,614 =$		$= 35,724$

The same point could be illustrated by other arithmetical operations; but the above example is sufficient to enforce the statement made above; and it must now be evident that the great merit of what we wrongly call "decimal" arithmetic depends on the system of Arabic numerals, and not at all on the number of digits it employs.

It was so when the Cartesian geometry gave a knowledge of the properties and relations of curved lines and surfaces before unsuspected. It was so when Newton and Leibnitz invented general methods of dealing with the so-called infinitesimal quantities of algebra and geometry, which led at once to the successful solution of the problem of central forces. It was so again, after Newton's death, when the consequences of the law of gravitation were developed in proportion as the resources of the new calculus were enlarged by the great mathematicians of the eighteenth century,—such men as Euler, Laplace, and Lagrange.

Mathematics, however, is a great deal more than an instrument for deductive reasoning. Just as logic has loftier aims than merely to dissect arguments and to lay bare their syllogistic forms and becomes in its larger expressions the science of thought, so mathematics is the science of quantitative relations wholly independent of their material expressions; and the so-called multiple algebra of our own day has been developed far beyond our positive knowledge of material relations, and it is at this moment waiting for some higher induction or broader generalization to open new worlds to conquer. Indeed, so transcendental are the abstractions involved that few educated men, not mathematical specialists, are able to follow them; although in some curious works of fiction attempts have been made to show the possibilities of conceiving of extension in more than three dimensions. In less abstract relations, on the other hand, mathematical analysis has not yet satisfied the demands of existing physical problems; and more satisfactory and exhaustive methods of solving equations of higher degrees would enable the physicists to broaden their deductions in many directions.

To a limited extent the symbolical language of chemistry may be used like mathematical formulæ, and has a similar value in facilitating deduction. But its terms have a far more restricted meaning, and are therefore less general; and moreover, the chemical formulæ, which we call reactions, only express the very simple relations of combination and decomposition.

As the use of the symbolical notation of chemistry is for the most part restricted to chemical students, a brief description of the system may be necessary in order to render the statement just made generally intelligible.

We recognize at the present time about seventy well-defined elementary substances, and in addition to these there are several others whose authenticity has not yet been satisfactorily established. From these elementary substances all known materials can be formed; and into these the various substances which exist on the surface of the earth can be resolved by processes with which all chemists are familiar. Moreover, when these elementary substances unite to form compound bodies, the combination takes place in certain definite proportions by weight.

The modern theory of chemistry, which we shall have occasion to discuss more at length hereafter, assumes that each elementary substance is an aggregate of exceedingly minute particles, called atoms, which are indivisible by any chemical means now known, and which are alike in every respect. Thus a mass of the elementary substance sulphur is an aggregate of atoms, all of which are exactly alike, but wholly different from the atoms of any other elementary substance. These atoms, being definite masses of matter, must have definite weights; all the atoms of sulphur, for example, absolutely the same weight, but a very different weight from that of the atoms of iron or from that of the atoms of oxygen, two other elementary substances.

If the mental concepts we call atoms are really entities, they must have a degree of minuteness which vastly surpasses our powers of observation. Granting the existence of such minute particles, there are known facts of physics and chemistry which compel us to assign limits to their magnitude on either side; and Sir William Thomson has estimated that if a drop of water were magnified to the size of the world, the atoms of which it consists would certainly appear larger than boys' marbles, and with equal certainty smaller than cricket balls. The almost inconceivable minuteness of the assumed atoms is, however, in itself no weighty argument against the atomic theory; for in a universe in which we recognize the infinitely great, why should we not expect to find also the infinitely small? If there be a macrocosmos around us, why should not there be also a microcosmos? And if creation be not limited by the powers of the telescope, why should it be limited by the powers of the microscope? The proof of the existence of atoms is solely a question of sufficient evidence, and may be reached in time; but as yet they can only be regarded as postulates of our scientific systems, the ultimate material units out of which the mind seeks to construct masses of matter. To our crude conceptions they are the bricks, as it were, of the material universe.

According to the atomic theory, when elementary substances combine, the union takes place between the atoms; and the groups of atoms thus formed are called molecules, and only like molecules aggregate together to form masses of different substances. Thus when oxygen gas unites with hydrogen gas to form water, one atom of oxygen unites with two atoms of hydrogen to form one molecule of water; and a drop of water is simply an aggregate of molecules of this kind, so numerous that they can only be counted when all the sands of the earth have been numbered; but all these molecules are exactly alike, each consisting of two atoms of hydrogen and one of oxygen.

If the atoms have definite weights, such a combination as we have just described must take place in the definite proportions of these weights. As the combined weight of two atoms of hydrogen is to the weight of one atom of oxygen, so and in just this proportion by weight must hydrogen gas combine with oxygen gas to form water; and the same general principle must hold in the combination of all other atoms, and in the production of all other compounds. Hence, according to the atomic theory, the combining proportions of chemistry are simply the relative weights of the atoms. Obviously, then, we can infer from the combining weights of the elementary substances, which can be accurately observed, the relative weights of those abstract units we call atoms; and in our modern chemistry the combining proportions of the elementary substances are called, under certain limitations, the atomic weights of the chemical elements. The smallest of these weights is the weight of the atom of hydrogen, which we take as the unit of the system. The atom of oxygen weighs sixteen of these units; the atom of sulphur thirty-two; and the atom of iron fifty-six of the same units. In general, the atomic weight of an elementary substance indicates how many times the atoms of which it consists weigh more than the atoms of hydrogen.

And here it must not be forgotten that although the atoms are wholly theoretical concepts, these relative weights are definite facts of observation; and, as already stated, are deduced directly from the definite proportions in which the elementary substances are known to combine. These values are independent of the atomic theory; but we can most easily make the facts intelligible in the terms of this theory, for the theory gives to the phenomena a concrete expression, and thus enables us to relate them to the rest of our knowledge.

If we know the number of atoms of each kind which enter into the composition of a molecule of any substance, we can find the weight of that molecule by simply adding the weights of the several atoms. Thus a molecule of water, consisting of one atom of oxygen and two atoms of hydrogen, must weigh $16 + 2 = 18$.

Now it will be obvious that if we arbitrarily select a symbol to stand for an atom of each element, we can readily represent the molecule of any substance whose composition is known, by simply writing together these symbols like letters in a word.

In our text-books of chemistry you will find a table giving, after the name of each elementary substance, the symbol which has been selected to represent its atom, and also the value of the atomic weight. Thus the atom of hydrogen is represented by H; and its atomic weight, as we have said, is the unit of the system. The atom of oxygen is represented by O, and its atomic weight is 16. The atom of carbon is represented by C, and its atomic weight is 12. The atom of nitrogen is represented by N, and its atomic weight is 14.

We represent, then, a molecule of water by H_2O, thus indicating that this molecule consists of two atoms of hydrogen and one atom of oxygen, as just stated; also indicating, further, that the weight of this molecule is $16 + 2 = 18$; and still further showing that in water oxygen and hydrogen are united in the proportions by weight of $16:2$.

In like manner we represent a molecule of carbonic acid gas by CO_2, a symbol which indicates, first, that the molecule of carbonic acid gas consists of one atom of carbon and two atoms of oxygen; secondly, that the weight of the molecule is $12 + 2 \times 16 = 44$; thirdly, that in carbonic acid gas carbon and oxygen are combined in the proportion of $12:32$.

We call these groups the symbols of the different substances.

Every chemical process may be regarded as the breaking up of the molecules of one or more substances into atoms, and the regrouping of these same atoms to form the molecules of new substances. In chemistry we technically call such processes reactions; the substances which concur in the process we call the factors, and the substances formed by the process we call the products of the reaction. As no atom can be destroyed, every atom coming from the factors, and none others, must be found among the products; and hence the total weight of the products must be exactly equal to the total weights of the factors. Therefore we can represent such processes by equations, writing on the left-hand side of the equation mark the symbols of the several factors connected by the sign of addition, and on the right-hand side the symbols of the products in a similar way. A few illustrations will make clear the meaning of such expressions.

$$\underset{\text{Grape Sugar.}}{C_6H_{12}O_6} = \underset{\text{Alcohol.}}{2C_2H_6O} + \underset{\text{Carbonic Acid Gas.}}{2CO_2}$$

This reaction expresses the well-known fact that in fermentation grape sugar breaks up into alcohol and carbonic acid gas. The one factor is the symbol of a molecule of grape sugar. This single molecule yields two molecules of alcohol and two molecules of carbonic acid gas, or four molecules in all. Notice how we write two molecules of alcohol, using figures to express several molecules, like coefficients in algebra; and notice also that there are as many atoms of each elementary substance in the one molecule of the single factor grape sugar, as in the two molecules of alcohol and the two molecules of carbonic acid resulting from the decomposition.

$$\underset{(2\times 14)+4+(3\times 16)=80}{\underset{N_2H_4O_3}{\text{Nitrate of Ammonia.}}} = \underset{(2\times 14)+16=44}{\underset{N_2O}{\text{Nitrous Oxide.}}} + \underset{2(2+16)=36}{\underset{2H_2O}{\text{Water.}}}$$

The second reaction expresses that the salt nitrate of ammonia yields, when heated, nitrous oxide gas and water. Here, as before, the atoms of the one molecule which is the factor of the reaction break apart, and rearrange themselves to form one molecule of nitrous oxide gas and two molecules of water. Since the symbols stand for definite relative weights, the reaction informs us further that from eighty parts of the salt we obtain forty-four parts of nitrous oxide gas and thirty-six parts of water.

$$\underset{(H_2SO_4+Aq.)}{\text{Dilute Sulphuric Acid.}} + \underset{Zn}{\text{Zinc.}} = \underset{(ZnSO_4+Aq.)}{\text{Zinc Sulphate.}} + \underset{H_2}{\text{Hydrogen Gas.}}$$

The third reaction represents the process by which hydrogen gas is made from dilute sulphuric acid and zinc. It gives in general, in regard to this chemical change, information similar to that we have learned from the two preceding examples. Moreover, it shows that the change consists essentially in this: that the atom of zinc replaces the two atoms of hydrogen in the acid; when these hydrogen atoms pair together to form molecules of hydrogen gas. It will be unnecessary for my present purpose to dwell on other and more abstruse points of signification which this symbolical language conveys. It is sufficient if I have made clear the more obvious meaning and prepared the way for a further inference, which can easily be drawn from the principles of the system which have been thus far explained.

It can now easily be seen that this symbolical notation gives an admirable basis for classifying chemical compounds; and further that it brings out analogies and enables us to draw inferences which otherwise would never have been suggested. If one substance undergoes certain changes it is probable that an allied substance, having a similar constitution and therefore represented by a like symbol, would partake of similar changes; and the analogy suggested by the symbols often leads us to test our inferences by experiment, and thus we are constantly led to the discovery of new truths.

There is, however, a most important difference between a chemical reaction and a mathematical equation, which should be always kept in mind. From a mathematical equation any result that can be deduced by the principles of algebra must in some sense be true. But in chemistry we have discovered no such far-reaching principles; and our chemical reactions merely express the known facts in regard to each process they represent; and we can draw no certain conclusions one step removed from the facts which the symbols signify. The notation is fruitful in suggestions, nothing more.

When the laws which govern the grouping of chemical atoms have been formulated we may hope for an all-embracing calculus of chemical operations; but from want of precise and exhaustive knowledge of these principles, all attempts in this direction have been thus far failures. Nevertheless, the conventional symbolism of chemistry has been of the very greatest value in suggesting possible relations and pointing out fruitful lines of investigation.

Of most subjects the fundamental conceptions and processes do not admit of more precise designations than ordinary language affords, and the arguments which arise are discussed under the conditions which the science of logic seeks to analyze and classify in the various forms of the syllogism. We may often thus arrive at as complete certainty as by mathematics, — although it is important not to wander far from the boundaries of known truth, and to verify every step of our progress by an appeal to observation or experiment. But whether the conclusions be reached by mathematical, chemical, or syllogistic reasoning, the method is essentially deductive; and implicitly the results were involved in the premises with which we started.

No fountain can rise higher than its source, and no process of reasoning, however conducted, can mount above the general principles or fundamental truths on which the reasoning rests. These are the essential conditions or premises of the mental process, and necessarily imply previous generalizations which were acquired by induction. While, however, we admit that the results of deductive reasoning, however conducted, were implicitly contained in the data of the calculation or the premises of the argument, we must not infer that knowledge cannot be increased by such means.

Before an Infinite Intelligence all the relations of truth must be open; but how far this is from being possible to a finite intelligence we have all sadly experienced; and to man the deductions of science are as much new truths as if they were direct revelations; and the greatest discoveries have been made by strictly deductive processes of investigation. Indeed, as I have already said, knowledge is enlarged chiefly by deductive reasoning, verified by observation and experiment. Nevertheless, as has also been said, deduction implies previous induction, and differs from induction, not in that its results are less real or less novel to men, but in that they are of a different order, and sustain different relations. What this difference is, we shall still further endeavor to illustrate.

If a general principle, like the law of gravitation, is absolutely true, everything that can be deduced from it by legitimate processes must be equally true. But in science we have constantly to deal with inductions which are only partial truths. Under such circumstances, entire reliance cannot be placed on the deductions; and hence the importance of testing each step of the argument by observation or experiment. In proportion as the predictions are verified, the greater confidence do we place in the universality of the principle on which the deductions were based.

Excepting, however, the axioms of mathematics, the laws of motion, and a few similar principles, there are no generalizations which can be regarded as absolutely beyond question; and it is conceivable that conditions may arise under which even the law of gravitation will fail. It is, therefore, only in pure mathematics and in simple physical problems, that we can feel safe in our deductions without submitting them to the test of experience.

Uncertainty in regard to the results of deduction may arise, not only from failure in the particular case of the general principle on which dependence has been placed, but also from inherent difficulties in the deductive process. In algebra, mathematicians have not been able, except in special cases, to obtain complete solutions of equations of higher degrees than the fourth, and the ingenious methods which they employ with problems which give equations of a higher order, yield at best only partial solutions. So also in chemistry, the methods of analysis give only approximate results, and for this reason the conclusions based upon them are more or less indefinite. Hence arises the importance, in all physical science, of the discussion of what is called the probable error of observations, and also of the personal error of the observer; and in this connection a few words on the errors which are inherent in all scientific methods, and necessarily affect their results, will not be out of place.

Even among scholars, who while familiar with the general results of science are strangers to its methods, there is a common misapprehension in regard to the certainty of scientific conclusions, or in regard to the infallibility of scientific evidence. Physical science is constantly spoken of as exact, and as yielding positive proofs, in contrast with the moral sciences, whose results are less definite and more questionable. As regards physical science all this is to a great extent true,—since a large mass of the facts which have been established in relation to the phenomena of nature are as certain as the axioms of geometry; but no results of measurements are absolutely exact, and the accredited values have every possible degree of precision. There are very few magnitudes of nature which are known accurately within a thousandth part of their value; and our knowledge of such fundamental quantities is often in error to the extent of one-tenth. To scientific experts this is a familiar fact, and in all their deductions they take into account the resulting uncertainty; but literary men are apt to reason as if they thought everything accepted in science was known with equal exactness, and are led into error by this unconscious assumption. A very small experience with the reality would dispel this illusion; and hence the importance to all scholars of that limited experience with scientific methods which will give an understanding, not only of the true relations of scientific facts, but also of the limitations of scientific results.

The unavoidable errors of scientific methods may be classed under two heads; and we must distinguish the constant errors, which are inherent in the process employed or in the observer himself, from the accidental errors, which are determined solely by chance. The last are as likely to be in one direction as another; while the first, under the same conditions, are always in the same direction.

Of the two classes of errors the accidental errors

are by far the less important, and to a great extent can be eliminated by multiplying observations. The arithmetical mean of several observations is always far more trustworthy than any single observation, and the theory of probabilities gives us in such cases a method of estimating, not only the probable error of any one observation of the set, but also the probable error of the mathematical mean. The discussion of probable errors is one of the most important applications of mathematics, which is generally known as the "Method of Least Squares;" and it is certainly a most remarkable result of science that what would seem to be at first sight so wholly accidental and utterly lawless, should be found to be regulated by definite principles and become a matter of exact computation. Yet this is strictly true. If, for example, we first eliminate from a series of observations of some definite quantity, as for example the value of an angle, all evident mistakes and known causes of error, there will still remain differences in the results, which will appear the more pronounced in proportion as we seek to secure greater accuracy in our measurements. Such differences we call accidental errors, and they are due to numberless causes which we cannot estimate, depending upon the imperfection of our instruments, or of our senses, or on the varying conditions under which all experiments must be made. Now if we take the arithmetical mean of all the numbers obtained as the most probable value, and call the difference between the mean value and each separate value the error of that observation, it will always appear,—

First, that small errors are more frequent than large ones.
Secondly, that positive and negative errors are equally frequent.
Thirdly, that very large errors do not occur.

Observations.	$v.$	$v^2.$
° ′ ″		
116 43 44.45	5.19	26.94
50.55	—0.91	0.83
50.95	—1.31	1.72
48.90	0.74	0.55
49.20	0.44	0.19
48.85	0.79	0.63
47.40	2.24	5.02
47.75	1.89	3.57
51.05	—1.41	2.00
47.85	1.79	3.20
50.60	—0.96	0.92
48.45	1.19	1.42
51.75	—2.11	4.45
49.00	0.64	0.41
52.35	—2.71	7.34
51.05	—1.41	2.00
51.70	—2.06	4.24
49.05	0.59	0.35
50.55	—0.91	0.83
49.25	0.39	0.15
46.75	2.89	8.35
49.25	0.39	0.15
53.40	—3.76	14.14
51.30	—1.66	2.75

$z = 116° \; 43' \; 49''.64 \qquad n = 24 \qquad \Sigma v^2 = 92.15$

$$v = 0.6745 \sqrt{\tfrac{92.15}{23}} = 1.''35 \qquad v_0 = \tfrac{1.35}{\sqrt{24}} = 0''.28$$

On these fundamental principles derived from experience all our reasoning on the subject is based.

An examination of tables of observations, such as are given in the Reports of our Coast Survey, may be very instructive as they exhibit in a most remarkable manner the principles we have been endeavoring to illustrate.

Thus, in a series of twenty-four measurements of an angle of the primary triangulation made at the station Pocasset in Massachusetts, and given in the Report for 1854, all the above principles are strikingly illustrated; and it further appears that while the largest difference from the mean value amounts to $5''.19$, the probable error of a single observation is but $1''.35$, and the probable error of the mean value only $0''.28$. The term "probable error," as thus used, has a conventional meaning, and simply signifies that there is an even chance that the true value is within the limit assigned.

But while such accidental errors as have been described are constantly reminding us of the limitations of our powers, they are limited in extent, and as also we have seen, can be to a large extent eliminated. Not so with the constant errors which arise from unknown causes of various kinds, or even from the idiosyncrasies of the observers. These may be very large, are likely to operate only in one direction, and may thus seriously vitiate our results. They are an insidious foe against which all our watchfulness and care cannot protect us, an enemy in the dark, of whose direction and magnitude we can form no estimate. These constant errors are the chief source of difficulty in all experimental investigation; they have occasioned incalculable loss of labor; and besides discouraging the investigator, they frequently introduce an element of uncertainty into his results. Years of conscientious and careful investigation have thus been rendered unavailing by an unsuspected error which has vitiated the whole work; and values which had been regarded as among the best-established data of science have subsequently been found to be erroneous, owing to the discovery of a source of error in the method by which they were determined. A remarkable example from my own experience will illustrate these important points.

The atomic weights are among the most important constants of science, and the accurate determination of these numerical values involves analytical work of great refinement and accuracy. In 1856 Schneider, of Berlin, made a determination of the atomic weight of antimony, and obtained the number 120.3. The work was done with all the skill and precision that a master of analytical chemistry could devise, and every known and conceivable cause of error appeared to have been foreseen and allowed for. Eight separate determinations were made, no one of which differed from the extreme value more than 0.23. Nevertheless, a year later Mr. W. P. Dexter, working with a different method, but with equal refinement, obtained as a mean of ten determinations 122.34, that is, a value two whole units greater than the first, — although here again the results of the several determinations agreed so closely with each other that the maximum difference from the mean value was only 0.14. At very nearly the same time the famous chemist Dumas made at Paris still a third independent determination of the constant under consideration, using a wholly different method from either Schneider or Dexter, and obtained 122.00, — nearly the same value as Dexter, and with a similar close agreement between the results of four separate experiments. The deserved reputation of Dumas for accuracy, skill, and judgment gave such authority to his result that it was at once adopted, and remained for twenty years the accepted value of the atomic weight of antimony.

In 1877 I was myself led to repeat the determination of Schneider, only reversing his processes, and obtained very closely his value of about 120. This led me to repeat the process of Dumas, when I obtained a still closer confirmation of the larger number, 122. What could be the occasion of this large difference? The discrepancy could not arise from the ordinary errors of analytical work, which in either process was far less than this; as the close agreement of the separate results obtained by the same process plainly showed. There must be some unknown constant error affecting one or both of the results. To confirm this conclusion I made a third determination of the atomic weight, by a process which had never been employed before and which admitted of great accuracy. This gave me with great exactness the first value, 120; and when a fourth determination by still another process also gave the same value, I felt convinced that the higher number, which had been so long accepted, was the one which had been affected by the constant error, but I did not feel satisfied until I detected the cause of the error and showed in what it consisted.

This experience is a fair illustration of what is constantly met with in scientific investigation, and indicates moreover the only general method of ferreting out constant errors. When determinations of a given value made by essentially different methods are accordant, we have a well-grounded confidence in their accuracy; but mere coincidences of numbers obtained in the same way are no proof of truthfulness, for constancy of results often arises from constancy of errors. I would that I could convey to you the full force of the impression which is left on the mind after repeated experiences such as I have described. The helplessness which one feels while thus working in the dark gives a reality to the sense of the limitations of our knowledge, of which so much is said and so little appreciated. If anything will lead man to hold his knowledge in humility and reverence it is the consciousness that results so laboriously obtained may be invalidated by circumstances over which he has no control, and of whose existence he is wholly unaware.

I would that I could also give an adequate conception of the great amount of conscientious work which is expended on the deductions of science for the sole love of truth. Were it possible, I am sure that your respect for the scientific investigator would be greatly increased and your belief in his sincerity established, however mistaken you may at times deem his opinions or his judgment. Of course in the cultivation of science, as in every other pursuit of life there is abundant room for the display of unworthy motives and ignoble passions; but I venture to assert that there is no class of men in the world among whom is found more unselfish devotion and more personal sacrifice than among the great army of scientific workers. The love of abstract truth may be a much lower motive than the love of man, but it equally calls forth the very noblest qualities of the mind. Moreover, in most cases the constancy and courage of the scientific investigator meet with no reward except the satisfaction which unselfish duty conscientiously discharged always brings; and, as Professor Tyndall has said, "There is a morality brought to bear on such matters which in point of severity is probably without a parallel in any other domain of intellectual action."

The difficulties of scientific deduction are further vastly increased by the circumstance that in the phenomena of nature the effects of various causes are usually so correlated and intertwined that the task of separating them or of determining their precise relations is well-nigh hopeless. Take such an apparently simple phenomenon as the rise of the column of mercury in the stem of such a thermometer as is universally used to measure changes of temperature. The height of the mercury column depends on a number of causes which combine to produce the result we observe. Besides slight effects arising from mechanical strain or irregularities of the tube, we must distinguish, first, the expansion of the mercury, of which the rate slowly increases as the temperature rises, and which tends to raise the column; secondly, the expansion of the glass, which is very irregular and tends to depress the column; thirdly, certain obscure changes in the texture of the glass itself which act slowly, but which on the whole tend slightly to raise the column. It is true that the last two effects are so inconsiderable as compared with the first that they do not seriously interfere with the use of the instrument as a rough measure of temperature in our houses. But when in scientific investigation we seek an exact measure, to the hundredth of a centigrade degree, they interfere most seriously; so that while small differences of temperature may be thus closely estimated under restricted conditions, we have no means of measuring large changes of temperature with any such approach to exactness; and beyond a certain limit of accuracy the use of this simple instrument is one of the difficult problems of science. Even in the ordinary use of the thermometer for determining the temperature of the external air, very considerable differences may be caused by radiation, from the ground, from the sky, or from surrounding objects, depending on the exposure of the instrument; and the discrepancies between neighbors on the state of the weather — which are often so amusingly paraded — are simple illustrations of what is very familiar to every scientific observer.

If, now, instead of using the thermometer as a measure of temperature, we seek to estimate each of the separate effects whose combined action the instrument registers, we are met at once with almost insuperable difficulties, and the approximate solution of this problem by Regnault was one of the triumphs of experimental science. By an ingenious method of experimenting, first devised by Dulong and Petit, he succeeded in measuring the absolute expansion of mercury, and when this was known he could estimate the expansion of the bulb and tube of which the thermometer was made.

As with the thermometer, so again with the barometer. The height of the mercury column in the barometer depends not only on the pressure of the air which the instrument is intended to measure, but is also perceptibly influenced by a variety of other causes, such as temperature, the force of gravity, and capillary attraction. For some of these effects we can make accurate corrections, but for others we cannot; so that the readings of a barometer made with the greatest refinement at Paris, are not strictly comparable with those of one made with equal care at New York; and the only way in which we could make an exact comparison would be by transporting the same instrument to and fro between the two places, as we might a metre measure.

These are but two examples of a universal experience. All the phenomena which we attempt to observe are obscured by other phenomena with which they are associated, and all the instruments with which we make our measurements are more or less fallible and faulty. Hence the general principles we deduce from our observations partake of the same limitations. This is no hair-splitting metaphysical refinement; for, with the exception of a few of the great primary principles of nature, like the law of gravitation or the conservation of energy, there is hardly one of the so-called laws of physics or chemistry which we should implicitly trust in circumstances widely differing from those under which they are established. As a rule, mathematical deductions are based not on actual qualities of bodies, but on ideal relations which have no exact material representatives. There are no such things as the rigid bars, the simple pendulums, and perfect fluids of our theoretical mechanics. These are as much abstractions as are points, lines, and surfaces; and in many respects the sciences of mechanics and astronomy are as much products of pure thought as geometry.

In order to bring the problems suggested by nature within the grasp of his analysis, the mathematician is forced to simplify them by leaving out of consideration every accessory circumstance. As the late Stanley Jevons has so strikingly said in his "Principles of Science," "The faculties of the human mind, even when aided by the wonderful powers of abbreviation conferred by analytical methods, are utterly unable to cope with the complications of any one real problem." Of course the mathematician endeavors to approach the natural problem as nearly as possible, and in most cases the differences do not alter essentially the character of the solution within reasonable limits; but they do narrow, and often most seriously, the scope of the deductions.

Many educated men who are familiar with the great definiteness of the elementary mathematics, form an exaggerated conception of the power and infallibility of mathematical analysis; and from their limited observation infer that mathematics has the power of solving, in a perfect manner, all problems which involve only quantitative relations. And when we consider what they have accomplished, the powers of such minds as those of Lagrange and Laplace do appear almost miraculous. But when we compare the simple problems which they have solved with the complicated relations which modern investigation has revealed, even the powers of such masters are seen to be inadequate; and to follow out the deductions from principles already known, appears to be a hopeless undertaking.

Jevons, whom we have just quoted, also says that "if a mathematical problem were selected by pure chance out of the whole variety which might be proposed, the probability is infinitely slight that a human mathematician could solve it." Let me cite a familiar instance.

The undulatory theory of light presents relations peculiarly favorable to mathematical analysis, and from which a great wealth of deductions has been drawn. But the colors of the rainbow, or more generally the whole range of phenomena attending the dispersion of light by refracting media, still remain essentially unexplained; and the most that Cauchy — perhaps the ablest mathematician of this century — was able to accomplish was to show that under certain assumed circumstances such a result might follow from the undulatory theory, and to make evident that the complete solution of the problem was beyond our present powers of mathematical analysis.

So also in regard to the finality of mathematical deductions. It is a common remark that figures cannot lie; but, as many have found to their cost, they may be made to bewilder the ignorant and cover up a great deal of error. Mathematical results are conclusive only as regards the assumed relations with which the analysis starts; and these may be so different from the relations of any real problem of nature as to render the conclusions inapplicable in any specific case.

It should be clearly understood that there is nothing mysterious about mathematics; that even when its processes cannot be followed except by adepts, its premises and conclusions can always be clearly stated. The operations or processes of thought which it combines by means of its admirable symbolism, are severally perfectly intelligible; but in the multiplicity of the possible relations confusion may readily arise, and it requires a keen intellect, with great power of abstraction and concentration, to trace out these relations to their consequences. Without the symbols the task would have been beyond the best human faculties, except in the simplest problems; and even with all the aids which an ingenious symbolism can give, the power of combination is very limited and wholly inadequate to grasp the complex relations which the real phenomena of nature invariably present.

In thus dwelling on the limitations of scientific deductions, I am not overlooking its grand results. These last speak for themselves, and are fully appreciated and honored. They have become an important element of our daily life, and have profoundly modified the thought of our time; and while we are thankful for the acquisitions of the past, we look for still greater rewards in the near future. It is well, however, at times, instead of looking back at what has been done, to look forward to what remains to be accomplished, and to compare our knowledge, not with what our fathers knew, but with the universe about us. Courage, enterprise, and confidence are great virtues, but so are also modesty, caution, and reservation of judgment. When men venture to frame theories of creation and claim that the existing order might have resulted from the principles of action now known, I am at a loss which most to admire, their unconsciousness or their boldness. My only attempt at refutation would be to ask these would-be world-builders to work themselves for a while in unravelling a web of material conditions in the darkness of the unknown. If they work faithfully I am sure that in distinguishing the ends of a few threads they will be rewarded for all their pains; but I am equally confident that at the same time they will gain the conviction that hidden causes, as yet unsuspected, may intervene in the commonest phenomena of nature. Do not think I am a pessimist because I feel it my duty to emphasize these well-known facts. In the admirable work of Jevons, to which I have referred, you will find the same general doctrine still more emphatically stated and more fully illustrated.

LECTURE V.

EXAMPLES OF SCIENTIFIC INVESTIGATION.

IN the present lecture I shall ask your attention to two examples of scientific investigation, which will give a better idea than can any general discussion, of the difficulties and uncertainties which perplex the student in almost every attempt to substantiate the deductions from scientific generalizations. I select the first example because it is within my own very recent experience; and although the history of science may present far more striking illustrations, I can speak of the perplexities incident to this investigation from personal knowledge; and as the results of the investigation have only recently been published,[1] this fresh example may have the interest of novelty.

The atomic theory is as old as Greek philosophy, and the best and most original exposition of the theory is still to be found in the famous heroic poem of Lucretius, "De Rerum Natura," which appears to have been written about 58 B.C. The adaptation of the theory to explain the definite combining proportions of chemistry was made by John Dalton, of

[1] Published in Proceedings of the American Academy of Arts and Sciences, vol. xiii. p. 119.

Manchester, in the early part of the present century, and since then these combining proportions have generally been called atomic weights.

It was obvious from the first that of all the elementary substances hydrogen gas must have the smallest atomic weight, and it was a natural inference that the atoms of all the elementary substances might be aggregates of this smallest indivisible unit.

Such a theory was in harmony with the philosophical conception that in the last analysis all materials could be reduced to the same ultimate essence, and that differences of qualities depended on the different affections of which this primordial material was susceptible. This theory was strongly advocated by Dr. Prout, an eminent physician in London, during the first half of this century, and the author of one of the well-known Bridgewater Treatises; and is known in science as "Prout's hypothesis." Obviously, if this theory be true it would follow that all the atomic weights must be multiples of the atomic weight of hydrogen; and if this last, as is usual, be taken as the unit of the system, the values of all other atomic weights must be expressed in whole numbers. Here, then, was an obvious deduction, which, if not substantiated by experiment must be fatal to Prout's hypothesis, an induction on trial.

At the time when Prout wrote, the accepted values of many of the smaller weights were in accordance with his views; and the methods of chemical analysis, by which the combining proportions of the elementary substances were determined, were not sufficiently accurate to distinguish, in the case of the higher atomic weights, even the difference of a whole unit. As analytical methods were improved, marked discrepancies with the theory appeared; but so strong a hold had the conception taken on the minds of chemical students that these anomalies were overlooked or attributed to errors of observation; and for many years it was customary in works on chemistry, to give as the values of the atomic weights the nearest whole numbers, instead of the actual mean of the observed values, and the practice is still continued in many works of accepted authority.

At an early period in the discussion, a marked exception to the theory had appeared in one of the smaller and best known of the atomic weights. The combining proportion of chlorine, which forms with metallic silver one of the best defined chemical compounds, could be determined with great accuracy; and all the experiments gave a value for its atomic weight closely approximating 35.5. This, and a few other similar facts, led the late Professor Dumas of Paris to entertain the idea that the atomic weights, if not all multiples of the whole hydrogen atom, might be multiples of the half or quarter atom; or, in other words, that the hydrogen atom might itself be an aggregate of two or more smaller masses, which were the real units of the system; and he was thus led to undertake the redetermination of a large number of the atomic weights, with the view of testing this modification of the original conception. His experiments were conducted with wonderful skill; and many of the new values he obtained for the atomic weights are still universally accepted by chemists. But the results had little bearing on the question at issue; for it is obvious that by taking the unit small enough any result could be regarded as an even multiple of this unit within the limit of experimental errors.

Soon after the publication of Dumas's paper, Professor Stas of Brussels undertook a work of still greater magnitude. Stas had never been a believer in the hypothesis of Prout, and his aim was to push the analytical work to such a degree of refinement as to show conclusively that the results could not possibly be reconciled with any modification of that theory.

Stas had been an associate of Dumas, and the latter always spoke of his former assistant in terms of the highest admiration, declaring that he was the most accomplished experimentalist he had ever known. Thus Stas brought to the new investigation the highest skill, and, moreover, his position as the director of the Belgian mint gave him command of means and appliances which enabled him to work on far larger quantities of material than any previous experimenter. As the error of an analytical process, other things being equal, is less in proportion to the quantity of material used, the advantage gained from the large scale of his experiments was very great. But at the same time these large amounts of material greatly increased the toil involved; and the amount of labor which Stas devoted to this investigation was extremely great; it can be appreciated only by those who are familiar with such processes. In this way however, Stas was able to reduce the merely accidental errors of the processes he employed within wonderfully narrow limits. He obtained values for several of the most fundamental atomic weights, which, though approaching whole numbers, still differed from a multiple of the hydrogen unit by quantities far exceeding the probable error. At first these results were accepted as conclusive, and it seemed as if the hypothesis of Prout had been forever consigned to the tomb of unverified theories.

Still, however, even from Stas's work the remarkable fact appeared that the atomic weights thus determined with so great labor and skill, though not exact multiples, approached very nearly to exact multiples of the atomic weight of hydrogen. If the several values were absolutely independent and distributed by chance, the probabilities that they would all so nearly approach whole numbers was exceedingly small, and there was not one chance in ten thousand that such a distribution would occur as Stas's results exhibited; so that on the whole Stas's work seemed to indicate that there might be some truth in the theory after all, if not in the exact form that had been supposed.

This feature in the distribution of the atomic weights became still more marked as accurate values of the atomic weights of additional elements were obtained. Professor Mallet, of the University of Virginia, was one of the first to call attention to the point just mentioned, in his admirable paper on the atomic weight of Aluminum, which his very accurate and accordant determinations had shown was very closely, if not exactly, a whole number; and Professor F. W. Clarke, of Washington, in his work entitled " A Recalculation of the Atomic Weights," after summing up the results of a careful collation of all the trustworthy determinations of these constants of nature, writes: " Enough has been said in this brief résumé to show that none of the seeming exceptions to Prout's law are inexplicable. Some of them indeed, carefully investigated, support it strongly. In short, admitting half-multiples as legitimate, it is more probable that the few apparent exceptions are due to undetected constant errors than that the great number of close agreements should be merely accidental. I began this recalculation of the atomic weights with a strong prejudice against Prout's hypothesis, but the facts as they came before me have forced me to give it a very respectful consideration." The following table from the writer's work on " Chemical Philosophy," will make clear the point we are discussing: —

ATOMIC WEIGHTS, MOST ACCURATELY DETERMINED.

Hydrogen	1.002	Chlorine	35.46
Lithium	7.01	Potassium	39.14
Carbon	12.00	Calcium	40.00
Nitrogen	14.04	Bromine	79.94
Oxygen	16.00	Silver	107.93
Aluminum	27.02	Antimony	120.00
Sodium	23.05	Iodine	126.85
Magnesium	24.00	Barium	137.14
Phosphorus	31.05	Thallium	204.11
Sulphur	32.07	Lead	206.91

This table includes all the values of atomic weights which up to 1882 could be regarded as known to within 1-1000 of their value; and with one or two notable exceptions, there is no instance in which the value differs from a whole number by a quantity greater than the possible error, though not always the " probable error" of the processes employed in their determination.

Were these numbers wholly independent of each other and distributed by no law, we should expect to find every possible intermediate value; and the fact that they so nearly approach whole numbers cannot fail to produce on the mind the impression that there is some influence which tends to bring about this result. It may be that the discrepancies are due to such unknown constant errors as we have already described, and which, as every experimentalist knows, are always greatly to be feared. Or it may be that there is in nature a tendency to whole multiples, which in many cases is not fully reached. This last view, to be sure, is not compatible with our present conceptions of the atomic theory; but nature is not bound by this theory, nor should be our philosophy.

The force of the evidence which such a distribution of values as the above table presents was brought home to the writer in his investigation on the atomic weight of antimony referred to in the previous lecture. After eliminating various causes of error, he was enabled to determine with great accuracy the atomic weights of antimony, silver, and bromine, in one and the same series of experiments, and it appeared that this ratio was —

$$120.00 : 108.00 : 80.00,$$

with a probable error of less than one in the last decimal place. Here, then, is a ratio of whole numbers, within the 1–100 of a single unit; and although the result may be no more impressive to others than many of the facts exhibited by the table, yet to the experimentalist who after long continued labor reaches such a result as this, the impression is inevitable that there must be something more than mere chance in such coincidences.

Since the ratio of the atomic weights of silver and oxygen have been determined with great accuracy, we can extend the above proportion to a fourth term, the atomic weight of oxygen, which appears also as a whole number, with a somewhat larger probable error. Still we have not reached the unit of the system, and when we attempt to extend the ratio to the atomic weight of hydrogen, we find that the most probable value from all experiments hitherto made gives the ratio, not of 16 to 1, but of 16 to 1.0025.

If now we wished to refer to the hydrogen unit the atomic weights of antimony, silver, bromine, and oxygen, whose ratios of whole numbers had been determined as above, it was only necessary to divide all the terms of the above proportion by 1.0025, when we obtain the series of values given below the others, and all semblance of conformity to the hypothesis of Prout disappears, although of course the second series of numbers bear the same ratios to each other as the first.

Antimony.	Silver.	Bromine.	Oxygen.	Hydrogen.
120.00	108.00	80.00	16.00	1.0025
119.70	107.73	79.80	15.96	1.

The numbers in the lower of the two proportions appear as incommensurable as Stas maintained that they were; and the same is true of most of the atomic weights when given, as is usual in recent text-books on chemistry, on the basis of the same hydrogen unit.

When, as the result of my investigation in the atomic weight of antimony, there were presented to me the ratios of whole numbers, as shown in the first of the above proportions, with the single exception of the atomic weight of hydrogen, the question was at once suggested, Is the ratio of the atomic weight of oxygen and hydrogen in fact that of 16: 1.0025, as the general average of all trustworthy determinations hitherto made seemed to indicate; or was there a constant error lurking in these results, which caused the very slight variation from the ratio from 16 to 1 required by the theory? I must confess that as I looked at the proportion as drawn out above, the conviction pressed upon me that this variation from the theory must be apparent, and I determined to ferret out the hidden error if possible.

The problem was easily stated, but as is usual in questioning Nature, her answer was not so easily interpreted, and it has required several years of work to reach a definite conclusion. The results were at first baffling, and it was not until grave experimental difficulties had been overcome that definite conclusions could be reached; and these conclusions were quite different from what had been anticipated. It is because this investigation is a good example of the methods of science, and an illustration drawn from personal experience of the general subject we are discussing, that I venture to ask your attention to some of its details.

On studying the methods by which the ratios of the atomic weights of oxygen and hydrogen had been determined, it was evident that they could be divided into two classes: first, the direct methods of determining the ratio, in which the proportions of oxygen and hydrogen uniting to form water were actually weighed; secondly, the confirmatory methods, to whose results small weight could be given independently of the first. Disregarding the last, as yielding no conclusive evidence on the question at issue, it appeared that all the trustworthy determinations had been made by essentially the same chemical process. This process consists in burning an undetermined amount of hydrogen by means of oxide of copper, and weighing the water which results, and further determining the amount of oxygen combined from the loss of weight of the oxide of copper.

The chemical process is a very simple one. Oxide of copper is a compound of simply copper and oxygen, and when hydrogen gas is passed over the heated oxide it takes up the oxygen to form water, and the copper is left in the metallic state.

By weighing the glass tube containing the oxide before and after the experiment, we can determine the weight of oxygen which has combined with the hydrogen; and by collecting the water formed, in appropriate desiccators, which are also weighed before and after the experiment, we can find the weight of this sole product of the process, with extreme accuracy.

NECESSARY CONDITIONS. 137

By subtracting now the weight of the oxygen found, from the weight of the water found, we have the weight of the hydrogen which has combined with the oxygen in the process; and the proportion between the weight of the oxygen and the weight of the hydrogen is one half of the atomic ratio we are seeking; because, according to our theories, one atom of oxygen combines with two atoms of hydrogen to form one molecule of water.

The proportion by weight in which hydrogen combines with oxygen to form water is about that of 1 to 8. The atomic ratio about that of 1 to 16.

Considering now the observed ratio of 1 to 8, it can be seen that the highest accuracy demands that each term of the proportion should be determined to an equal degree of exactness. Thus, if in a given experiment we have 8 grams of oxygen uniting with 1 gram of hydrogen, it is of no avail to weigh the oxygen to a tenth of a milligram, unless we can weigh the hydrogen to the same proportionate degree of accuracy; for an error 9–10 of a milligram in the weight of the water, or of 8–10 of a milligram in the weight of the oxygen, will have no more influence on the resulting ratio we are seeking than an error of 1–10 of a milligram in the weight of the hydrogen. Remembering now that 1–10 of a milligram is about the extreme limit of accuracy of our best balances, when loaded with more than a few grams of material, it can easily be seen that there is an obvious source of error in the determination we have described.

The weights actually observed are, first, that of the water formed, and secondly, that of the oxygen used.

The weight of the water can be determined to within a few tenths of a milligram; that is, with all the accuracy with which our problem requires that the larger term of the proportion 8 to 1 should be known; and for the moment this weight may be regarded as established.

It is quite different with the weight of the oxygen; this last is found by weighing the glass tube containing oxide of copper, before and after the experiment, and between the two weighings the tube is heated to a low red heat for several hours, while a stream of hydrogen gas is passing through it; and there are several causes which might lead to a slight variation in these weights, independently of the loss of oxygen, which has been used up in the process. It is unnecessary to discuss here what these causes are, but their effect would be unimportant if they only led to a small error in the observed weight of the oxygen. Unfortunately, this is not the case; for in order to find the weight of the hydrogen, we subtract from the weight of the water, accurately known, the weight of the oxygen, which may be for the causes referred to, slightly erroneous; the whole error appears in the weight of the hydrogen thus found, and in the opposite direction. If, for example, the weight of the oxygen is too large, the weight of the hydrogen will be too small by exactly the same amount; and although the error may be an inconsiderable part of the weight of the oxygen, it may be a very appreciable quantity in the weight of the hydrogen.

On the other hand, if a means could be devised for weighing the hydrogen, leaving the oxygen to be determined by subtracting this smaller weight from the weight of the water, then a small error in the observed weight of the hydrogen would have no appreciable effect on the weight of the oxygen.

Professor Dumas, who made by far the most extended series of observations by the old method, fully recognized the source of error to which I have referred, and in his paper on the subject wrote as follows: —

"Of all analyses which a chemist can undertake, that of water is the one which offers the greatest uncertainty. In fact, one part of hydrogen unites with eight parts of oxygen to form water; and nothing would be more exact than the analysis of water, if we could weigh the hydrogen as well as the water which results from its combustion.

"But the experiment is not possible under this form. We are obliged to weigh the water formed and the oxygen used to produce it, and to calculate the weight of the oxygen consumed in the process from the difference of these two weights. Thus an error of 1–900 in the weight of the water, or of 1–800 in the weight of the oxygen, affects the weight of the hydrogen by a quantity equal to 1–90 or 1–80 of its value. As these errors are in the same direction they are added to each other, and we shall have an error amounting to 1–40."

On entering upon the investigation it was evident from the outset that no advantage was to be gained by multiplying determinations by the old methods. The work had repeatedly been done by the best masters of the science, with all the accuracy of which the method was capable. The only hope of improvement lay in finding some method of weighing the hydrogen with sufficient accuracy; and it was essential to determine this weight to within 1–10,000, or at least 1–5000 of its value.

A gas can only be weighed by enclosing it in a glass globe or some similar receiver, and hydrogen is so exceedingly light that its total weight can only be a very small fraction of the containing vessel; moreover, as the buoyancy of the air is fourteen and one half times as great as the weight of the hydrogen, the variations in buoyancy caused by changes in atmospheric conditions have an all-important effect in the apparent weight. The late Professor Regnault, of Paris, devised a very ingenious method of compensation which could readily be applied in this case. It consisted in balancing the globe containing the hydrogen, hung to one arm of the balance, by a second globe of exactly the same volume and made of the same material, hung to the opposite arm, and so arranging the balance-case that both globes should hang in the same enclosure and therefore be equally affected by atmospheric changes. This method I applied in the problem before us, and after a number of trials I found it possible to make the compensation so accurate that the weight of my globe holding five litres of gas did not vary more than 1–10 of a milligram through large changes of temperature and pressure. In order now to weigh the hydrogen with this degree of accuracy, it was only necessary to exhaust the air from the glass receiver, and after balancing it as described, to fill it with hydrogen, when the increased weight (only about 4-10 of a gram with my apparatus) was the weight of the hydrogen required.

In order to burn this hydrogen I used essentially the same apparatus as previous experimenters, passing the gas over heated oxide of copper, collecting the water formed, and determining its weight. Every detail of the apparatus was the result of careful consideration, and in many cases was only reached after numerous experiments.

There were many difficulties to be overcome, but the result left nothing to be desired, and thus far the method was as perfect as the conditions required.

Everything now turned upon introducing into our globe absolutely pure hydrogen, and here the greatest difficulties were met.

Fortunately at this point I secured for my work the assistance of a young chemist, Mr. T. W. Richards, my former pupil and present assistant, of whose experimental skill I can speak as warmly as did Dumas of Stas.

A part of the difficulties of filling the globe with pure hydrogen were wholly mechanical, and the only ones which it is important I should mention here are the difficulties we met in procuring absolutely pure gas.

It will be obvious that an exceedingly small amount of impurity would be fatal to the accuracy of my method. If the hydrogen we introduced into our globe carried with it only 1-10,000 part of its volume of atmospheric air, — an impurity which it is exceedingly difficult to avoid, on account of the rapid diffusion of hydrogen and the pervasiveness of our atmosphere,— this impurity would increase the apparent weight of the hydrogen by 1–10 of a per cent, and cause an error that would be fatal to the degree of accuracy we were seeking.

In our earlier determinations we drew the hydrogen gas from a large self-acting generator charged with sulphuric acid and zinc. We used in the generator pure, but not the purest materials, which it would not have been practicable to procure on the scale on which we then expected to work; and we trusted to a complicated system of purifiers to remove the traces of sulphurous oxide or other chance impurities which the gas might contain. With hydrogen thus prepared and purified, we made a large number of determinations. We give only a few of these in the table on page 148, but those here exhibited are a fair specimen of the whole. In each case the numbers express the atomic weight of oxygen referred to hydrogen as unity; and it will be noticed that these values are not only far below the average of the previous results, 15.96, but also that they differ widely from each other.

PRELIMINARY RESULTS.

| 15.793 | 15.850 | 15.835 |
| 15.790 | 15.937 | 15.820 |

It was now obvious that the varying values must result from impurities in the hydrogen, and as we knew that our purifiers did their work efficiently, we were persuaded that the impurity must be the nitrogen of the atmosphere which entered our apparatus by diffusion at its many joints. We sought to stop such leaks by every means possible, and we thus succeeded in obtaining better and better results, but there was still far too great irregularity to make the determinations of any value, and we were finally forced to reduce the scale of our experiments.

We then constructed an apparatus in which hydrogen was prepared on a smaller scale from chemically pure zinc and hydrochloric acid. The extent of the purifiers was greatly reduced; and the number of joints also greatly reduced to only two or three, and these were carefully sealed with impervious cement. With this apparatus we made the first five determinations given in the table on page 148. In this table we give, in the first column, the weight of the hydrogen burnt; in the second column, the weight of water obtained; in the third column, the atomic weight of oxygen deduced from these weights after making allowance for the buoyancy of the air; and in the last column, the difference between each atomic weight and the average of the five.

It will be seen that we had now reached a very different result. All the values are closely concordant, the maximum difference from the average corresponding to less than 1-10 of a milligram of the hydrogen weighed; and also this mean value very closely agrees with 15.96, the average deduced from previous results.

Indeed, the agreement was as close as we could possibly expect. If there was an error it could not arise from any fluctuating cause, like the diffusion of air which we had previously encountered; it must be some constant error depending on the process. Moreover, we felt equally sure that the error, if any, could not arise from our method of weighing the hydrogen, for our result was essentially the same as that obtained by the older process, in which the oxygen, and not the hydrogen, was weighed. Still, to trace out any error, if existing, we next sought to vary the process of preparing the hydrogen, and constructed an apparatus with equal care in which hydrogen was evolved by electrolysis, that is, by the action of a current of electricity on a mixture of water and hydrochloric acid. With the gas procured from the new apparatus, we made five additional determinations, which follow the first five in the table just referred to. By inspecting the column of differences, it will be seen that the concordance in this second set is even greater than in the first. Apparently, then, we had reached a maximum which we could not exceed by varying the process; but that there might be no question on this point, we set up an apparatus still simpler than the last two, by which hydrogen gas was prepared from the metal aluminum, and a solution of caustic potash; and with hydrogen thus obtained, we made still five other determinations, whose results are given below in the same table. Here again, the average given is essentially identical with the averages of the other two series.

The evidence now seemed to be conclusive; the average of these fifteen experiments must be the true value of the atomic weight of oxygen, within a very small limit of probable error. The process had been varied in every conceivable way, and with the same identical result. Nevertheless, these results were affected by an important constant error, which, although so obvious when pointed out, had been overlooked in spite of all our care. The publication above referred to was already in print when our attention was called to the point by Lord Rayleigh, who had been working on a similar problem.

In adopting the method of Regnault for weighing the hydrogen gas subsequently burnt, we had assumed with this eminent physicist that the volume of the globe remained invariable after the air had been exhausted, when of course the pressure of the air on the exterior surface was no longer balanced by the tension of the gas within. As Regnault had himself experimented on the compressibility of glass, and as the least change in the volume of the ten litre globe which he used must have most seriously affected the values he obtained for the densities of the aeriform substances on which he experimented, — namely, air, oxygen, nitrogen, hydrogen, and carbonic acid, values which have since been regarded as among the most accurate constants of science, — it seemed safe to assume with him that the effect of the atmospheric pressure on the globe when exhausted was insensible. And it should be remembered that the investigator must always build on previous work, and that there could be no progress if he felt obliged to verify all the data which he necessarily employs. He must accept data which are regarded as well-established, and in selecting these data he is necessarily guided by authority. There could be no better authority than Regnault on the point in question; his results have been hitherto accepted without question, and a vast amount of experimental work has been based upon them.

Nevertheless, the globe which Regnault used in his determinations of gas densities, when exhausted, must have been sensibly compressed by the atmospheric pressure; and must, therefore, have appeared to weigh more than when full of gas, in consequence of the diminished displacement, and hence the lessened buoyancy of the atmosphere. This increase of weight must have been about 1.29 milligrams for every centimeter by which the volume of the globe was compressed; and the observed weights of this globe-full of the different gases on which Regnault experimented must, therefore, have been too small by the same quantity.

Unless the globe which Regnault used has been preserved it is not now possible to correct his results; since the amount of compression of a glass vessel under a constant pressure depends on conditions which vary widely and must be separately determined for each vessel. Fortunately, in our work the same glass globe had been used from the first, and there was no difficulty in determining the exact amount by which our results had been influenced by the effect under discussion. For this purpose it was only necessary to weigh the globe under water, first when exhausted, and afterwards when full of air. Under these circumstances, if there was any change of volume, the difference of buoyancy would become very marked, and could be accurately estimated.

A description of the details of these additional experiments would be out of place here. It is sufficient to say that the shrinkage of the glass balloon we used, when exhausted, amounted to nearly two cubic centimeters, or about 0.0004 of its exterior volume; that in each of our determinations the true weight of the hydrogen gas burnt was nearly two milligrams greater than the apparent weight; and that after making correction for this altered weight the atomic weight of oxygen deduced from our experiments is 15.869, instead of 15.953 as before given.

After such a catalogue of difficulties encountered, and errors avoided, it may well be asked, How can we be sure that there may not be still other causes of constant error invalidating our results? Obviously we cannot be sure. All we can do is to work earnestly and conscientiously for the truth, and leave the future to revise our results and correct our mistakes. In this way the truth will be finally reached, although the progress may be slow and halting, and our individual labor may appear to have been lost.

But although the exact value of the atomic weight of oxygen may hereafter be found to differ more or less from the number we have finally reached, the general result of our work has been to invalidate the hypothesis of Prout. This theory appears to fail at the most critical juncture. Is there then no significance in the analogies we have pointed out? Has the close approximation of the ratios of so many of the atomic weights to a proportion between whole numbers no meaning? I feel persuaded that there is a significance in the analogies, and a meaning in the coincidences; but it is not a significance or meaning that we can as yet interpret, and we must be content to wait for more knowledge and larger views.

ATOMIC WEIGHT OF OXYGEN.

First Series.

Weight of Hydrogen.	Weight of Water.	Atomic Weight of Oxygen.
0.4233	3.8048	15.977
0.4136	3.7094	15.937
0.4213	3.7834	15.960
0.4163	3.7345	15.941
0.4131	3.7085	15.954
		15.954 ± 0.0048

Second Series.

0.4112	3.6930	15.962
0.4089	3.6709	15.955
0.4261	3.8253	15.955
0.4197	3.7651	15.942
0.4144	3.7197	15.953
		15.953 ± 0.0022

Third Series.

0.42205	3.7865	15.943
0.4284	3.8436	15.944
0.4205	3.7776	15.967
0.43205	3.8748	15.937
0.4153	3.7281	15.954
0.4167	3.7435	15.967
		15.952 ± 0.0035

Total Average 15.953 ± 0.0017'.

After correcting for shrinkage of balloon under the atmospheric pressure, —

Final result . . . . 15.869 ± 0.0017.

The history of physical astronomy since the publication of the "Principia" furnishes abundant illustrations of the various features of scientific deduction on which we have dwelt in this lecture. There has been a continuous development of the deductions from the law of gravitation, and in this work the mathematical genius of two centuries has found abundant employment. The law of gravitation is one of the few fundamental principles of nature of which we feel confident that we have found the exact expression. Most of the laws of physical science are only laws of approximation; that is, laws with which the phenomena of nature closely agree, but which exhibit certain discrepancies that lead us to believe that with larger knowledge we may reach more accurate representations of the truth. But the law of gravitation appears to be exact, and we have every reason to believe that in the progress of science it will remain essentially unaltered. It is, moreover, a very simple relation. In consequence of the mode of action which we call gravity, and which is as mysterious an agent now as when first recognized, a pull is exerted between any two masses of matter in the universe, or the parts of any two masses, which is proportional directly to the products of the two masses, and indirectly to the square of their distance apart, — as may be expressed by the very simple algebraic formula:

$$F = \frac{MM'}{D^2}$$

Unlike any other physical forces with which we are familiar, this attraction is not influenced by the nature of the material of the masses, by the nature of the medium interposed, by the proximity of other masses, or by any other conditions, except solely the quantity of material in the masses and the distance between them. Newton himself made these points the subject of an experimental investigation, and his results have been confirmed by other astronomers, who, like Gauss, have been ready enough to question the finality of the law; and it is only after repeated doubts have been resolved in its favor that we have settled into the belief that it is precisely correct. Still, simple as the law is, to trace its action between the heavenly bodies becomes at once a problem of great difficulty.

So long as astronomers limited themselves to the question of central forces and considered only the action of the sun on the individual planets, the problem was comparatively simple, and admitted of the elegant solution which Newton gave in the "Principia;" but when the universality of gravity came to be recognized, and it became a question of the mutual action and reaction of all the bodies in the universe, not only of the sun on the planets but of all the planets on each other, the problem assumed a complication with which no human power could grapple, and whose complete solution was impossible. But setting aside for the time the more general problem in which many of the forces acting were so slight that they could be overlooked, there was in the fore-front of astronomy the case of the moon, acted on strongly by both the earth and the sun; and thus arose the famous problem of the three bodies, which alone has exhausted the powers of the mathematicians from Newton's time to our own. When only three bodies simultaneously attract each other the complication of effects is so great that only approximate calculations are possible, and the complete solution of this comparatively simple astronomical problem has yet to be given. Newton himself grappled with this subject, and so far succeeded as to give a tolerably accurate representation of the moon's motions; and the only open bitterness shown during his life appears to have been displayed towards his contemporary Flamstead, the first Astronomer Royal, who showed unwillingness to furnish him with the observations he needed to compare with his theory.

The consideration of the mutual attractions of the planets and the sun brings us to the more complex problem of planetary perturbations. The complete solution of this problem even in its simplest form is hopeless, and the principle on which the calculation of planetary perturbations proceeds is to reject every effect which does not lead to a quantity appreciable in observation. The quantities thus rejected are indefinitely more numerous and complex than the few larger terms which are retained; and in combining these last, numerous assumptions have to be made in order to simplify the problem. The solution reached therefore is merely partial, and the results approximate; but by such tentative methods great perfection has been reached in the theory of the planetary orbits.

One of the greatest triumphs of astronomical deduction, and yet one of the most striking illustrations of the incompleteness of its methods, was the discovery of the planet Neptune. For many years the observations of the planet Uranus, discovered by the elder Herschel in 1781, had differed markedly from the theory of its orbit, even after making every allowance for the perturbations caused by its nearest associates, Saturn and Jupiter; and what was more note-worthy, the error had gone on increasing rapidly from year to year. That this effect might be due to the disturbing influence of an unknown outer member of the solar system was a reasonable supposition; and if so, the theory of astronomy ought to be able to predict the elements of the orbit, and, therefore, to point out at any moment the position of the disturbing body. Here, however, as in other problems involving the mutual action of several bodies, a complete solution was impossible, and the tentative methods of calculation were long and tedious; so that astronomers were slow to undertake the work. But in 1843 the investigation was begun by Adams at Cambridge, England, and also, at about the same time, by Leverrier at Paris, and the issue is well known.

Leverrier communicated his result to the astronomer Galle, by a letter received at Berlin September 23, 1846; and the same evening the planet was found, nearly in the place pointed out. By a fortunate coincidence, a map of that portion of the heavens—one of the sheets of Bremiker's Berlin star map, then recently published—facilitated the search; and Galle quickly found a star of the eighth magnitude, not on the map, which the observations of the next two days showed must be the object sought. A year previously, however, Adams had communicated to Professor Challis of the Cambridge Observatory, the results of his independent calculation, which subsequently proved to correspond closely with those of Leverrier; but although search had been made, and, as afterwards appeared, the planet had been seen, it had not been recognized from want of such a map as the Berlin astronomer possessed.

Thus two separate mathematicians, without concert with each other, reached the same solution of this difficult problem, and their prediction appeared to be precisely verified. Could there be a more striking confirmation of theory, a greater achievement of human intellect? And yet in its greatest triumph mathematical analysis displayed its weakness.

On March 16, 1847, within six months of the discovery of the new planet, Professor Benjamin Peirce stated to the American Academy of Arts and Sciences, in words which I quote from their Proceedings, "The planet Neptune is not the planet to which geometrical analysis has directed the telescope." This declaration, first received with distrust, proved to be fully justified. The planet of the theory had a mean distance from the sun of from 35 to 37.9 times that of the earth, with a corresponding period of revolution of from 207 to 233 years. The actual Neptune has a mean distance of only 30, with a period of about 168 years. At the time of the discovery, the planet of the theory and the actual Neptune had approximately the same apparent position, or, as astronomers say, were in conjunction.

But this was a "happy accident," and to this chance the discovery of the actual planet must be ascribed.

As Professor Peirce clearly showed at the time, this singular result depended on the approximate and tentative character of the method of calculation necessarily employed. Had the conditions been exactly known, and had the mathematical analysis been exhaustive, the actual planet which caused the perturbations would doubtless have been at once pointed out; but several approximate solutions of the problem were possible. Of these the theoretical planet was one, the actual planet was a second, and still others might be distinguished.

The problem could not be approached without making an assumption in regard to the solar distance, and as both mathematicians were led, by the so-called law of Bode, to make the same assumption, they came to the same approximate result. Unfortunately, the law assumed to regulate the relative distances of the planets from the sun conspicuously failed in the case of Neptune, and we have heard but little of it since. According to this law, the solar distance of Neptune should have been about 39.6 times the earth's distance. Leverrier tried successive assumptions, beginning with 39.1, and finding that with a diminishing value the conditions of the problem were at first better satisfied, while afterwards the discrepancies increased, he concluded that the value must be within the limits stated above. Adams followed in part the same course, although his calculations were less full. The planet found had a distance of 30 only, and if the calculations had been

METHOD OF CALCULATION. 155

extended to this limit, another solution of the problem would have appeared which proved to be the true one. But the second solution was not suspected; because at an assumed distance of 35.3 there was a singular point which introduced peculiar disturbances. In a word, the theoretical planet was an approximate solution of the problem for the field of research covered by the analysis; while the real planet was outside of this field, and separated from it by a barrier which the partial analysis could not overstep.

You cannot find in the whole history of science a more striking illustration than this, both of the power and of the limitations of deductive thought. The discovery of a new planet appeals strongly to the imagination of men; and the story of the mathematician who from his study directed the astronomer where to find a predicted member of the solar system, is constantly told as an evidence of intellectual power,—less frequently as a signal instance of mental limitations and human fallibility; and yet the last is the more impressive lesson. Here, however, as so often in human affairs, weakness was made strength. Through striving, the planet was discovered and the boundaries of knowledge were extended.

Obviously there was a large element of chance, or — as I prefer to call it — Providence, in the discovery of Neptune; and such chances have been repeatedly the turning-points in the history of science. The accidental breaking of a crystal of Iceland spar revealed to Haüy the structure of crystalline bodies. A chance reflection of light from the windows of the Luxembourg Palace in Paris disclosed to Malus the laws of polarization. The twitching of the legs of a frog first made known to Galvani the existence of low tension electricity. The swing of a compass-needle on his lecture-table opened to Oersted the phenomena of electro-magnetism, and was the simple beginning from which have come all the wonderful applications of electrical currents. In the remark that Lagrange is said to have made of Newton, that "such accidents happen only to those who deserve them," there is a deeper philosophy than was probably intended. It must be remembered that to a higher intelligence there can be no such thing as accident; and that "the fortuitous concourse of atoms," like any other event, would be seen to have its antecedents and causes if our imperfect perceptions could take cognizance of their existence. Moreover, even on our plane, numbers would fail to convey a conception of the utter hopelessness of the chance, on the doctrine of probabilities, that the right accident would happen to the right man at the right time.

On the other hand, such experience as I have narrated should show us that close coincidences of approximate results are in themselves no sure test of truthfulness, and carry with them but little weight. Men of science are familiar with this principle, and almost every investigator could enforce it by numerous examples. But on most men such coincidences make an extraordinary impression; and many of the delusions of society, including the astrology of the past and the pseudo-spiritualism of the present, find their chief support in the apparent coincidences which a wide latitude of variation permits.

Lastly, such experience should teach us how unsafe it is to rely implicitly on popular statements of scientific deductions. An impression widely prevails that however important a knowledge of the general results of science may be, it is not necessary that the literary man or the general scholar should acquaint himself with scientific methods. But it is obvious, from what has been said, that no accurate knowledge of the facts of nature is possible without a knowledge of the methods by which the facts have been established. The phenomena of nature are so complex, and the simplest effects so modified by concurring agencies, that they cannot be fully comprehended unless studied in their natural relations. The phenomena described in text-books are often not realities of nature, but ideal relations which are as much abstractions as the conceptions of geometry. As systems of science such books have their value; but their necessarily general statements are not often a sound basis for theological arguments. We cannot safely reason from the facts of nature until we know them with all their limitations; and if I have enabled you to realize this truth, my chief object in this lecture has been gained.

LECTURE VI.

LAWS OF NATURE.

IN the previous lectures we have endeavored to make clear the distinction between induction and deduction in scientific investigation. Induction is the discernment, recognition, and verification of a general principle of nature previously unknown. The discernment may be more or less accurate, the recognition more or less satisfactory, the verification more or less complete; but the process is essentially an intuitive act of the mind working upon previous knowledge or experience, and familiar acquaintance with natural phenomena. Hence, under favorable conditions, it is more or less spontaneous, and cannot be regulated by methods or directed by rules. It is, in a word, the product of genius.

Deduction is the evolution by logical processes, mathematical or otherwise, of the consequences, inferences, or implications which a general principle includes or suggests. It may be more or less direct, more or less difficult, more or less exhaustive; but in any case the results were implicitly involved in the premises established or assumed. It is a creature of methods, a slave to rules, and deals with syllogisms, equations, observations, experiments, and measurements of every kind. It is the task of the many, the work of the great army of scientific laborers.

Induction raises the level of human knowledge; deduction expands that knowledge. Induction opens new fields of investigation; deduction explores these fields. Induction discloses hidden treasures; deduction appropriates and uses them. Induction soars; deduction creeps. Induction aspires; deduction contemplates. Induction is imaginative; deduction is realistic. Induction is theoretical; deduction is practical. Induction is bold and confident; deduction is cautious and sceptical.

I am well aware that the position I have taken is not wholly in harmony with the mechanical view of induction which the authority of Bacon has so strongly impressed on English thought; but I still feel confident that I am in sympathy with the great body of scholars who are practically familiar with scientific methods.

Professor Jevons, who as a logician classified induction as inverse deduction, thus wrote in regard to the nature of the process itself: "All induction is but the inverse application of deduction; and it is by the inexplicable mental action of a gifted mind that a multitude of heterogeneous facts are caused to range themselves in luminous order as the results of some uniformly acting law." This is the best authority I could quote; and I now pass on to consider certain distinctions among the results of induction, which I hope will serve to make our conceptions of the subject still clearer.

Of all the results of induction there are none so

familiar or so striking as the laws of nature; and of the aspects of the material universe there is none which is more appalling to the religious mind than the reign of law. Law and Providence seem incompatible and mutually exclusive. "The wind bloweth where it listeth," without regard to the tempest-tossed ship freighted with the hopes of nations. The laws of motion do not spare precious lives when a broken rail turns the rushing train from its appointed track. The law of gravitation made no discrimination among the victims on whom the Tower of Siloam fell; and so fire and blood, pestilence and famine, tornado and earthquake, have ever involved the good and the bad alike in common ruin.

Law is inexorable, cruel, pitiless; and no wonder that as thus viewed the conception of law should be a hindrance to faith. But this view of nature is a misconception which arises from a superficial knowledge of the facts; and the law of the text-books, or of the popular imagination, is for the most part an ideal phantom. Correct views on this subject are of such supreme importance in natural theology that I propose to devote this lecture to a discussion of some of the distinctive features and manifold variations which the so-called laws of nature present.

A law of nature is simply a declaration or statement of a certain order, sequence, or relation, observed among material phenomena. Jevons says, "The laws of nature are simply general propositions concerning the correlation of properties which have been found to hold true of bodies hitherto observed." And again: "A law of nature is not a uniformity which must be obeyed by all objects; but merely a uniformity which is, as a matter of fact, obeyed by those objects which have come beneath our observation." Thus the first law of motion declares that any mass of matter continues in its state of rest or motion until acted on by some force external to itself. The law of Mariotte affirms that the volume of a given mass of gas is inversely proportional to its tension. The law of gravitation states that any two masses of matter attract each other with a force directly proportional to the product of the two masses, and inversely proportional to the distance between them; and so we might multiply examples. Notice, nothing is affirmed in regard to the mode of action in either case. *The phenomena observed may be the effect of a single cause, or the resultant of several causes;* but the law takes no cognizance of any such feature. It only recognizes the order, sequence, or relations it describes. This is a most important point, to which I would ask your special attention.

The laws of nature are simply statements of observed relations. They are not efficient causes or modes of action of any kind; and whatever features with such an aspect may be superimposed upon the formal propositions in the description or by the imagination, is something superadded to their only real sanction as laws of nature.

There may seem to be in the statement of the law of gravitation, as usually given and as enunciated above, something conflicting with the positive position here laid down. When it is said that one mass of matter attracts another, or, as Newton himself enunciated the law, every particle of matter in the universe attracts every other particle, it might appear as if a mode of action was declared in the proposition; and I have no doubt that the law is so understood by nine out of ten of the students who repeat the statement. But Newton intended to convey no such conception; and no such conception was received by the scholars for whom he wrote.

It is true, however, that one mode of explaining the law is to assume that there resides in the ultimate particles of matter some unknown virtue which determines the attraction. But this is a pure hypothesis, one of those redundancies referred to above, for which the law must not be held accountable. When Newton himself was asked whether he had any conception of this kind he is said to have replied: "Hypotheses non fingo."

Moreover, the whole tendency of modern science is entirely opposed to any theory which assumes an inherent potency in the particles of matter; and, in the case of gravitation, such an hypothesis, as we shall see in the next lecture, is beset with insuperable difficulties and objections. It would be better if we could enunciate the law without using the word "attract;" but this cannot be done without an awkward circumlocution. Of course what is meant is simply that two bodies, if free to move, would act as if they were pulled by a force varying according to the well-known law; and what is true of this proposition is equally true of the statement of every recognized law of nature. All such propositions are intended to declare solely a relation between phenomena; and in any case if the language implies more, there is something accessory, which careful criticism will distinguish and eliminate.

When such propositions are briefly enunciated in ordinary language there is always danger of misapprehension and confusion; and hence one of the objections to unguarded popular statements of scientific principles to which I have referred. For instance, from the ordinary statement of the law of inertia — every mass of matter continues in its state of rest or motion until acted on by some force — I know by experience that a large majority of students derive the idea that an original state of motion must have been the effect of some force; and yet this is precisely the reverse of the impression that the words were intended to convey; and in general I may say that it is rare that students acquire from text-books on physics correct conceptions of the fundamental principles of mechanics.

The popular conception which so constantly associates causation with a law of nature undoubtedly arises from the figurative use of the word law in this connection. Law in human relations implies a law-giver; and therefore we associate with human laws the personal attributes of the law-giver. The laws of the Medes and Persians were inflexible; the laws of the Romans were equitable; the old laws of England were cruel; the modern English laws are more merciful, — simply because, each and all, they reflected the character of the men who made and administered them; but to call the law of gravitation pitiless is like calling the multiplication table inexorable, or a prisoner's chains cruel. Of course it will be said such language is figurative; but the difficulty is that the distinction between the figurative and the real is not always kept clear; and this is not the only case in which mental confusion and logical fallacy have arisen from the use of familiar terms.

Still, while all must admit that the definition of a law of nature as here given is conformable to the best usage among scientific scholars, it may be said, the awful fact remains that amidst the misfortunes of man, the whole aspect of external nature is hard and pitiless, and fine-drawn distinctions do not relieve the suffering that the relentless march of natural phenomena entails. Certainly not! We cannot solve the terrible problem which the evil of the world everywhere presents. This is a fact of nature, as well as law. But do not confound it with law. Its sources are far deeper, among those hidden springs of being whence flow also the equally mysterious relations of personality and free will. Do not then by any perversion of thought associate malevolence with the laws of nature. To a finite being, law means reliance, confidence, and repose. It is heaven-born, beneficent order; but it has no potency in itself, and may be used by the powers of evil as well as by the powers of good.

Another popular misconception of the relations of a law of nature appears in the trite argument so often urged as a disproof of the Christian miracles. It is impossible to conceive, it is said, that a law of nature should be broken. Certainly it is, and so it is impossible to conceive that the qualities of metallic gold should be changed. Were the properties of gold changed in the least degree the material would be no longer gold; and so, were the relations predicated by the law of gravitation altered, we should at once have a different law. I do not say that either of these changes is possible, much less probable; but I do maintain that they are both conceivable, and not so inconsistent with our actual knowledge of the order of nature as to render the supposition inherently absurd. So far from this, the transmutation of the metals was the favorite problem of the elder chemists; and it is well known that Sir Isaac Newton, whose scientific sobriety cannot be questioned, devoted a great deal of time to experiments in this direction; and, although in a somewhat different form, the question has been reopened in our own day. So also, as before said, the most eminent men of science have seriously considered whether the law of gravitation might not be modified under new conditions.

Could each law be traced to a *single* definite cause, it is obvious that a change in the law would imply a corresponding change in the cause, and, therefore an alteration of purpose, or method, inconsistent with our philosophy either of an intelligent first cause or even of a self-evolving, self-sustained cosmogony. But these are not the conditions. The laws of nature are relations of phenomena which, in most cases, at least, are obviously resultants of *many causes* whose action is inextricably commingled; and it is perfectly possible to conceive of a new element introduced into one of the chains of causation which would utterly alter the final result. I do not say that this is possible; but I do say that we have no positive knowledge which makes such a contingency impossible.

Man cannot increase by the smallest fraction either the material or the energy he employs; but he can introduce conditions into the chain of causation, by which he is able to control and determine events, and even to alter the face of the earth. Why, then, may not new issues appear in nature? Why may not a new force overrule an old one? Why indeed may not unrecognized agencies, which have always existed, and whose effects have been slowly accumulating, at any moment appear as important factors in human affairs and relations? Not only do I see no reason for believing that we possess an exhaustive knowledge of nature's powers; but on the contrary I am persuaded that even in the most familiar fields, there may at any time appear indications of forces hitherto undiscovered, which may be capable of momentous effects. Remember that it is only a century ago that the first indications were noticed of a power which is now one of the chief agencies of our civilization. And what were these indications? Only the momentary twitching of a frog's legs!

Let it be understood that I make no claim to substantiate or explain miracles; but I do maintain that we cannot disprove Divine interference in the course of nature; and that the scientific probabilities against such occurrences may be fairly set off against the moral presumptions in their favor. To me it seems to be a question of evidence, upon which our knowledge of the laws of nature has no bearing. Moreover, to my mind the marvellous in these events is no weighty evidence against their credibility. What could be more marvellous than many of the revelations of modern science? As I distinctly remember, the revolving of the vanes of Crooke's radiometer, seemed to me, when I first saw the instrument, as much out of the ordinary course of nature, as would the turning of water into wine. Investigation showed that the motion was the normal result of a force which had always been acting, though unsuspected; and so at any moment a strange phenomenon may put us in possession of a new force which will overrule all the powers of the world, and make more than the dreams of Aladdin sober realities. Nothing is too marvellous to be believed, provided it is substantiated by satisfactory evidence.

Why, then, it may be asked, do you not believe in mind-reading, clairvoyance, faith-cure, and other so-called spiritual manifestations, with which the popular mind is from time to time deluded? Simply because they are not attested by satisfactory evidence. It is upon this ground, and not on account of their strangeness or improbability, that we hesitate to accept them. There are doubtless facts, and very incredible facts, concerning these matters, that are well attested; and there may be agencies which have never been recognized. But the phenomena claimed to exist are so complex, and so obscured by unconscious self-deception, or by actual imposture, that no undoubted truth, or definite relation, has as yet been established.

Societies have been formed, both in this country

and in England, for the promotion of psychical research; but it may be questioned if, in the presence of so many problems of nature which are within our grasp, it is good policy to expend energy on those which, for the time at least, are hopelessly involved; and also whether it is wise to concentrate public attention on abnormal states, or diseased conditions of mind, which will certainly be excited and spread thereby. Nevertheless, if a single clearly new phenomenon were elicited by such investigations, who can question that it would be studied with the same zest as was Crooke's radiometer?

Of course I do not forget the paralyzing impression of desolation and despair which in some moods the uniformity of nature forces on the mind; but this impression, though an unquestionable feature of human experience from the earliest times, has no pertinency to the laws of nature. This aspect of nature affects most strongly minds of an imaginative temperament, and is one which the study of science rather tends to soften and elucidate. It is seen as clearly by the poet as by the philosopher; and it inspires fatalism more often than scepticism. It is a part of the discipline of life, to which all sorts and conditions of men must bow. This aspect of nature has, then, no special relations to our scientific knowledge; only the facts of science are often perverted to sustain the terribly gloomy philosophy it suggests. Moreover, science has pointed out the one consideration which may solve the mystery.

The insect's life is often only a summer's day whose sunshine knows no change; and may not the uniformity of nature during human life be like a shifting scene to Him with whom we have to do? Such a doctrine is wholly consistent with our knowledge of the laws of nature; and the point has been so forcibly put by the late Charles Babbage, in the "Ninth Bridgewater Treatise," the most profound of those celebrated works, that I cannot do better than to quote his words. After describing the calculating machine, which is so inseparably associated with his name, and showing that such an engine might work invariably by one law of action, during any finite number of steps however great, and yet at a predetermined point introduce a break in the series,— for instance, after counting up the natural number to a term expressed by a hundred million digits, — he writes: " If every letter now before the reader's eye were changed into a figure, and if all the figures contained in a thousand such volumes were arranged in order, the whole together would yet fall far short of the vast induction the observer would have had in favor of the truth of the law of natural numbers; yet shall the engine, true to the prediction of its director, after the lapse of myriads of ages, fulfil its task and give that one, the first and only exception, to that time-sanctioned law." What would have been the chances in favor of the perfect continuity of the series immediately prior to this break? Certainly, we may add, as great as are the chances that the sun will rise to-morrow.

Now this same machine, as Mr. Babbage also showed, may be so constructed and set as to change its law after an appointed number of terms, and then proceed to follow a new law as invariably as before. Thus, after giving the natural numbers for a certain period, it might suddenly begin to give square or cube numbers; and it is possible to conceive of a machine by which such transitions might be indefinitely repeated.

If such things are possible in human mechanism, why not in the scheme of nature? That in the short history of science we have not observed such changes is no proof that they may not take place. If they do come to pass we should expect from all analogies that they would come with extreme slowness, according to our measures of time, and without observation. And certainly during the geological ages changes have come to pass for which we can give otherwise no clear account.

Of course such considerations as Babbage has so eloquently urged are no arguments, but they do help the imagination; and this is a question in which the imagination has raised all the difficulty, and is therefore chiefly to be addressed.

We have tacitly assumed thus far that the laws of nature are all equally definite and equally exact; but this is very far from being true. In most cases, at least, the phenomena correlated under a law admit of a more or less wide variation; and the proposition which we call a law is an ideal rather than an actual relation,—an abstraction, rather than an entity. This is the next point to which I wish to ask your attention; and its bearing on the previous considerations is obvious. For if it shall appear that the laws of nature vary with different relations, and are not the hard and fast rules which have been assumed; that they are modes of thought, and not modes of action; then all that has been said in regard to the independence of causation, and the possibility of interference, will be seen to have still greater force than at first appeared.

Very few of the recognized laws of nature are absolutely definite; and of these few, with the exception possibly of the law of gravitation, the invariability must be assumed; for it cannot be proved, at least absolutely. In the present state of knowledge we should class as among these definite laws, the law of conservation of mass, the law of conservation of energy, the laws of motion, and the law of gravitation. Now, although we may have no question that all these laws are absolutely fixed, and can never be expected in the least degree to alter in their manifestation, yet there is not one of them which is susceptible of experimental proof, except, to a limited extent, the law of gravitation.

Take, for example, the first law of motion, the law of inertia, as it is also called, and which we have before more than once enunciated. We cannot demonstrate experimentally that a body will continue in a state of motion until acted on by some external force. On the surface of the earth, even under the most favorable conditions, all motion is soon arrested by friction, or by some other mode of impact; and the most we can do is to show that in proportion as such resistances are removed, the longer the motion continues, — a form of inference which has been called " the principle of successive approach," but which is obviously no proof. Could the law of inertia be verified experimentally, perpetual motion would be possible; but even with all our experimental skill we have not made the most distant approach to such a condition.

It is a mistake of ignorance to infer that perpetual motion means unlimited work; and yet it is this very erroneous inference which alone gives a popular interest to the question. Work done by a moving body necessarily involves loss of motion; and the effects of friction are merely examples of this general principle. Perpetual motion is theoretically possible, but work without the loss of motion, or the expenditure of energy in some form, is inconceivable; and the assumption implies a confusion of mechanical conceptions. It is unnecessary for our purpose to dwell on this point, and we allude to it only because it serves indirectly to illustrate the character of the law under consideration. Nor need we do more than refer to the grand displays of perpetual motion revealed to us by astronomy, which seem at first sight to be most conspicuous illustrations of the principle. But the law is here so overlaid and obscured that observations on the motions of the planets cannot be regarded as a direct proof of its validity. Indeed, originally the law was an assumption made to explain these very motions, and is, therefore, an induction based on astronomical facts, not a deduction that can be demonstrated by them.

As with the law of inertia so is it with the law of conservation of mass. We cannot demonstrate that the amount of material in nature has never been

CONSERVATION OF MASS. 173

increased by the smallest amount. All we can do in any case is to show that the amount of material with which we experiment is not perceptibly altered in the various transformations through which it passes,—assuming of course that the amount of material, or to use a technical term, the mass, is accurately measured by the weight. In a chemical process, when we can weigh all the materials concerned, we find that within the unavoidable experimental errors, often very large, the sum of the weights of the products of the process is exactly equal to the sum of the weights of the factors; and after a very wide experience with similar results we assume that the two sums are always exactly equal. Hence we represent every chemical process as an equation, writing on the left of the sign of equality the several symbols which represent the weights of the factors, and on the right the corresponding symbols which represent the weights of the products. Obviously, however, we can never demonstrate the exactness and universality of the law which our chemical equations assume. The constancy of the law is of necessity a question of inference. Still, as in the case of inertia, we can appeal to phenomena which render the inference in the highest degree conclusive.

There are, for example, a very large number of chemical processes which it is possible to conduct in an hermetically closed vessel,—as in a sealed preserve jar; so that by weighing the vessel before and after the experiment, it can be shown that no change of weight has come from the chemical process which has taken place inside, — a result which we should confidently expect, since nothing could get in or out of the sealed vessel.

The burning of charcoal in oxygen gas, under such conditions as just described, furnishes a very striking illustration of the principle under discussion. When a lump of charcoal burns, a solid material, the fuel, is converted into an aeriform substance, the smoke; and the result seems at first sight glaringly to contradict the assumed law; but when we burn the coal in a closed jar it is obvious that as there has been no change of weight, there can have been no loss of material; and it is further evident that the substance of the coal must have been absorbed by the oxygen gas to form the aeriform product we call smoke.

We can now pass to the earth as a whole; and regarding our dwelling-place as a globe isolated in space from which no material escapes, and into which none enters, — except an occasional meteorite, — we can at once recognize relations similar to those of a sealed jar, in which all terrestrial nature appears as a grand illustration of the conservation of mass. But obviously such illustrations, although they may be the basis of well-founded inferences, are no proofs of the absolute exactness and invariability of the law; and a study of either of the other laws we have classed as exact would bring out the same features. But this is a subsidiary point, and it is not necessary to dwell upon it further.

The laws classed as exact present also another character worthy of your consideration, which, although it cannot be definitely formulated in the present state of our knowledge, is probably fundamental; and it distinguishes these special cases from the great body of the laws of nature whose relations we shall study later. Such principles as the laws of motion, and the laws of conservation, whether of mass or of energy, seem to be fundamental relations of the material universe; and not the modes of action of external agencies. They are like the essential qualities of matter, — extension, impenetrability, mobility, — and not like the accidental qualities, which may be regarded as superimposed upon matter by the action of some mode of energy, — such as color, temperature, or magnetism. Consequently they are simple instead of complex relations.

Consider, for instance, inertia, which is often classed as a quality of matter. This is not an active but wholly a passive relation, as the common use of the word "inert" indicates. Matter has no power within itself to change its state or condition in any way. Such changes in all cases imply an external agent, and an expenditure of energy, which is to be distinguished from the passive mass on which it acts.

It has been said that the original atoms contained the potency of all possible being; and if by this is meant that they were the beginnings of things, —

" . . . rudis indigestaque moles,
Nec quicquam nisi pondus iners, congestaque eadem
Non bene junctarum discordia semina rerum, — "

the proposition is harmless enough, if we accept the general theory that atoms are the final result of the analysis of matter; but if it is meant that the atoms have actual creative potency, and all future being involved in their substance, in the same sense that the flower is infolded in the bud, then it is a sufficient answer to all such speculations to say that they are wholly at variance with the manifest tendency of modern science. If there be one thing more marked in that tendency than another, it is to distinguish energy and matter as two distinct and separate entities; and to regard matter as wholly inert, utterly lifeless and dead, except in so far as it is controlled and energized from without. We believe this to be the correct view, not only in regard to such manifestations of material bodies as we refer to heat, light, and electricity; but also in regard to those seemingly inherent forces which hold the parts of a body together, and determine the effects of cohesion, elasticity, and the like.

For example, we distinguish among the conditions of magnetic phenomena what we call the "field of force." Masses of iron brought into that field — that is, into any space thus conditioned — become at once magnetic, and attract or repel each other as the case may be. Now it is a plausible conception that we live in a space conditioned not only by magnetism, but by various other agencies, which may determine the cohesion and structure of solid bodies. Every year I show to my class an experiment which I never witness myself without being strongly impressed by the wonderful relations which it illustrates, and the still more wonderful relations it suggests. On the top of a board, resting on the poles of a powerful electro-magnet, I place a large, loose pile of wrought-iron nails. When the current of a dynamo-machine passes through the coil of the instrument, a magnetic field is established throughout all the space in the neighborhood of the poles; and with this the board in no way interferes, although it keeps the nails from direct contact with the magnet itself. As soon as the current passes, and the field is established, the loose nails, by their mutual attractions, — thus determined, — become a tough, plastic mass, which can be moulded into the form of an arch, or of any similar structure. But when the current is broken the magnetic virtue of the field disappears, and the structure that had been reared, crumbles into nails. Analogy suggests that the atoms of matter, inert in themselves, are similarly conditioned, and that all structures would be resolved, and all forms of matter disappear, if the Presence which sustains them were withdrawn.

Now, just as the first law of motion appears to be merely a declaration of a passive quality of matter, so it seems to me all the other laws we have classed as exact are fundamental attributes either of matter or of energy. This may not appear as the laws are usually stated; but an analysis of the relations thus enunciated will always show their true character. Thus in regard to the law of conservation of mass, to which we have just referred in another connection, — it would be easy so to state the law as to make it appear arbitrary and anomalous. That in every chemical change the sum of the weights of the products formed should be exactly equal to the weights of the factors consumed; for example, that when water is resolved by an electrical current into oxygen and hydrogen, the combined weights of these two aeriform substances should be exactly equal to the weight of the liquid water used up in the process; or, what is still more remarkable, that when coal or wood burn, the weight of the smoke added to the weight of the ashes will be, to the smallest fraction of a grain, exactly equal to the weight of the fuel which has disappeared, and for the most part flown up the chimney, — all this does seem at first sight to be such a precise conformity to weights and measures as could never have been secured unless specially ordained; but a few moments' consideration will show that this law, so far from being an ordinance superimposed as it were upon matter, is a relation necessarily arising from its very constitution. In any mechanical process you at once recognize that there can be no real loss of material. When silver and gold bullion are coined or made into ware and trinkets, you confidently expect, from your knowledge of material relations, to find all the metal in the manufactured articles, — of course excepting a small loss from dispersion by attrition, abrasure, or otherwise, for which you can readily account. Why should not the same be true in a chemical process? If there be no loss of precious metal when one hundred pounds of silver are coined at the mint, why should there be any loss when the same amount of bullion is converted into nitrate of silver by the manufacturing chemist? Certainly, not only can we find no "sufficient reason" for expecting a change of relations under such circumstances, but also the more we study material relations the more evident does it appear that conservation of mass is simply the manifestation of the persistency of the mode of being we call matter. In other words, the study of the relations of matter, and even our own familiar experience, has produced the conviction that beneath the evanescent qualities of changing substances and the decaying forms of organic structures, there is a material substratum which is permanent and unchangeable; and that the law of chemistry we have been studying is simply the manifestation of this fundamental essence of matter. The illusion which is produced by the escape of colorless aeriform matter in the burning of fuel, and in many other less familiar chemical processes, is easily corrected by conducting the experiment in an air-tight vessel, as we have before described.

The same essential feature appears in the second of the great laws of chemistry, which we have already described as the law of combining proportions. That hydrogen gas should combine with oxygen gas to form water in the exact proportions of 2.000 to 15.869, as was shown in the last lecture, does seem at first sight as accidental or arbitrary a relation as could well be imposed on these elementary substances; but if we look at the subject from another point of view, it will be seen that some definiteness of relation is implied by the other essential attributes of matter, even though our present knowledge may not enable us to see the reason of the precise value of the proportion in a given case. It is obvious, for example, that assuming the supply of oxygen unlimited, we should expect to obtain twice as much water by burning twice as much hydrogen; and so, on the other hand, were the supply of hydrogen unlimited, we should expect the same result by using twice as much oxygen; otherwise all our knowledge of material relations would be confounded. But this implies that the relative weights of hydrogen, oxygen, and water, which concur in the familiar process of burning hydrogen gas, must be definite,— although we have no means of predicting that the definite proportion should be exactly that of 2.000 to 15.869 to 17.869.

Take, as another example, the simple chemical process which results when we bring together carbonate of soda, hydrochloric acid, and water. The products of this process are common salt, carbonic acid gas, and a small additional amount of water. Here again common-sense, as we might say, tells us that we must proportion our carbonate of soda to the amount of carbonic acid gas we desire to make. If we need three times as much gas we must take three times as much soda, and so in regard to any of the other materials concerned in the process; but this implies a definite relation between the several factors and products of the chemical change, or, in other words, this familiar experience and common-sense imply the law of definite proportions.

In the two cases last cited these so-called laws of chemistry are evidently, as we have before said, merely fundamental relations of matter, and not the modes of action of external agents. To the same category belongs the law of conservation of energy, and so obviously that I need not press the point; but in regard to the great law of gravitation there is a manifest difficulty of interpreting the phenomena from this point of view. As we have already pointed out, the usual statement of the law implies an attractive force, and therefore an active power of great potency. Nevertheless, I am inclined to the opinion that here also the facts are best explained on the view that gravitation is simply a manifestation of a fundamental relation between energy and mass.

There are several circumstances which would support the opinion thus expressed, although I have only time to allude to them here. In the first place, gravity is the only attractive force which is directly proportional to the mass. Magnetic and electrical attractions follow wholly different and far more complex laws. In the second place, the diminution of gravity with the square of the distance is simply the law of the diffusion of any radiant energy through space; as may be seen in the intensity of illumination on screens at different distances from a luminous source. In the third place, the attraction of one mass is not in the least influenced by the proximity of similarly attracting masses. Thus, each of two weights on a scale-pan exerts its specific effect independent of its association; but two magnets or two electrified bodies when placed in juxtaposition do not exert the same invariable concurrent action. In the fourth place, the attraction of gravity is wholly independent of the intervening medium. Two bodies on the opposites sides of this globe would attract each other with the same force whether the earth were in the way or not; while electrical or magnetic attraction is very greatly influenced by the nature of the dielectric or diamagnetic which intervenes. In fine, activities which are superinduced, like electrical or magnetic attractions, follow wholly different and vastly more complex laws than the simple relations to mass and space which gravity exhibits. Hence the grounds of the opinion expressed above that the law of gravitation is a proposition which expresses, not the mode of action of a special force or agency, but simply a fundamental and necessary relation between energy and mass.

I freely admit that the opinion I have expressed in regard to the laws classed as exact may be open to philosophical objections, and I do not advance it as a well-grounded, much less as an accepted doctrine. Since, however, I expect to show in my next lecture that the great body of natural laws, as enunciated in our systems of science, are merely ideal relations, which the phenomena of nature approach, but which are rarely if ever realized, I felt it incumbent on me to give a clear account of those fundamental principles that appear to be more exact. My one object is to make clear to you the aspect of the laws of nature as seen from the standpoint of a student of physical science, with all the indefiniteness which the view presents, and with the impenetrable clouds which limit the prospect on every side. Do not, however, accept my opinions, or rely on my judgment; but study the phenomena for yourselves, not as drawn in sharp outlines by popular writers, but as exhibited by nature, with all their limitations, all their variations, and all their obscurity. Make sure of the actual facts; so that you shall build your philosophy on a firm and enduring basis that cannot be moved.

LECTURE VII.

DETERMINATE AND INDETERMINATE LAWS.

OF the great body of the laws of physical science which are described in the treatises on physics or chemistry, I could not select a fairer illustration than the law of Mariotte. This law was discovered during the last half of the seventeenth century, wholly independently, by the Abbé Mariotte in France and by the famous English philosopher Boyle, and is often called by English writers "the law of Boyle." Since that time all the relations of the law have been repeatedly and carefully investigated, and there are few principles of science in regard to which our knowledge is more precise. According to the usual formula this law declares that *the volume of a given mass of gas is inversely as the pressure to which it is exposed;* or in other words, that as the pressure increases or diminishes, the volume contracts or expands in precisely the same proportion. For example, if we have a perfectly flexible balloon, partially inflated, the volume of the confined gas will contract or expand in absolutely the same proportion as the pressure of the air on the outside is increased or diminished. We can also enunciate the law in another form, which applies to any mass of aeriform matter, whether confined or not,— saying that the density of a given atmosphere is directly proportional to its tension. But since the tension of a gas must necessarily balance the pressure to which it is exposed, and since the density of a gas must increase as its volume diminishes, the last statement only describes another phase of the same principle.

This law discovered by Mariotte is of fundamental importance in many departments of chemistry and physics, especially in meteorology; but in nature its simple working rarely if ever appears. The volume and density of a mass of aeriform matter not only varies with the external pressure or internal tension, but similar and as great changes are caused by variations of temperature. Considerable although less marked effects are produced by moisture, and in passing from one place to another a sensible change may be caused by the variations in the intensity of gravity. In any case the observed phenomenon is the resultant of all these partial effects, which may either concur or tend to balance each other. Constantly, then, in practice, the law must be disguised and its action obscured. The same is true of all similar laws. The phenomena of nature are usually very complex results, and such laws as the one we are discussing are the simpler elements into which we attempt to analyze the phenomena. But this, although a perplexing, is only an incidental circumstance, and we must consider the aberrations of the law itself.

Even when abstracted from all concomitant conditions, so far is the law of Mariotte from exact that it holds absolutely in no single instance, unless inferentially as a passing phase of a continuous change. When we study the subject minutely and pay regard to small differences we find that each distinct aeriform substance has a rate of its own, and is, as it were, a law unto itself. At the common temperature most gases, as nitrous oxide, carbonic acid, ammonia, oxygen, nitrogen, and the mixture of the last two we call air, contract under pressure to a perceptibly greater extent than the law authorizes. At high pressures the deviation becomes very marked, and as we approach the pressures under which the gases are condensed to liquids no semblance of the law is left. Hydrogen, on the other hand, the lightest condition of aeriform matter, alone contracts less than the law requires. Hydrogen therefore seems to present unique relations, and to stand apart by itself. But the experiments of Regnault indicate that this relation depends to a large extent on temperature. He observed that although carbonic acid deviates widely from the law of Mariotte at the freezing-point of water, it conforms almost precisely to it at the boiling-point. So also he noticed that air deviates from the law much less at an elevated temperature than at the ordinary temperature of the atmosphere; and he concluded that a temperature could easily be attained at which the deviation would become insensible to our means of observation. He even thought it probable that at a very high temperature the air would again deviate from the law, but in the opposite direction, like hydrogen at the ordinary temperature. Generalizing these observations it is supposed that the same would be true of all gases, — namely, that with each aeriform substance there is some temperature at which it conforms to Mariotte's law; that at all temperatures below this point the gas is compressed more than the law authorizes, and at all temperatures above this point it is compressed less than the law demands. In a word, the law is an ideal relation, which is realized, if at all, only under the concurrence of conditions which it is impossible to command.

Mariotte's law illustrates in a very forcible manner the character of the large class of the so-called laws of nature we are considering, and its history furnishes one of the best examples of refined scientific investigation. I could readily multiply examples, but further discussion would be tedious, and would add nothing to the force of my argument; for I feel confident that it will be generally allowed that I have selected as fair and as typical an illustration as I could find. In my work on "Chemical Physics" I have given at some length the history of the law of Mariotte, and I would refer you to that book for the details; feeling confident that while they fully bear out the impression I have endeavored to give here in a few words, a careful study of the particulars will give you a much larger comprehension of the subject I am seeking to illustrate. In bare outline the history can be briefly told.

The compressibility of gases was in the first place studied with a comparatively rude apparatus, and a simple law was discovered, which was accepted as the absolute truth. Later, when the methods of investigation had become more accurate, it was found that the law was not general; but it was still maintained in regard to air, until finally the refined experiments of Regnault proved that it failed here also. Still the law remains as an ideal truth toward which nature tends, but which is never fully reached, and we can even trace the action of the agents which produce the perturbations. So it is with most physical laws. They are not realized with mathematical exactness, but are ideal truths always more or less false in each particular case. When we are able to go behind the phenomena to their proximate causes, we shall undoubtedly find that the law and its variations are merely different phases of the workings of one complex system; but it is doubtful whether by man's limited powers the anomalies of nature will ever be fully explained, or its discords resolved. More probably, as we go forward in our investigations, and continually widen our generalizations, the last generalization of all will bring us into the presence of that Intelligence of which all natural phenomena are the direct manifestation.

When a physicist can discover no simple relations between conditions or phenomena obviously interdependent, his usual method of proceeding is to plot his observations on paper, on some system of coordinates, and draw a curve through the points thus found. The process is a simple one, and with the aid of an example can easily be made intelligible, even to those who do not understand the technical terms with which the so-called graphical method is usually described.

The solubility of a substance in water varies with

the temperature, usually increasing, but sometimes diminishing, as the temperature rises, and at rates which vary with different substances between wide limits. There is an obvious connection between the weight of a substance which will dissolve in one hundred parts of water and the temperature; but no definite law connecting these quantities can be discovered. Assume that we have determined experimentally the weight in grams of some salt, for example, nitre (KNO_3), that will dissolve in one hundred grams of water at various temperatures between its freezing and boiling points, and that we have tabulated the results. Assume also that we have a sheet of what is called "co-ordinate" paper, divided off into little squares like a multiplication table, as in the accompanying figure. On the lower horizontal line, called the "axis of abscissas," we mark off the temperature in degrees, and on the left-hand vertical line, called the "axis of ordinates," we mark the weight in grams. Taking now the data we have tabulated, and noticing that at 0° thirteen grams of nitre (KNO_3) dissolve in one hundred parts of water, we follow up the vertical line marked 0°, until we come to the horizontal line marked thirteen grams, and there fix the first point. Seeing next that at 15° one hundred grams of water dissolve twenty-five grams of nitre, we follow up the vertical line marked 15° to the horizontal line marked twenty-five grams, and the intersection fixes a second point. As at 30° one hundred grams of water dissolve forty-five grams of nitre, we find a third point by following up the vertical line marked 30° to the horizontal line marked forty-five grams ; and so we proceed with each of the experimental data we have found. Thus we obtain as many points as there are observations, and then with a free hand we draw a curve as nearly as possible through all the points. On the diagram we have given, a number of curves showing the varying solubility of several chemical compounds in water have been thus drawn. Such curves represent to

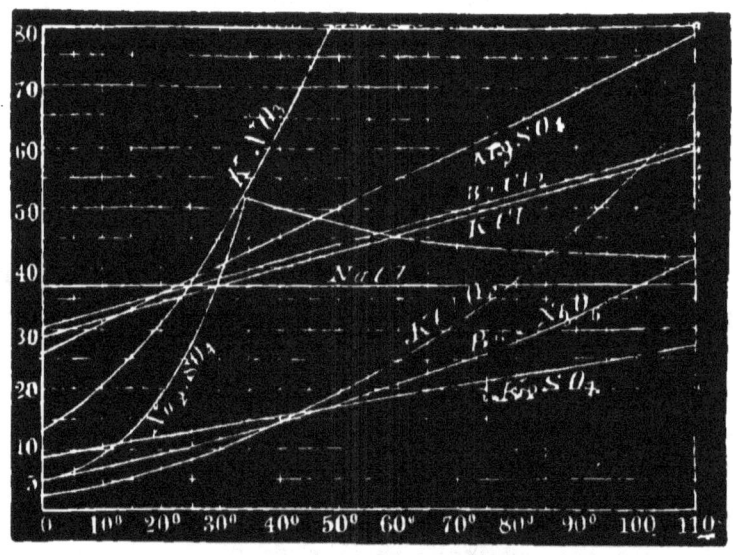

the eye what has been called the "law of the variation," using however the word "law" in a still less definite sense than we have as yet employed it. They not only exhibit the general order of the phenomena, but they enable us to fix with close approximation values between the points at which the observations were made. Thus we see from the figure above that while the solubility both of potassium chloride (K Cl) and of barium chloride (Ba Cl$_2$)

increases slowly, but at a uniform rate with the temperature, the solubility of nitre (KNO_3) varies very rapidly, and at a constantly increasing rate. Again, the solubility of sodium sulphate (Na_2SO_4) presents what is called a singular point, increasing rapidly up to 34° and then diminishing. Lastly, if we wish to determine the solubility at a given temperature of any of the salts here represented, we have only to follow up the vertical line corresponding to the temperature, until it intersects the curve of the substance in question. Then on following from the point of intersection the horizontal line to the left, we read off on the vertical axis, the number of grams of the substance which will dissolve in one hundred parts of water at that temperature. Other physical phenomena can be plotted and interpreted in a similar way.

Every algebraic equation involving two variable quantities corresponds to some kind of plane curve; and so, on the other hand, every plane curve may be represented symbolically by an algebraic equation of a more or less complex character, containing the unknown quantities. Thus, for example, the solubility of nitre graphically represented by the curve above described, may also be expressed by the equation —

$$S = 13.32 + 0.5738 t + 0.017168 t^2 + 0.00000035977 t^3$$

in which t stands for the temperature in degrees centigrade, and S for the number of grams of salt which at this temperature will dissolve in one hundred grams of water. In this expression the value of one of the variables, the quantity sought, is given in the terms of the ascending powers of the other variable, in this case the temperature, — each term being multiplied by a numerical coefficient, whose values are deduced from experimental data. Equations of this general form are the simplest, although not always the most concise, means by which such relations can be algebraically expressed. The science of mathematics, however, gives us the means of treating the subject exhaustively, so that after distributing the errors, we can express our results in the most concise manner of which the observations admit, as well as in the form best adapted to computation. It furnishes us with methods and guides for interpolating, — that is, of calculating from numerical results of definite experiments, what would have been the value of intermediate results, — or even for assigning values beyond the limits of the experimental data, exterpolating, as Airy called it. But in its details this subject cannot be understood without some knowledge of mathematics; and further discussion would be out of place in these lectures. It is only with the broader relations of the subject that we are here concerned; and it is obvious that such algebraic expressions as I have described represent what we may call an indeterminate law. Such expressions are sometimes called empirical laws, because they are really conventional expressions of the results of experiments, and can never be trusted far beyond the limits of the experimental data. From another point of view these formulæ may be regarded simply as methods of approximation to indeterminate results.

Still, in discussing the nature and character of the laws of nature, these important modes of representing physical relations must not be overlooked, and they may be regarded as a third class of laws; so that we have to distinguish the fixed laws, like the laws of motion, the determinate laws, like the law of Mariotte, and the indeterminate laws, such as we have just described. That these last are in the fullest sense mere abstractions is sufficiently evident from what has already been said; but after all, they do not differ essentially from the more determinate laws, as will appear from this final consideration.

In those laws which can only be geometrically or algebraically expressed, we find the greatest differences in the complexity of the relations which the curves or formulæ exhibit; and sometimes the expression is so simple that it might well be questioned under which of the two artificial categories we have made, the given relation should be classed. Between classes which thus blend there are not usually any essential differences, and such differences as we find probably depend on the greater or less complexity of the phenomena under consideration. The distinction between the fixed and the variable laws appears to be more fundamental; and the first, as we have before said, seem to be expressions of the essential properties or relations of matter and energy.

The conception of the distinction I have drawn as it exists in my own mind, may be readily illustrated by the well-known Jacquard loom, which with numerous modifications is used for weaving almost every kind of fabric having inwrought designs. In such a machine, a carpet-loom for example, although the parts work in harmony, we may distinguish between the essential machinery of a loom common to all looms, and the ingenious devices of Jacquard by which the pattern is determined. Without these additions, the loom would weave a perfectly uniform plain fabric, with fixed and unvarying relations of the woof and warp; but Jacquard's perforated cards determine a selection of the threads, and through a combination of these variable conditions, so complex that the observer cannot follow their intricate workings, the pre-designed pattern appears.

So is it, as it seems to me, in the loom of nature. Mass and energy are the woof and warp, with their commingled tints, out of which the tissue of events has been woven; and these fundamental relations are fixed and invariable. But ten thousand changing conditions, fore-ordained by Omniscience and directed by Unerring Wisdom, select the threads, and thus gradually the great design is unrolled.

I might push the analogy further; but such similitudes are of value only as suggestions to thought, and I leave the subject to your reflections.

From the very necessities of the case the analysis of the laws of nature, which I have given in this lecture, is far from complete; and I cannot, therefore, hope that it is conclusive. Only in proportion as one sees clearly is it possible to describe clearly what appears; and when peering through a mist all outlines are ill-defined. But such is the condition under which the investigator must work, and he can only tell you faithfully what he thinks he discerns. Sometimes, however, the clouds break, and he gains a vision of the truth in its glory; and I trust one conclusion at least remains clear to you after this discussion.

From no point of view can the laws of nature be regarded as efficient causes; and this ruler which a materialistic philosophy has attempted to enthrone over the universe is no potentate in any sense, but merely a very intangible, indistinct, and protean mental image of man's abstraction.

As has already been intimated, this sophistry of materialism has been very widely disseminated in consequence of our imperfect methods of education. The only knowledge of material relations which most even of our educated people acquire is derived from elementary text-books, whose formal statements constantly convey false impressions; and hence arises much of the fallacy which prevails. It may not therefore be out of place to devote the remainder of the hour to a short discussion of the educational aspects of our subject.

One of the most brilliant and influential writers of our day, while fully conceding the very great importance to the scholar of the general results of science, as furnishing an essential part of the materials of modern literature, has expressed the opinion that the details and methods of science are of value chiefly to experts, and are unfit materials to form the basis of liberal culture.

With the general spirit of Mr. Matthew Arnold's address on "Literature and Science" (first delivered as the Rede Lecture at the University of Cambridge in England, and afterwards often repeated in this country) I entirely sympathize. I freely admit that as a means of liberal culture that knowledge is most important which, to use Mr. Arnold's striking expression, can be most directly related to the sense for beauty and the sense for conduct; as well as I should add to all the senses which make up that wonderful composite we call character. Character is the great end of education; and that which arouses in man elevated thoughts and conceptions, and that which stirs within him great resolves that lead to noble deeds, has more influence on character than any special knowledge however profound, and however valuable in itself considered to the welfare of society.

The term "science" was used by Mr. Arnold in its broadest sense, to include any body of systematized facts, whether of nature or of any department of human learning; and I wholly agree with him that the mere acquisition of knowledge, however useful, is a very insufficient means of liberal culture; and also that it is equally unimportant to the great mass of educated men whether the products of the combustion of a wax taper be carbonic acid and water, or whether the genitive plural of *pais* and *pas* take the circumflex on the termination. The practice in so many of our schools of cramming immature minds with heterogeneous information, which they at least are unable to relate to the sense of beauty, to the sense of conduct, or to the sense of fitness of any kind, is to my mind a waste of golden opportunities, and productive of no permanent good.

But while conceding all this, I claim for the study of physical science, if rightly pursued, the highest value, even when judged by the very criteria which Mr. Arnold has so acutely laid down. The grand results of physical science are most closely related to the sense for beauty, and to the sense for conduct; and as a matter of fact they have satisfied the needs of the noblest men for beauty, for conduct,— and for holiness also, — as fully as any earth-born knowledge ever can. The beauty of God's creation loses none of its loveliness to him who knows the fitness of all the parts. Beauty, as we have before said, is simply that harmony of proportions and qualities which results from the most complete fitness of all the parts in a perfect whole, and becomes the more apparent, and the more commanding, in the exact proportion as that fitness becomes known and appreciated through study and investigation. His mind must be dull indeed whose noblest impulses are not awakened, and aroused to action, by the revelations of intelligence and forethought which come from the study of the material universe; and we can aptly quote, though with a somewhat different interpretation, the refrain of Mr. Arnold's noble address, — " no wisdom, nor understanding, nor counsel, against the eternal!"

Passing now for a moment from the subject matter to the methods of science, I may venture to assert, as the conclusion from an unusually long experience as a teacher, that no one can acquire an adequate knowledge of scientific results without such an acquaintance with the methods by which the results were obtained as will give a correct appreciation of the limitations under which the conclusions must be received; and that in many cases no language, however skilfully used, is adequate to convey an accurate conception of the truth. A student must observe and experiment for himself if he would acquire clear and correct ideas of natural phenomena. Every teacher of experience knows that the conceptions acquired from elementary text-books and popular lectures are constantly erroneous, and often absurd.

Take such a simple result of chemistry as that water is composed of oxygen and hydrogen. I am sure from my own experience that not one in ten of the young men and women who learn to repeat this statement at our high schools and academies have any clear idea of what it means. For many years I have asked questions on the examination papers for admission to Harvard College to test this very point, and it has been the rarest exception to receive an intelligent answer. Although I have repeated the same question year after year, the result has been uniformly unsatisfactory; and not until experimental teaching was introduced into some of the preparatory schools was there any improvement. To most of the men the names oxygen and hydrogen conveyed no conception of definite substances; and in what sense it could be said that the familiar liquid water was composed of two aeriform substances, and on what evidence this remarkable scientific conclusion is based, almost no one had clear ideas. The laboratory student, however, who has actually made oxygen and hydrogen gases from water, and who has satisfied himself with this evidence that these aeriform products came from the material of water and from nothing else; who also has mixed two volumes of hydrogen gas with one volume of oxygen gas, and after exploding the mixture with an electric spark has seen that the result is two volumes of vapor which condense on cooling into liquid water, and must therefore be steam, — has a knowledge of a wholly different kind. He knows that the conclusion so tersely stated in his text-book is far from self-evident; he has experienced the difficulties which had to be overcome before the truth was established; he has seen the limitations under which this truth must be held; and his knowledge is complete and final.

In literature the printed record is the final appeal; but in science books are at best only a secondary authority, and can never supply the place of direct observation and experiment. All descriptions of natural phenomena are necessarily partial and imperfect; and in elementary works they are as a rule so inadequate as to be constantly misleading. Any one who relies upon them is liable to be led into serious error. Hence it is that students of nature often hold in such slight esteem popular expositions of scientific subjects, feeling that they often convey false impressions and inculcate error in spirit, if not in substance. Nevertheless, such popular expositions have their proper place, and are of the greatest importance, not only by awakening interest in scientific subjects but also by exhibiting large views of scientific relations. They are avenues to knowledge which men may wisely follow, and by which many have been led into the sanctuaries of truth; but the scholar must worship at the shrine and wait on the altars, if he would interpret the oracles aright.

One of the great educational needs of our day is such a training by the schools in experimental methods as will enable the great body of our educated men to weigh scientific evidence, and thus to protect the community from the frauds and sophistries of which otherwise intelligent, instructed, and even shrewd men are now so frequently the dupes. Of the common-school system, so early established and carefully fostered by our forefathers, we are justly proud; but let us not be blind to the fact that this system has grave defects, and has been excelled in several countries whose governments entered on the great work of popular education long after ourselves. In many respects our methods of elementary education are inferior to those of Germany, of Sweden, or of Italy. Two very obvious reasons may be assigned for this result. In the first place, the details of our system are ordered by the average, and not by the highest intelligence of the community; and in the second place, our school boards are greatly hampered in all efforts for reform by the cost of labor.

The ingenuity of our people has not failed to devise expedients for economizing the labor of the teacher, and thus for enabling one man to control the greatest possible number of pupils. In almost every subject taught in our secondary schools books are provided in which each day's lesson is exactly proportioned, and the questions to be asked definitely appointed. The teacher's work is made as mechanical as possible, and the pupil's task becomes a mere exercise of the memory. Under such conditions there is no need that a teacher should have any special knowledge of the subject taught; and untrained persons are employed, whose whole knowledge of the subject is bounded by the covers of a school-book; which too often has been prescribed by a school committee, under the influence of interested publishers. Thus education is cheapened in our country, like so many other products of labor, at the expense of refinement and finish.

It is no wonder that the overworked and underpaid teachers should oppose any change which necessarily involves a large increase of labor, even when they fully recognize the ruinous effects of the mechanical system under which they are compelled to work. Obviously, however, this substitution of indiscriminate cramming, in place of intelligent acquisition is fatal to the efficiency of our school system, and a reform should be demanded at any cost.

Fortunately, our political system is as flexible as it is crude; and if the demand is seriously made the reform is sure to follow. But let it be remembered that the changes required will be necessarily costly, and we must be prepared to bear the increased expense. Do not, however, be deceived by any makeshifts which are often paraded as scientific education. If teaching is to be simply a process of loading the memory with more or less useful, as well as more or less ephemeral, information it makes little difference in the end what are the materials used in the process of cramming. The material may as well be the long list of exceptions to the rules of prosody, required in the Latin schools of former days, as descriptions of experiments in physics or chemistry so glibly recited by the pupils of our modern high schools.

No teaching of science is of any value which is not a direct appeal from the mind of the teacher to the intelligence of the pupil. The teaching must be direct and personal, and this necessarily implies a large expenditure of time and patience, a special training on the part of the teacher, and a great increase of teaching force.

The successful teaching of natural science also requires that the teacher should be independent of all books. The great object of science-training is to enable the scholar to interpret nature; and the book of nature is the only text-book which should be prescribed. As in the study of ancient classics the one great aim is to acquire such a command of Latin or Greek, such a knowledge of the circumstances and relations of these elder nations, as will enable the student to render not only the general sense, but also the delicate shades of meaning and the coloring of the language of their writers; so in the study of science the great object is to interpret the meaning of natural phenomena, to decipher the significance of every feature, and to show forth the intelligence of which nature is the expression.

Books have their value chiefly as guides, and as records of what has already been accomplished; but in the study of nature they hold a secondary and subordinate, and not a chief place. To train young minds to interpret nature is a perfectly practical scheme. The power can be acquired as readily as the ability to translate Virgil or Homer, although of course with limitations which are similar in both cases; and it is this power, and not the mere acquisition of scientific knowledge, at which the so-called "new education" aims. This all-important statement cannot be too often repeated, or too strongly emphasized. The advocates of an exclusively classical culture constantly describe the new education as an attempt to substitute the acquisition of useful knowledge for mental discipline; or, at best, to replace serious intellectual work with superficial object-teaching; and, as we have before intimated, there has been an attempt on the part of some schools to satisfy an obvious demand with contemptible shifts. Let me then repeat that the great aim of scientific training should be the ability to interpret nature; and this is an intellectual exercise which in its higher forms may tax the most gifted intellects, but which in its more humble phases is within the power of every educated man.

That such training is of the highest value and is a legitimate aim of education, must, I think, be universally admitted; but it cannot be secured without trained teachers, without well-appointed laboratories, and except at a cost proportionate to such requirements. Certainly we cannot afford to fall behind the most favored nations of the earth on the very ground which we first occupied; and it is equally certain that no investment will yield a larger return than the money expended in the acquisition of real knowledge.

The distinction between real knowledge and formal

knowledge is one of paramount importance, which should never be overlooked in our plans of education. That knowledge alone is real to a student which is obviously related to some need of his life, or to some phase of his intelligence. All other knowledge, however valuable in itself considered, is to him formal. Obviously, the distinction here insisted on is purely a relative one; for the same knowledge which is formal to one man may be very real indeed to his next-door neighbor. The paradigms of grammar are formal knowledge to the young student who memorizes them for the first time, but are very real knowledge to the grammarian. Even formal knowledge has its right place; and there are exigencies under which its acquisition is to be encouraged or even enforced. Man is a creature of habit, and his usefulness requires that certain essential truths should become so woven into his nature as to be always at hand on every emergency. Certainly the multiplication-table and the spelling-book represent formal knowledge of this sort; but I do maintain that it should be the great object of education to relate all knowledge, so far as possible, to the pupil's understanding.

I know that on this point I differ from many old experienced teachers whom I greatly respect. It was formerly held almost universally, and even now it is believed by many teachers, to be best for a child to acquire knowledge at first in a formal way, and to wait for the development of his intelligence to exhibit its relations. On this theory, boys preparing for college in my own school-days were compelled to learn the Latin grammar by rote before they understood the meaning of one half of the terms employed. The vivid remembrance of my own experience may lend undue proportions to this abuse of the memory; still, after a long experience as a teacher myself, I cannot but regard such discipline as a great waste of mental energy, if not absolutely cruel; and no one can deny that the acquisition of any knowledge is greatly facilitated when the relations of the knowledge are understood. I have granted that in certain cases the acquisition of formal knowledge is necessary; nevertheless, it should be the study of the teacher to lessen the requirement as far as possible; and certainly in science, formal knowledge is wholly without value.

Some years ago, while working in the mineralogical cabinet under my charge at Cambridge, I was addressed by two lady visitors who had evidently found great interest in the collection, and asked some very intelligent questions in regard to several of the more common mineral species. It gave me great pleasure to answer their inquiries, and I passed a pleasant hour in pointing out some of the characteristic features of quartz, feldspar, mica, pyroxene, hornblende, and similarly familiar minerals which are the constituents of our common rocks. At the close of this improvised lecture, one of the ladies said to me in an apologetic tone, — evidently deeming some excuse required for such an unusual feminine taste, — " We are teachers in the —— High School," naming a town not one hundred miles distant from Boston, " and I have been taking a class through the sections on mineralogy, introductory to Dana's Geology; and I was interested to see some of the minerals described in them."

I think this incident, without further comment, will illustrate what I mean by a formal knowledge of elementary science, and will also show how utterly worthless all such acquisition must be. The incident has an amusing side, but it also exhibits a very sad aspect of our secondary education. This lady was evidently a conscientious teacher, who had a conception of something better than the mechanical routine in which she was forced to work, and this had led her to seek some real knowledge of the subject she had to teach. I know that there has been a great improvement in our schools during the last few years; and the practical classes supported by the Lowell Fund, under the direction of the teachers of the Boston Institute of Technology, as well as similar courses under the auspices of the adjacent Natural History Society, have done not a little to hasten the reform. But our best teachers are still constrained by over-crowded class rooms, and the mechanical routine which this condition of things necessarily implies. Of this I know. There is not a more devoted or more conscientious class of workers in our community than the teachers of the secondary schools; and if our people realized how much mental energy was wasted in these schools by just such senseless tasks as attempting to teach mineralogy from a book, the teachers would soon be relieved from such profitless and thankless duties.

What I have said in regard to the teaching of science, applies with almost equal force to literary studies as well. Real knowledge has the same great worth in every department of learning, and formal teaching the same deadening influence; and let it not be inferred from anything I have said, that I desire to exalt scientific culture at the expense of literary or artistic culture of any kind. All mental culture is alike good; and it is not by a one-sided growth, but by a symmetrical development of all its powers, that a community can secure the largest productiveness and acquire the widest influence.

I have elsewhere expressed myself so strongly on this point that it does not seem to me necessary that I should guard the language here used against any misinterpretation ; but that I may make the declaration still more emphatic, let me repeat that I still believe the old forms of literary culture to be for the large majority of scholars the best preparation for useful lives. I merely claim that there is an important class of the students who now seek a college education, for whom, on the other hand, a scientific culture will best secure their future usefulness; and I have already indicated sufficiently clearly what I mean by scientific culture in this connection. Let not scientific culture be confounded with technical training, and let it not be misjudged by any counterfeits which have assumed its name. Several of the sciences have opened lucrative fields for professional labor; and the engineer, the chemist, and the electrician follow as learned vocations as the lawyer or the physician. For each of these new professions, as for those of the elder triad, special training is required; and in all of them some of the subjects involved are the same as those studied in view solely of a general education. The difference between technical training and liberal culture depends, not chiefly on the subject-matter studied, but on the purposes and spirit with which the study is pursued. Thus, chemistry studied with the object of manufacturing chemical products, or of directing other chemical industries, or of solving the numerous sanitary and technical problems which constantly arise in every highly civilized community, is a legitimate and learned profession; but when studied for the sole object of interpreting nature and extending knowledge, it is one of the liberal arts. I do not say that one object is more worthy or more noble than the other; but I do maintain that any country becomes more enlightened and more honored in proportion as liberal culture is fostered and maintained. That it will have its proper place in our community is already assured; and the movement recently inaugurated by Harvard College is already producing visible effects.

To this reform in education, and to the substitution of real for formal knowledge which it involves, I look more than to anything else for the reconciliation between science and theology. When all the wisdom and learning of this world has been related not only to man's need of beauty and to man's need of conduct, but also to man's need of understanding and man's need of religion, the harmony between material and spiritual truths will plainly appear; and thus it is that this discussion of what seemed at first a purely educational problem, has an important bearing on the larger subject we have in hand.

LECTURE VIII.

THEORIES OR SYSTEMS OF SCIENCE.

IN my last lecture I defined a law of nature as a declaration or statement of a certain order, sequence, or relation observed among natural phenomena, and aimed to show that such propositions could be regarded from no point of view as efficient causes. It is not in the study of nature alone that the mind of man does not rest satisfied with laws. In social relations as well as in science, men demand to know the meaning of laws, and their demands are the more imperative in proportion as they become more enlightened. The scientific investigator is not content with a knowledge of the outward relations of phenomena. He seeks to discover the proximate causes of the order he has observed, and although he may not be able to reach certainty, he is not satisfied until he has framed some explanation by which he can classify his facts, and which at the same time will give the form and body to his thoughts so indispensable for successful study. Hence arise of necessity the hypotheses, theories, and systems of science.

Using the term in its broadest sense, an hypothesis is a postulate imagined or assumed to account for what is not understood. Its derivative meaning from ὑπόθεσις (a supposition) is closely followed in the meaning here assigned to the word. These suppositions may be based on a larger or smaller knowledge, they may be more or less in harmony with natural phenomena, they may more or less fully agree with generally accepted systems of science; but they differ from the laws of nature in that they seek to go behind the external relations of things, and explain how this order might have been produced. The word "hypothesis," unfortunately for our purpose, has acquired a coloring which suggests a depreciatory inference. A plausible supposition is sometimes spoken of contemptuously as "a mere hypothesis;" and possibly for this reason the term "theory," although often branded in a similar way, is frequently used by scientific writers to distinguish such hypotheses as they regard as more credible or more fully established. But until the truth of an hypothesis has been placed beyond doubt, — when of course it ceases to be a supposition, and is classed among fixed facts, — the degree of credibility must be to a great extent a matter of opinion, and no definite line of distinction can be drawn. Moreover, the word "theory" has a very important use, corresponding also to its derivation, which we cannot afford to have compromised. We shall use, therefore, the word "hypothesis" to designate any assumed explanation of natural phenomena, without any implication as to the plausibility of the supposition.

As is well known, it is a fundamental doctrine of the positive philosophy that man can know nothing of efficient causes. Hence all hypotheses are vanities, and the only reasonable course for helpless man is to limit his attention to determinate relations of phenomena; that is, to natural laws. But this philosophy utterly ignores the only power by which the level of human knowledge can be raised; that is, induction: and as we have shown in previous lectures, the whole history of science is simply the story of verified inductions. Guesses at truth are not to be despised, for they have been again and again divinations.

We cannot expect fruitful suggestions except from men who are thoroughly acquainted with the subject they are studying; but to gain any insight into nature's processes, something more than erudition is required; call it genius, call it intuition, call it inspiration, or by whatever other name, there is an element, although we may not be able to define it precisely, which we all recognize in such creative minds. Man's discernment and God's inspiration blend together, and no one can distinguish the point where they meet.

There is a certain sense in which the suggestions of gifted minds may be said to be the oracles of God; and there is another sense in which they must be regarded as the conceits of very fallible and short-sighted men; and it is no wonder that their value will be very differently estimated according as they are regarded from one or the other point of view. I have the greatest respect for the love of truth and accuracy which the positive philosophy so strongly inculcates; but, as it seems to me, this doctrine finds its chief disciples among scholars who have been so engrossed in deductive methods as to overlook the mental visions by which the broader relations of truth have been discovered.

To my mind there is a deeper and nobler philosophy than positivism, which explains that mysterious sympathy between mind and nature so evident in the great discoverers, — a philosophy proclaimed in the declaration of Holy Scripture that man was created in the image of God. Only in proportion as man partakes of the Divine intelligence can he understand the Divine creation, and just in proportion as he is in sympathy with the Divine mind will he recognize the Divine thought which has been manifested in nature. And even if we take no higher view than that man has grown into harmony with his environments through the influence of what is called natural selection, we must at least recognize in such antecedents a close relationship with the rest of nature; and this affinity alone would help to explain the power of genius to frame fruitful hypotheses.

As we have already explained, there is but one satisfactory test of the Divine afflatus in such imaginings; and that is the test of experience. Hypothesis is of value only in so far as it explains facts, and by pointing out consequences directs investigation, — as has been already fully illustrated. In this way hypotheses have been the chief means by which science has been advanced. The great discoverers have been the men who were the most fruitful in hypotheses, and at the same time most skilful and conscientious in submitting them to the test of observation and experiment,—men like Copernicus, Kepler, Galileo, Huygens, Newton, Oersted and Faraday.

I have already shown out of what copious and often grotesque fancies the laws of Kepler were educed; and Faraday, although far more sober-minded, was equally distinguished by exuberance of fancy; but, like Kepler, he submitted his hypotheses to the severest tests. So also Newton, while emphatically expressing his contempt for idle speculations in his celebrated aphorism already quoted, constantly made use of legitimate hypotheses in his own investigations,—as both his "Optics" and his "Principia" give abundant evidence.

The word "theory"—from $\theta\epsilon\omega\rho\epsilon\omega$, to see or contemplate—is correctly used in speaking of a system of science, as the theory of music, or the theory of the moon; and to this meaning it is best limited. In this sense a theory may involve many principles and complex relations. It may be based on known laws or definite facts, as is, for example, the theory of sound; or it may rest to a greater or less extent on hypotheses, as does the undulatory theory of light on the assumption of an adamantine ether. It is therefore plainly to be distinguished on the one hand from a law, which is the declaration of known relations, and on the other hand from an hypothesis, which is an assumption of unknown conditions. Indeed, it often includes both laws and hypotheses, and attempts to correlate them in a consistent system. The theories of science are of the very greatest value, and chiefly in two ways.

In the first place, a good theory has a very great

educational value. It classifies facts, it unfolds phenomena in logical sequences, and exhibits events in intelligible relations. As thus presented, the mind is able to grasp the subject as a whole, to view it in many relations, and through their relationships to gain a command of a mass of facts which otherwise the most retentive memory could not hold. We are all acquainted with this use of theory. We know how completely our working knowledge in almost any department of learning is associated with the system in which it was acquired, and many of us know by experience how difficult it is to work with a new system when the progress of knowledge demands a change. Theories are thus necessities of our mental constitution, and essential conditions of effective thought.

In the second place, theories are of the very greatest use in directing investigation, and in natural science their efficiency in this respect is their chief merit. The highest recommendation we can give to a system of science is to say that it is a good working theory; and in saying this we do not necessarily pass any judgment on the credibility of the system as abstract truth. As I shall soon show, we have good working theories whose postulates cannot for a moment be regarded as realities; but so long as the theories direct us to new discoveries it would be the height of folly to abandon them simply because they cannot be squared with our speculative philosophy. There has been a great deal of misunderstanding on this point which, in the interest both of religion and of sound philosophy, ought to have been avoided. Sober-minded men have been accused again and again of being false to religion because they entertained theories which the Church at the time regarded as inconsistent with sound doctrine; and, in defending their position, I have known men of great power driven into extreme positions by an intolerance which forced a mental conflict where none need to have followed. If in the study of nature there is one truth more than another which it is important for the student to learn, it is that in a great many cases reservation of judgment is the only honest attitude of the mind; and that man is to be honored, and not persecuted, who can use his theories for what they are worth and keep his faith in eternal verities pure and radiant.

As we cannot expect a theory fully to harmonize with our philosophy, so we cannot expect that its predictions will always· be verified. Of course the failure of a theory to account for well-established phenomena shows that either the theory or our powers of deduction must be at fault; but this is no reason for rejecting the system, until we can find a better theory to take its place. How foolish it would have been for Columbus to throw overboard his compass-needles when he discovered that they did not point exactly to the north pole. Like all human inventions, systems of science are imperfect; and we must accept them for what they are worth, and use them only so long as they give us essential help in our search for knowledge. It has been repeatedly the case in the history of science, that theories have failed so completely to do their legitimate work that they have been deposed and new theories enthroned in their place; but so intimately are theories associated with our processes of thought, that the change has usually been attended with an intellectual revolution. As I have shown in these lectures, it was so when the Ptolemaic theory was set aside; and we have had a similar experience in chemistry since I have been a teacher of the science.

We have said that a system of science might involve postulates wholly inconsistent with sound philosophy, and yet remain a good working theory; we have now to add, what is still more surprising, that such a theory may give us accurate measurements of magnitudes which are wholly hypothetical, and of whose relations we have otherwise no positive knowledge. Such, for example, are the absolute lengths of the so-called waves of light, and the relative weights of the chemical molecules and atoms. There cannot be a question that the values obtained are real magnitudes; and, although we have made our measurements in the dark and have not known certainly what we were measuring, yet the definiteness of the results gives us the strongest assurance that our theories contain an element of truth, although the truth may be clothed with much error.

We have already seen what a mighty influence the Ptolemaic system and the "Organon" of Aristotle exerted over the intellectual world for more than a thousand years; and at the present day, besides the many subsidiary theories, there are four great systems of science which possess a similar authority. These are the Theory of Universal Gravity, the Undulatory Theory of Light, the Molecular Theory of Chemistry and Physics, and the Theory of Organic Development; and I propose in this lecture to show that these famous systems of science exhibit in a most striking manner the characteristic features of all human theories to which I have referred.

In my last lecture I not only pointed out the clear distinction between the law of gravitation and the theory of universal gravity, but I also discussed some of the incongruities which this assumed mode of action presents, showing that the idea of independent attractive forces exerted by separate particles of matter was not only inconsistent with the fundamental conception of inertia, but also entirely out of harmony with our knowledge of other attractive forces, like those exerted by electricity and magnetism. Remember that each particle of matter of this earth is assumed to attract each particle of the planet Jupiter, each one every other, as if there were no other material in the universe.

Now besides the improbability and incongruity of such independent action, the whole idea is at utter variance with a principle which in all philosophical thought has always been regarded as a prime condition of every mode of action, and which is expressed in the aphorism "Nulla actio in distans." This principle has been universally recognized in other systems of science. It was recognized by Newton himself in his emission theory of light, which ascribed the luminous power to small projectiles darting through the intervening space and carrying the energy from the luminous body to the point of application; and to these projectiles Newton gave form and imparted rotation in order to explain what he called "fits of easy transmission" or reflection. The same philosophical necessity for a medium of transmission led Huygens, in framing his wave theory of light, to fill all space with an elastic medium, through which the waves might be propagated. This medium, which to his conception was an indefinitely attenuated but highly elastic condition of aeriform matter, as its name denotes, the demands of modern science, as we shall soon see, have converted into an adamantine solid. It was again the same necessity of thought which, in a most memorable investigation, led Faraday to search for the medium through which electrical attractions and repulsions are exerted, and to distinguish, as he did with so much skill, the qualities and relations of the dielectric. While, however, we have met the necessity by interposing a medium through which a particle of sodium at the sun sends to our spectroscope an intelligible signal, that same particle is assumed by the theory of gravitation to exert an attraction on every particle of that instrument at the distance of ninety millions of miles, not only independent of any medium, but also irrespective of any conditions or relations except mass.

Although I feel strongly the philosophical objection to the theory of gravitation which I have endeavored to present; and although I feel under the constraint of the same limitations of thought to which I have referred,—yet sometimes I cannot but fear that we are influenced by the old aphorism more than we ought to allow ourselves to be; and that, after all, we may be but repeating the experience of the Aristotleans at the time of Galileo. Who can question that Nature's abhorrence of a vacuum was as much a philosophical necessity to them as " Nulla actio in distans" is to us. Man cannot act where he is not, or where he cannot reach,—although the electrical nerves of modern science enable him to reach across oceans and continents, and almost even to clasp the globe itself.˙ Moreover, on the earth we cannot transmit energy without an adequate medium. The falling water acts directly on the turbine, but power cannot be transmitted from this water-wheel to the spindle and looms except through adequate shafting, pulleys, and belts. So also the power of steam, however far the steam may be carried through pipes, must do its work ultimately against the piston of the motor. Even the more modern dynamo-machine, by which power can be transmitted to greater distances than by any other means, must have a line of electrical conductors through which the energy passes. In all these cases power is lost in the transmission in such a way as to show that the transmission takes place from point to point along the line. All such analogies give a strong support to the doctrine that no action can take place except between contiguous masses; but should we not be careful not to limit in our thoughts the possibilities of nature by our own experience? It seems to me that such an attitude of the mind is required by philosophical sobriety; and although I have given a very different interpretation to the seeming non-conformity, it is possible that gravitation is the first exceptional phenomenon which has· shown the short-sightedness of our philosophy. Still the main fact which I have been endeavoring to illustrate remains. This grand theory of universal gravitation, from which has been developed the wonderful deductions of modern astronomy, presents anomalies which our philosophy has been wholly unable to reconcile.

Of the four great theories of modern science, the one which is to me the most fascinating is the undulatory theory of light. As a student of crystallography and of crystal optics, I have been charmed by the completeness with which it not only explains the general order of these phenomena, but also predicts the magnitude, intensity, and other relations of each minute detail. Moreover, the remarkable prediction of conical fraction first made known on theoretical grounds by Hamilton, and afterwards verified by Lloyd, will always be cited as one of the most striking examples of the prescience of physical science. Nevertheless, in spite of all its elegance and efficiency, the undulatory theory of light is imperfect, and demands postulates which even the wildest imagination cannot reconcile with common-sense.

The earlier exposition of the undulatory theory was published by Huygens nearly contemporaneously with that of the emission theory by Newton; but although from the first much more elegant in mathematical form, the theory of waves did not for a long time acquire nearly as great authority as the theory of corpuscles; and even down to the middle of this century the two theories were described as rival systems in most text-books on optics. Sir David Brewster, one of the most successful students of optics in this century, who died in 1868, defended the Newtonian theory to the last. Unquestionably, the paramount authority of Newton in astronomy gave greater weight to his hypothesis in optics than it intrinsically merited; for there are not to be found in the whole history of science more elegant demonstrations than those which Huygens originally gave, deducing the fundamental principles of optics from the theory of the wave motion, — such principles, for example, as the rectilinear path of a beam of light, the laws of reflection and refraction, and above all, the phenomena of double refraction, then recently observed by Erasmus Bartolinus in Iceland spar.

Huygens was undoubtedly led to his wave theory by the analogy which the phenomena of light and sound exhibit, and conceived of waves of light as transmitted like waves of sound in the atmosphere, only through a vastly more attenuated, but at the same time more elastic, medium which he called the "luminiferous ether." But in an aeriform medium, elasticity, the force by which waves are transmitted, can be developed only by compression. Of course compression at one point must be attended by expansion at contiguous points, and waves of sound consist in alternating states of compression and expansion spreading from every centre of disturbance. Such alternating conditions must produce variations of pressure at the surfaces which the medium touches, and the phenomena of wave motion result from the concurrence or interference of such partial effects, as Huygens so beautifully showed.

Although the general order of the appearances

observed in the double refraction of light by Iceland spar was beautifully explained by the wave theory of Huygens, yet there remained certain features of this striking phenomenon — described both by Huygens and Newton — which were inexplicable until in 1810, when Malus, while looking through a double refracting prism at the light of the setting sun reflected from the windows of the Luxembourg Palace at Paris, first observed the most fundamental of that remarkable series of phenomena which he afterwards developed and referred to what he called the "polarization of light." Malus, who was a disciple of the emission theory, ascribed all these effects to a polarity in the light-bearing corpuscles; and hence arose a name which is meaningless, and indeed confusing, on the basis of the theory of undulations. As soon, however, as the new facts came to be studied in the light of the undulatory theory, it was seen that the essential feature of the condition which had been called "polarization" was the transmission of the luminous energy in a definite plane; and that the elementary motions in that plane which constituted the wave motion must take place at right angles to the direction of the rays of light. These considerations led to a profound alteration of the wave theory, first recognized by Thomas Young, but afterwards worked out with great ability by Fresnel. The wave motion could no longer be regarded as transmitted through an attenuated gas by the elasticity of compression, and it became necessary to conceive of the ether with parts held in definite relative positions, as in a solid, through which the waves are transmitted by the elasticity of tension. In a word, the theory now filled space with an attenuated solid, whose parts are bound together far more firmly than those of steel.

Consider now the apparently contradictory qualities which it has been found necessary to attribute to the ether of space, in order to explain the known phenomena of light and heat. In the first place, as the ether does not give rise to any sensible perturbations in the motions of the heavenly bodies, we must assume that it has no perceptible mass; so that a solid block of ether of the size of this room cannot weigh more than a fraction of a grain. But while having such an excessive tenuity, we must in the next place assume that this singular solid consists of parts bound together with such an incredible force that, as the waves in passing through this medium tend to part or force together the ultimate particles, the action and reaction over each inch of surface must be measured by millions on millions of pounds.

Why it is necessary to ascribe such an incredible elasticity to the luminiferous ether will in general appear from two considerations. In the first place the immense velocity of light requires this great elasticity. Assuming that two media have the same density, their elasticities are proportional to the squares of the velocities with which a wave travels through them. The velocity of the sound wave in air is 1100 feet a second, or about one fifth of a mile, and that of the light wave about 183,000 miles a second, or nearly one million times faster; so that in proportion to its density the ether must have an elasticity a million million times greater than air. In the second place, this great elasticity is required in order to transmit power from the sun. The earth is but one of a number of great machines which are run by the sun. There is no form of energy manifested on the earth which cannot be traced to the sun. The sun is the great motor from which all this power comes, just as directly as the power which runs the spindles and looms of a manufactory is transmitted by shafts, pulleys, and belts, from a turbine wheel in the basement. Now these connections must be strong in proportion as the power to be transmitted is great; and so the ether which transmits the power from the sun must be strong enough to do the work; and if you reduce the material in it to next to nothing you must make what is left proportionally strong,—that is, ascribe to it this immense elasticity. Of course the imagination knows no bounds, and you may ascribe to the ether any extravagant relations you please; just as you can imagine materials so strong that the power of Niagara could be transmitted with shafts no larger than wires, and belts no larger than horse-hairs. And if you are not to take into any account the harmonies of nature, one supposition is as reasonable as the other.

It is not, therefore, without reason that, following the authority of Jevons, I have called the luminiferous ether an adamantine solid; and yet in the midst of this adamantine mass we live and move without perceiving the least resistance. In general two explanations have been given to show how motion in such a solid medium is possible. In the first place, it has been suggested that the molecules of a body may pass between the ultimate particles of the ether; just as a flock of birds, regarded as constituting one mass, would pass between the branches of a forest, — the body not displacing the ether but, as it were, penetrating it. I need not say that besides the difficulties of conception, there are insuperable philosophical objections to this view. The second suggestion is that the ether is a semi-liquid, which, like pitch or ice near the melting-point, has a great elasticity associated with an equally great degree of liquidity.

Ice, as is well known, flows down-hill in the glacier's streams; and so will pitch, although masses of either substance have marked elasticity, and will break with a conchoidal fracture like glass. Now conceive of the ether as pouring round a body, passing through it, without a parting of the ultimate particles of the medium, which continue to cling together with the immense force I have mentioned, — and you have the most recent conception that has been advanced of the relations of this inconceivable material. But obviously, such devices of the imagination do not in the least degree remove the difficulty of the conception. Fundamentally, this difficulty consists in associating great extremes of qualities which from our experience seem to be incompatible. In ice or pitch a very small degree of liquidity is associated with elasticity of tension; but in similar semi-liquids the elasticity diminishes in proportion as the liquidity increases, while in the ether we are asked to associate indefinitely great elasticity with indefinitely perfect liquidity.

Such utterly incongruous and irreconcilable relations may not discredit a theory as a system of science, but they must shake our faith in its credibility as a reality of nature. As we have already said, there is nothing in science so improbable, or so inconceivable, that it may not be realized. With all the unknown relations of nature it is not safe to say that anything is impossible, unless it absolutely conflicts with fundamental laws. We are doubtless safe in expressing the opinion that no form of matter or energy can be produced without a corresponding expenditure; and that those who stake ventures in processes for making materials or obtaining work from nothing are deluded; but much further than this it is not safe to prophesy. It is within our own experience that steam navigation, ocean telegraphy, and electrical lighting, were pronounced impracticable by men of large knowledge and great intelligence; and we have lived to witness their confusion in the accomplished results.

In all such cases, however, when the improbable has been once realized, it has been found to be in harmony with the rest of our knowledge; and it has been seen that the seeming incongruity arose from our ignorance of general principles, or other links through which the relationship became evident. Therefore, while repeated experience of this kind should make us cautious, it cannot but increase our confidence in the general trustworthiness of the analogies by which the student of nature is so greatly guided. But the same experience should also make us duly sensible of the limitations of our knowledge, and inculcate largeness in thought and reservation in judgment.

That such an adamantine medium as the ether of our theories actually exists I cannot for a moment believe; but that the ether is our crude conception of some reality which bridges the celestial spaces I have no question. Perhaps in time the fulness of knowledge will come; perhaps it is incomprehensible to our limited faculties; but that there is something corresponding to the ether of our imaginings, I feel as confident as that there is a solid crust of earth under my feet. In some way illimitable power crosses the immense gulfs of space; and what we catch glimpses of in the darkness, and try to express in our material symbols — whose inadequacy appears in the extravagances of our theories — is simply an order of being recognized as fully in the infancy of our race as now; and of which it may be said as in the days of Job: "Where is the way where light dwelleth? . . . Knowest thou the ordinances of heaven? Canst thou set the dominion thereof in the earth?"

It is undoubtedly in consequence of the large element of truth which the great systems of science contain, in spite of all their philosophical absurdities and formal inconsistencies, that they have led us in several cases to a knowledge of magnitudes which, although entirely beyond our powers of direct observation, have been measured with the greatest accuracy. In the undulatory theory this is true in regard to the lengths of the waves of light; and although there is such large room for doubt in regard to the nature of these magnitudes, our knowledge of their values is so exact that it has been seriously proposed to use them as standards of linear measurement. Remember that the longest of the luminous waves only measure 1-39,000 of an inch — counted as with a water-wave from crest to crest — and you can see what such a proposition implies, and also what must be the order of the unknown quantity which we are able to measure so accurately. And not only do we know the values of those magnitudes, but we have followed out their relations through most intricate conditions, and found our deductions most completely verified at every step of our inquiry. That these values are the magnitude of real things, we can have no more question than that the measurements given by Piazzi Smyth, in his work on the Egyptian Pyramids are the dimensions of actual blocks of stone, however much archæologists may question this learned astronomer's theory in regard to the purposes for which these blocks were originally wrought.

But besides presenting in its postulates the philosophical and formal incongruities I have pointed out, the undulatory theory is by no means perfect in its appropriate relations; for there is a most important and conspicuous class of optical facts which it has as yet essentially failed to explain. I refer to the beautiful phenomena on which spectrum analysis is based. Newton's earliest experiment, in which he separated the colored rays composing white light by means of a glass prism, still challenges the undulatory theory. I have already referred to the remarkable investigation of Cauchy on this very point, which has been justly regarded as a monument of mathematical skill; but this investigation wholly failed in its main purpose. The most that Cauchy accomplished with his profound mathematical analysis was to show that such effects might follow from wave motion on certain assumptions in regard to the molecular structure of the dispersing media; so that when our knowledge of molecular structure is more complete, the undulatory theory may possibly be able to explain the phenomena in question. He did not in any proper sense bring the phenomena of dispersion under the control of the theory; and to the average student they remain to the present day as inexplicable as ever. If, however, Cauchy's analysis gives us good reason for expecting that with larger knowledge we may be able to include the phenomena of dispersion in our system, there are also equally strong grounds for the opinion that before this can be done the present undulatory theory must be profoundly modified.

I fear that in thus dwelling on the inconsistencies and imperfections of the undulatory theory, it may seem as if I were aiming to discredit the system; when on the contrary I desire to exalt it. The last word has always such undue force that, to avoid misapprehension, it is almost necessary to reiterate the opinion I expressed at first, — that the undulatory theory of light is one of the noblest creations of science, one of the greatest achievements of the human intellect, and that its value can not be overestimated. I believe that the system is no more imperfect than is necessarily implied in saying that it is a product of human thought, that it involves human conceptions, and must necessarily be subject to human limitations. My aim has been to exhibit the system in its true relations, and to show that we must be content to use it for what it is worth, and not expect to reconcile it at all points with either our speculative opinions or our limited experience.

We come now to the third of the three great systems of science which we have called the Molecular Theory, and this presents two very distinct aspects, according as we study the theory from a physical or from a chemical standpoint. On certain features, however, both the physicists and the chemists agree. By students of both classes the mass of material bodies is regarded not as uniformly and continuously distributed through the spaces they seem to occupy, but as segregated into an innumerable number of excessively minute masses called "molecules," each of which is a separate unit,— as much so as a planet.

There must be as many different kinds of molecules as there are distinct substances, but all the molecules of the same substance — as, for example, the molecules of water — are assumed to be the exact counterparts of every other. Of the absolute size of the molecules we can only form a very rude estimate, but the estimates made in different ways quite closely agree, and a conception of the order of magnitudes with which our theory deals is best given by means of the illustration already cited, which we owe to Sir William Thompson, who said that if a drop of water were magnified to the size of the earth, and the molecules of water magnified in the same proportion, they would certainly appear larger than "marbles," and smaller than cricket-balls. Wonderfully small as these magnitudes must be, the theory does not on this account present any insuperable difficulties of conception; for it only asks us to believe in a microcosmos beneath us, in some measure comparable with the macrocosmos which astronomy has shown to exist above us. The difficulties appear when we come to consider the attributes and relations which our theory compels us to ascribe to these minute masses.

In physics the molecules are regarded as the points of application of forces; as for example, when a body is expanded, melted, or volatilized by heat. Indeed, limiting our attention in this direction to thermal phenomena, heat itself is regarded as molecular motion, and it is an established fact that a given quantity of heat corresponds to a definite amount of mechanical work. On the molecular theory, quantity of heat means simply quantity of molecular motion, and temperature is the average moving energy of individual molecules. Molecular and mechanical motion are interchangeable. When a cannon-ball strikes a target and buries itself in the iron plate, the increased temperature of the united metallic masses is the result of the transfer of the motion of the ball, as a whole, to the molecules of which both ball and target consist; and on the other hand, the piston of a steam-engine receives all its power from the molecules of steam which rebound from its surface.

Sir William Thompson used the word "atoms," meaning the units which chemists now distinguish by the word "molecules;" but both atoms and molecules are of the same order of magnitude.

Motion is thus transferred between large and small masses indifferently, as it would be transferred between two elastic billiard-balls; and indeed the well-known laws of collision between elastic bodies were the basis of the analogy which led to the molecular theory. But in transferring our conceptions from ivory balls to molecules we are obliged to call on the imagination to take one of those extreme flights which all similar theories demand. Balls of ivory or steel, although made of the most elastic materials with which we are acquainted, would very soon come to rest in knocking about among each other; but our molecules must be so perfectly elastic that though each one makes millions of collisions every second, yet throughout all time no moving power is lost.

If we think only of their minuteness, the moving power of molecules may seem insignificant; but the molecules are as numerous as they are small, and their aggregate moving power is enormous. When a quart of water is heated from the freezing to the boiling point, as in the familiar process of boiling a teakettle, an amount of moving power is imparted to the molecules of water which, if transferred to a pound cannon-ball, would impart to it an initial velocity of 4,715 feet a second.

In a solid body the molecular motions are limited by the various forces which determine its structure, and are supposed to be restricted to a definite orbit. In a liquid the motion is less constrained, but is limited by the boundaries of the liquid mass. In a gas, however, the molecular motions are supposed to be entirely free, limited only by mutual collisions, or by the walls of the containing vessel. In both solids and liquids the relations are both so complex and obscure that the molecular theory has not been able to solve, except to a very limited extent, the difficult problems which they present; but with aeriform matter the theory has been far more successful, and gives a very satisfactory explanation of most of the observed phenomena. The tension or pressure exerted by a gas is the effect of molecular bombardment; and the well-known laws of Mariotte, of Charles, and of Avogadro, which define the condition of aeriform matter have been shown to be necessary consequences of the molecular theory.

Like the undulatory theory, the molecular theory has also led us to a knowledge of magnitudes which must ever evade our senses, and which almost defy our imagination. Thus we can calculate with great accuracy the average velocity of the molecular motion in any gas under given conditions,—that in hydrogen gas at the freezing-point, for example, being 6,099 feet in a second. And what is still more singular, we can calculate the average number of collisions per second, as well as the average length of the molecular path between two successive collisions, of course under definite conditions. In hydrogen gas, under the standard conditions of temperature and pressure, each molecule strikes against its fellows 17,750 million times a second; and the average molecular path is only 31 ten-millionths of an inch. This last seems incredibly small, but it is at least 136 times the average distance between two molecules; and in an assembly of men such an allowance would be regarded as very liberal.

These few data, which might be greatly multiplied, will show how definite are the conceptions which the molecular theory involves; and my brief description will give some idea, although very imperfect, of the scope of the theory itself. I can only add that in its relations to aeriform matter the theory has been developed mathematically by such men as Rankine, Clausius, and Maxwell; and that it gives a satisfactory account of the efficiency and mode of action of all thermo-motors, which, like the steam-engine, are such important factors in our civilized life.

But while in that special field known as the "kinetic theory of gases," the molecular theory is one of the best elaborated systems of modern science, it involves difficulties of conception fully as great as those we met in connection with the undulatory theory of light. Not only must we ascribe to the molecules a perfection of attributes, like perfect elasticity, which we only find in material bodies to a very limited degree, but also we must associate together attributes which from our experience seem to be incompatible. We must, in a word, give up all our ordinary prepossessions, and accept provisionally what seem to us monstrous hypotheses because they explain facts and relations which would be otherwise isolated phenomena, and because they are parts of a system which as a whole is a good working theory.

Having discussed similar difficulties of conception in the undulatory theory of light, it is unnecessary for me to dwell on the corresponding features in the system now before us. They obviously result from the same incompleteness of knowledge, and teach the same lessons already sufficiently enforced. Any one, however, who desires to study the details, will find them very clearly stated by J. B. Stallo, in his admirable book on "The Concepts and Theories of Modern Physics,"— a volume of the International Series to which I take great pleasure in referring.

I wish next to ask your attention to the chemical side of the molecular theory; for it is in this direction that it has run into the greatest extravagances; and yet, singular as it may seem, it is just here that it has proved of the most value as a working theory. In addition to molecules, the chemist is obliged to distinguish a still smaller subdivision of matter, which he calls "atoms." The ultimate analysis of the physicist goes no further than molecules; but the ultimate analysis of the chemist breaks up the molecules and gives us atoms. There must be as many kinds of molecules as there are distinct substances; but only as many kinds of atoms as there are elementary substances, some seventy at most. In a physical change in which the distinctions of substance remain unaltered the integrity of the molecules is preserved; but in a chemical change, which necessarily involves a change of substance, the molecules are broken up, and the atoms regroup themselves to form the molecules of the resulting products.

Thus when water is converted into steam, the molecules of water remain unchanged, and are only driven more widely apart; but when under the action of an electric current water yields oxygen and hydrogen gases, the molecules of water are broken up into atoms of oxygen and hydrogen, which regroup themselves to form the molecules of these aeriform products.

In fact the chemist regards the molecule in quite a different light from the physicist. To the latter, molecules are chiefly centres of force; while to the chemist they are more or less complex structures on which depend the distinctions and relations of substance. The qualities of substances are all referred to the molecules. The properties which distinguish water from alcohol, or sugar from salt, depend, not on the relations of any perceptible masses of these substances, but ultimately on the constitution of their molecules. Divide up a lump of sugar, and you may still distinguish the qualities of sugar in the smallest visible particles; but the chemist declares such a subdivision could not be carried on indefinitely, even if our senses could follow it. We should soon come to the smallest possible mass of sugar, which on pushing our subdivision further would break up into atoms of carbon, hydrogen, and oxygen, three well-known chemical elements. This smallest possible mass of a substance is the chemist's molecule; and hence his definition, — " the smallest mass of a substance which can exist by itself."

The forces which bind together atoms into molecules we distinguish as chemical forces, while such as determine the aggregation of molecules to form material masses are said to be physical, although we have no sufficient reason for assuming that there is any essential difference between the two; and all such forces, whatever may be their nature, are overcome by heat. At the intensely high temperatures which rule at the sun or at the fixed stars, it is supposed that the elementary atoms are isolated and intermingled, if not still further resolved; and as in the process of evolution of our system the planetary masses have cooled, it is held that the atoms have united to form the molecules of various substances, and that similar molecules have then aggregated to form definite material products. When, now, on the surface of the earth we heat such materials to the highest temperatures we can command, the process of world-building is to a limited extent reversed, presenting us with a remarkable class of phenomena known as dissociation. But why in the process of evolution unlike atoms should unite by preference to form molecules, while in the further aggregation to form material products only like molecules should associate together, remains an unexplained enigma.

A confusion often arises from the use of the word "elementary" in connection with substances as well as with atoms. The atoms are the only true chemical elements. An elementary substance like oxygen gas, sulphur, or iron, is an aggregate of molecules like any other substances, and externally presents no characters by which it can be recognized as elementary. But on analysis we find that its molecules are formed by the union of atoms of the same kind only, while the molecules of compound substances consist of atoms of different kinds. The molecules of oxygen gas, for example, are aggregates of atoms, as well as the molecules of water; but while the first consist of oxygen atoms only, the second contain atoms of hydrogen united to the atoms of oxygen.

Upon the distinction between atoms and molecules the philosophy of modern chemistry rests, and its symbolical language is based. Each one of the seventy chemical symbols stands for an atom. By grouping these symbols together, like letters to form a word, we represent the infinite possible varieties of molecules; and then all chemical changes are represented by an equation, writing the symbols of the substances concurring to produce the change in the first member, and the symbols of the substances resulting from the change in the second member. Such an equation declares that the process consists, as already said, in the breaking up of the so-called factors into atoms, and the regrouping of the resulting atoms to form the molecules of new substances, the products.

In the vapor of mercury immediately above the boiling-point, the atoms appear to be completely dissociated, so that this aeriform substance must be regarded as a mass of isolated atoms; but this is a very exceptional condition on the surface of the earth. In a few of the elementary gases or vapors, and in some of the simpler compounds, we are able to recognize — when the substances are aeriform — molecules consisting of only two or three atoms. But the molecules of most bodies are far more complex; and although as the complexity increases, our confidence in our inferences diminishes, yet with a considerable degree of confidence we can say that the molecules of some of the most familiar materials are aggregates of more than a hundred of these assumed ultimate elements of matter.

It was formerly assumed that the qualities and chemical relations of a substance depended on the nature of the elementary atoms of which its molecules consisted, and resulted from a blending of the qualities of the chemical elements in some mysterious way; but we now recognize that the chemical properties of substances depend in great measure, at least, on the manner in which the atoms are grouped in their molecules; and the order in which the different atoms are grouped in the molecules of substances is not only a legitimate object of inquiry, but is a subject which has nearly engrossed the attention of the chemists of the world for the past twenty-five years.

It would be impracticable in this course of lectures to give any clear conception of the nature of the evidence on which our knowledge of the atomic structure of molecules is based, or of the course of reasoning by which the accepted conclusions have been established. The subject is abstruse, and could not be made intelligible without entering largely into the details of chemistry.[1] In any modern work on organic chemistry, you can see our conceptions of the atomic structures of the molecules of various substances exhibited by placing the atomic symbols in definite relations to each other and connecting them by dashes supposed to represent the atomic

[1] I have endeavored to present the subject in a popular form in my " New Chemistry," and to that book I must refer any one who desires such information.

bonds. Such graphic representations are called structural formulæ, and are supposed to show at least the order in which the several atoms are united in the molecule. A single example of a structural formula will suffice as an illustration: —

Alizarine.

To one who realizes what is thus represented, but who is not familiar with the evidence, or imbued with the spirit of the matter, it must seem incredible that these apparently fanciful groupings should be sober results of science; and yet a reason can be given for the position of every symbol and of every dash, which — if the postulates are granted — must be admitted to be cogent. Moreover — what is the more remarkable fact — by following out the indications of such structural formulæ chemists have succeeded in preparing artificially a very large number of exceedingly complex compounds whose production under such circumstances could not but inspire the greatest confidence in the general correctness of the reasoning on which the structural formulæ were based. Some of these products, like alizarine, the coloring-matter of madder-root, — now prepared artificially from anthracene, one of the constituents of coal tar, — have such great commercial importance that these theoretical investigations have completely revolutionized large branches of human industry. Indeed if certainty of prediction is to be regarded as the test of validity, there is not one of the great systems of science, excepting the theory of gravitation, which has so completely vindicated its legitimacy as has this molecular theory of chemistry.

But although our structural formulæ have this wonderful power of prediction, and are therefore of the highest value as a system of science, yet no philosophical chemist thinks of regarding them as more than conventional symbols of relations which are at present incomprehensible. I would urge this point with special emphasis; because, although the same feature appears, as I have shown, in connection both with the theory of gravitation and with the undulatory theory of light, it has been said that the difficulties of conception, which an inherent gravitating force or an adamantine ether present are of no weight in view of the so general accordance of these theories with observed facts. In the present case no such claim can for a moment be maintained. All the conceptions are obviously conventional; and yet we have the same wonderful gift of prophecy. Is not the lesson plain? Man must work under limitations; he must often be content with the shadow instead of the substance of realities; but he may with confidence follow his earth-born systems of philosophy, if only they are grounded on experience and established in loyalty to truth.

And if this course of conduct be safe and legitimate in one realm of thought it certainly must be equally so in every other. Spiritual experience can be no exception to the general principle.

> " Finding, following, keeping, struggling,
> Is He sure to bless ?
> Saints, apostles, prophets, martyrs
> Answer, ' Yes.' "

Of the four great dominant systems in modern science to which I referred at the opening of this lecture I have as yet spoken of but three. The fourth during the last twenty-five years has attracted more attention than all the rest combined, and is inseparably associated with the name of that chief of naturalists, Charles Darwin. All these systems have been in their turn the subject of controversy; and too often the introduction of irrelevant theological issues has added acrimony to the debate. I say irrelevant because, if the position I have taken in regard to the relations of scientific systems to actual knowledge be correct, there can be no real issue between theology and the theories of science, — any more than between theology and the theory of music. In my view of the subject it is as useless to seek for theological antagonism in Darwinism as it would be to look for it in the Calculus.

In regard to the other systems, whatever differences of opinion may remain, all feeling about the matter has long since disappeared; but in regard to Darwinism, while the blaze of theological protest with which the theory was first received has died down, the embers of the excitement still remain; and it is more difficult to discuss the subject dispassionately. In another place I have before strongly urged the irrelevancy of theological issues on this question; and I will only add here a few remarks, which may be deemed pertinent because showing how the subject is viewed by a student familiar with the bearings and use of theories in a very different department of science. Further than this I do not feel that it is within my province to discuss the subject; for my special studies have been limited to a very different field; and I have not that detailed knowledge which alone would entitle me to express an authoritative opinion on the merits of the system.

The theory of Darwin rests on three distinct postulates. The first is that the existing species of plants and animals are not independent creations, but the results of a gradual evolution from earlier forms. The second is that while in the provisions of nature for the propagation of all living beings there is evidently a strong striving for the conservation of types, there is also a manifest tendency to variation, which although barely perceptible in single steps may go on increasing in successive generations to an unlimited extent. The third is that in the struggle for existence those variations are preserved which are best adapted to the environment, and which therefore protect the individuals possessing them in the midst of the terrible mortality which the struggle for existence entails.

However many facts or considerations may be

urged in their support, there is not one of these propositions which has been demonstrated beyond reasonable doubt; so that this theory, like the other great theories of science, rests on hypotheses, and must be judged as a scientific system by the completeness with which it explains the phenomena of nature.

In regard to the first proposition it seems strange that with all the attention which has been directed to the point during the last twenty-five years the fact of a transition between two well-marked species has not yet been established conclusively. For, admitting all that has been said in regard to the slowness of the transition, or the imperfection of the geological record, yet considering the extent of the field that has been surveyed, it seems very strange that more of the missing links have not been found. We can point with great precision to definite geological horizons — to use a now familiar technical term — on which certain species of well-marked types appeared on earth; and certainly, on the hypothesis we are considering, it is strange that we can in no case point unhesitatingly to other species in lower strata from which they descended, on the evidence of an unbroken series of the intermediate forms between the two.

Take the case in which we are the most interested, that of our own race. Assume all that is claimed in regard to the antiquity of man. Still, there is a definite horizon of the tertiary epoch below which man is not, but above which his remains are found in ever increasing abundance, with all the features of man and his works as strongly marked as they are to-day. Skeletons of these primeval men, and their belongings, are to be seen in our ethnological museums; and there are no greater differences of structure between them and ourselves than between the different races which inhabit the earth at the present day. But if man be descended from "an anthropoid animal of arboreal habits," it is passing strange that so far as any direct evidence goes, he should have appeared on the earth thus suddenly, and that we can find no traces of his progenitors either of the first, second, third, or of any other generation.

Nevertheless, the hypothesis of a gradual genesis of organic types seems to me not only reasonable in itself, but also in harmony with what we know of nature's workings. Growth, and not spasmodic effort, is the usual order of the divine government both in the material and in the spiritual world; and, reasoning from analogy, it is the method by which we should expect a new race of plants or animals would be introduced into the world. Indeed, from a scientific point of view any other mode is wholly unthinkable. Conceive of an elephant suddenly appearing in a tropical jungle, like a jack in a box, without any antecedents except a fiat; and see if the thought does not put to confusion every dictate of your experience, and every principle of your intelligence. You will then clearly see that if by mortifying reason the doctrine of independent creations can be accepted as a wonder, it cannot possibly be reconciled with the rest of your knowledge. Attempt further to realize in imagination the genesis of the first man. Was he suddenly created in his full development and strength, prepared to subdue nature? or did he come into the world as an infant, as have come all of his race since,—even the Saviour of the world?

Do not deem such questions irreverent. They are asked in that spirit of truth and soberness which sanctifies any inquiry. They ought not to be further pushed in this place; but the suggestions they make, if followed out in your own reflections, will bring you to the point of view from which a naturalist is compelled to look at the question of the origin of species. Roman mythology provided the heaven-born founders of their state with a foster-mother; and it is a similar necessity of thought which has led to what is usually regarded as the most objectionable feature of Darwinism. And apart from the authority of any undoubted declaration to the contrary, why should we be shocked by the hypothesis here involved?

On the other hand, it may be said, You admit that any prodigy must be accepted in science on adequate evidence; why not then receive the plain doctrine of independent creations taught by the Hebrew Scriptures? To this the Christian naturalist replies that all such inferences from the Scriptures must be to a very great extent questions of interpretation; and that in this case, as in so many instances before, the interpretation will be reconciled with the facts as soon as the truth plainly appears. And in the second place, he will add that while in science no wonder is so great that it may not be realized, so also no marvel is so sacred that it may not be reverently investigated; and that, whatever the event, the showing forth of the truth can only redound to the glory of God. Again, he may urge that this is a question between the interpretation of Nature on one side and of Scripture on the other, and that it ought not to be prejudged by assuming the infallibility of our rendering of either of these two co-ordinate authorities.

Moreover, this is not a question of creative power nor of Divine Providence. After all has been granted that any one can claim in regard to the constancy of the laws which we fully understand, there is, as has been plainly shown, abundant room left for interference; and it is more consistent with our conceptions of the Divine method to suppose that God works by introducing new conditions into old chains of causation than by spasmodic acts of creation, which must inevitably confuse and confound the intelligences he holds so dear. That such interference has taken place, it seems to me that the transition from a geological to an archæological museum as plainly shows as any record can whose meaning has been left to human interpretation. And when with every Yuletide the Christ Child becomes the emblem of all that is lovely, pure, and holy, why should we be alarmed at the supposition that as the Child of Mary "grew and waxed strong in spirit" so in the beauty of innocence, human intelligence at first slowly awakened to the wonders of this earth?

In regard to the second postulate on which Darwinism rests, we must admit that this also is to a great extent in harmony with well-established facts. No one can study the aspects and characters of a family of children without being struck with the undoubted truth that while minute details of features both of body and mind are wonderfully preserved, striking variations from the parent type are equally conspicuous. The same is seen to be even more markedly true of the lower animals when we watch them as closely; and when we think of it, the wonder is that the variations are not greater than they are.

There is nothing in our actual knowledge of nature which makes it any less strange that an acorn should always grow into an oak than that a race of monkeys after unnumbered generations should assimilate to men; and we know of no reason whatever why, with an equal experience, one change should not appear as natural as the other. Indeed I feel confident that, with all our knowledge of embryology, any one who reflects on the mysteries which the beginnings of life both in plants and animals present, will conclude that it is a far more remarkable fact that every creature should produce of its kind, than that occasional variations should occur. Nor is there any reason why we should be surprised to learn that in successive generations the variations should become cumulative, and lead to such a departure from the original type as to amount to a difference of species.

As before said, however, it is strange that the evidence of such a transition is so limited and inconclusive; and moreover, as was so strongly urged by the late Professor Agassiz, that the variations produced by domestication — which have been so carefully studied by the propagators of plants, and the breeders of stock — all tend to revert to the original wild condition.

Coming lastly to the third postulate, we find in this also a general principle which appears to a student of nature highly plausible. The struggle for life among the lower animals is a condition, the violence and destructiveness of which is wholly unappreciated except by those who have made a special study of the subject. The survivors of this internecine warfare who finish their allotted span of life are frequently not one in a hundred, often not one in a thousand. Tennyson quite understates the condition when he speaks of —

"finding that of fifty seeds
She often brings but one to bear."

Even in our own race the mortality is frightful to contemplate, — as Malthus has so vividly depicted it in his great work on population. Professor Wallace, who, independently of Darwin, and almost at the same time, originated the doctrine of natural selection, has distinctly said that it was the work of Malthus which gave him the key to the problem; and it is well known that Darwin himself was also strongly influenced by the facts so powerfully set forth in that remarkable book. I only repeat what some of you must have heard from Professor Wallace's own lips when I say that until one realizes the prodigal destructiveness of nature it is impossible to appreciate the strength of the doctrine of natural selection. Wallace also has stated that the generalization came to him as a sudden thought,—when, overpowered with what he was constantly witnessing in the East Indies, he stopped to reflect on the necessary issues of such fearful mortality. The "survival of the fittest" was to him a fact of observation; and by the indiscriminate slaughter of all others, a selection was seen to be made of those creatures whose features best fitted them to cope with their surroundings. The conclusion was that any accidental variation in color or form which better equipped the animal for the inevitable fight must be preserved; and that thus came the gradual adaptation to the environment in which natural selection consists.

All this is plausible, and to most naturalists conclusive; and that the struggle for existence must tend to perpetuate varieties seems to be beyond question. It still remains, however, to determine how far variations thus caused can proceed; and whether they can ever lead to fundamental differences of type. The assumption that all forms of plants and animals may have been thus produced from a few germs is as yet an hypothesis, to be judged, like any other hypothesis, by the extent to which it explains and correlates facts. Let it not be prejudged on any theory of Divine government, or on the basis of any speculative views about the nature of causation; for, were the hypothesis established without reservation,—a most improbable event, judging from the past history of science,—the new truth would only serve to enlarge our views of the mode of the Divine government; and there is abundant room for causation left.

Assume that the variations preserved by natural selection are all accidental, a point on which naturalists greatly differ, still what is the result? An adaptation to the environment. According to the theory, then, the conditions of the environment are a determining cause; and unless we believe that all nature was the result of a fortuitous concourse of atoms, we can find in these conditions abundant opportunities where intelligent causation can act. And the thought which the terrible facts implied in our theory force on the mind, are they not wholly in harmony with what we believe in regard to the Divine plan? Everywhere in this world are not beneficent results worked out through suffering? And to the lines of the English poet which I have just quoted, must I not add the anti-strophe from preceding stanzas? —

> "O yet we trust, that somehow good
> Will be the final goal of ill,
> To pangs of nature, sins of will,
> Defects of doubt and taints of blood.
>
> "That nothing walks with aimless feet,
> That not one life shall be destroyed,
> Or cast as rubbish to the void,
> When God hath made the pile complete."

Finally, looking at the Darwinian theory of development for a few moments as a whole, I would remark that it has not the completeness of the other dominant theories of science; and that the modes of action which it predicates have not been worked out. It is a doctrine rather than a complete system of science. Nevertheless, it is a doctrine which exerts very great power. It owes its influence over natural history students solely to the wonderful effect it has exerted in directing and stimulating investigation, as well as to its capability of exhibiting order and harmony among many classes of facts whose relations before were very obscure, if not wholly unrecognizable. Its influence on the religious thought of the student will depend very greatly on the manner in which its philosophy is presented by his religious teachers; and I therefore greatly deprecate hasty judgment or indiscriminating censure. Remember that, though not proven, it is a useful and admirable theory of science, and can be made an influence for good instead of for evil, if only set forth in the right light, and candidly accepted for its great worth within its proper sphere and just limitations. Set at naught all questions of intelligent or unintelligent causation as irrelevant, on which scientific theories have no bearing. The character of the First Cause cannot be judged from the mode of action of any secondary agencies. One mode of action is as mysterious as another, so far as any relations to a First Cause are concerned. The intelligence of the First Cause can only be judged from the result. Each man has grown from a germ; and we do not disown creative power when, for the sake of a consistent system, we assume that the species grew as well.

I myself deprecate the present domination of the Darwinian theory, not on account of what it is in itself, but because it has for a time thrust to one side, and cast into the shade, the doctrine of "organic types" so ably and so forcibly advocated by my late teacher and colleague, Professor Louis Agassiz, and which I believe to be the more valuable system of the two, at least in one important respect.

The conception that each of the four great families of the animal kingdom is a definite plan, a specific design, a creative thought, worked out in infinite variety, and adapted, possibly through the principles of natural selection, to varying conditions of soil or climate, is to me a far grander and more comprehensive doctrine than the one which now so exclusively prevails. The idea that types of structure are forms of thought is moreover an hypothesis which has very great intellectual reach and educational value; and for this great virtue of the older theory, Darwinism offers no sufficient substitute. When now we consider that the educational power of a scientific system is its chief element of strength, we cannot but regret that the present generation will lose much of the charm which the grand conceptions of Cuvier and Agassiz imparted to the study of natural history.

It is to be expected that a theory at once so original and so fruitful of suggestions as Darwinism should for a season control thought, and engross attention. But time may be trusted to place all human systems in their true relations; and I feel confident that the doctrine of organic types will before long exert its just influence. The new and the older conceptions are not mutually exclusive. Whatever is true in each will survive; whatever is false will be forgotten; and out of the limited hypotheses of to-day will grow the larger views of coming generations.

Having discussed the more characteristic features of the dominant systems of science, I will next add a few words in regard to the attitude of scientific scholars towards these systems, as there are marked differences in this respect which strikingly illustrate a point I desire to emphasize.

In the first place, then, we distinguish a very large and efficient class of scientific scholars who are wholly wedded to the system of science by which their studies are directed. They are men to whom the system gives strength and motive, and their whole intellectual life has been moulded by their guide. No wonder that they value the system, for it has made them what they are, and without it they would be to a great extent helpless. They are not men who originate systems or strike out new paths of discovery, but they are men who with a well-defined aim work zealously and efficiently. The system has opened to them new fields of investigation from which they have reaped an abundant harvest. They have thus extended the boundaries of knowledge, and are in consequence deservedly highly honored by their fellow-men. It is impossible that a system through which they have realized such great results, should be at fault or even have a blemish. Imperfections, which to other men appear glaring, they refer to errors of observation; inconsistencies are overlooked or ingeniously explained away, and mere philosophical objections are laughed to scorn. By such men the obvious symbolism of the system often comes to be regarded as a likeness of real things; and they dwell with equal emphasis on the essentials and the non-essentials of these arbitrary signs. Sometimes they even parade the extravagances of the system in order to testify more conspicuously their allegiance to their leader.

Such men are apt to be dogmatic, and to demand conformity to their well-grounded opinion as well as deference to their long experience. They do not readily brook dissent, especially from younger men; and when they have the power, they are sometimes tyrannical. The tyranny of a system is often as cruel as the tyranny of a despot, and may be exercised with complacency and self-respect by the "mens sibi conscia recti," who thinks he holds the keys of knowledge. We must not overlook what is often noble and worthy in these men. They are actuated by the power of conviction which a successful system inspires, and the intolerance of conviction is often associated with all that is pure, lovely, and of good report. There is a still nobler charity, which never faileth; but scholars are not always saints, and ostracism is a form of persecution which requires no sanguinary edicts. The noblest martyrs of science are not those who have braved great dangers and succumbed only before the unattainable; but rather those who have suffered even unto death, in consequence of depreciation, deprivation, and neglect. I have known of such, and among them the founders of one of the now dominant systems of science. Boycotting did not originate in Ireland; and among men of learning supercilious sneers may cause more suffering than blackballing. Scientific societies are probably no worse than other associations of men; but they have often been subservient to the intolerance of doctrine, and the domination of system.

A very much smaller class of scientific scholars display a habit of mind the very reverse of that I have just described. These men are superior to systems, of which, however, they speak with respect and condescension as the necessities of weak minds. They boast of their freedom from prejudice, and of their eclecticism in thought. They magnify inconsistencies of doctrine, or incompleteness of evidence. They expose the extravagances of the assumptions, or the unsoundness of the philosophy on which the dominant system is based. They are apt to be severe critics, and not to make due allowance for the limitations of methods or the necessary imperfections of all material results. They deal with negations rather than with affirmations, and see blemishes more readily than beauties. They are largely tolerant in theory, but they esteem the freedom of dissent more than the freedom of conviction. Such persons are usually prone to speculation, and are often fruitful in ingenious suggestions; but they have seldom the inclination or the patience for the tedious experimental work required to verify their hypotheses. They are, as a rule, highly imaginative, and their fancy paints with glowing colors every subject which they study; but their deductions are not always trustworthy, and their generalizations are often more subtile than profound. They are sanguine students, and their enthusiasm invests their teaching with a peculiar charm; but their zeal is not always tempered by prudence, and they are apt to be better expositors of what is known than investigators of what is unknown. Men of this temperament are not unfrequently truly liberal-minded, capable of large views, and fitted to be leaders; and have exerted more influence on the advancement of knowledge than many a harder student or deeper thinker.

Then there is another class of scientific students quite different from either of the two types we have sketched, and one which the specialism of our day is tending very greatly to multiply. Among this class are to be found many of the exact anatomists in natural history, the accurate analysts in chemistry, the untiring observers in astronomy, men who do much of the hard work of science, and on whose unswerving truthfulness and scrupulous exactness entire confidence can be placed. Minds which are occupied with minute details, which delight in delicate distinctions, and find pleasure in pushing observations to the extreme limit of accuracy, are apt to overlook the broader relations of truth, and value only definite results; and it is among such students that the positive philosophy finds most of its disciples. The class of men to whom we refer includes not only those who actually avow the doctrines of positivism, but also those who cherish a similar habit of mind, — men who worship facts and have little faith in ideals; men who never had any visions themselves, and therefore regard all visions as hallucinations; men to whom the material is the only reality, and the spiritual a dream. Such men often condemn as idle speculations the very hypotheses by which their own studies have been guided, and despise the theories which alone give significance to the facts that have cost them so dearly. These are worthy men and sincerely devoted to the truth; but their range is narrow, and their prospect restricted. They have always dwelt in a narrow valley amid pleasant pastures and beside still waters. They have never ascended unto the hills around them; they never have been awed by the mountain torrent; they never have been oppressed by the mountain gloom; they never have been gladdened by the mountain vision.

These are not ideal sketches which I have attempted to draw. They are lineaments of real men, whose biographies you may read in the history of science; whom you may meet to-day in every large society of scholars; whom you all must have known. Such characters are not the products of scientific study only. They are equally marked in every department of learning. In politics they are conservatists, liberals, or bureaucratists. In philosophy they become realists, nominalists, or positivists. In theology they are classed as low, broad, or high church; and they are recognized as conventionalists, impressionists, or preraphaelites in art. We must seek for the origin of such distinctions far down in the varying dispositions of the human mind and in the influences of education. However much they may be exaggerated by passion, or misguided by evil counsel, these traits of character are all good in themselves; and when blended in due proportion, they make the Solons, the Washingtons, the Shakspeares, the Miltons, the Newtons, the Faradays, of history. But so rarely are such qualities of mind combined that we often regard them as incompatible. You do not expect to find in a poet that attention to minute details which marks the man of affairs; nor in a wise counsellor the imagination of an artist; yet in the great pioneers of science such opposite faculties have been united in a most remarkable degree. They have been men of ideals, but men whose vivid imaginations were regulated by education, and chastened by wisdom. They have been men of courage and perseverance, who followed out their convictions through every discouragement. They have been men of entire truthfulness who have never hesitated to submit their doctrines to the test of crucial experiments and to abide by the issue. They have been men of the most scrupulous conscientiousness in attention to minute details, regarding themselves as responsible to the Giver of all truth for accuracy in every observation, and for exactness in every statement. Finally, they have been men of modesty and of reserve in judgment, realizing, as no other men ever have, how boundless is truth; how limited knowledge; how intricate the problem of nature; how weak in comparison the intellect of man.

LECTURE IX.

PREDOMINANT PRINCIPLES OF SCIENTIFIC THOUGHT.

WE have already in the preceding lectures discussed at some length the validity and character both of the inductive and of the deductive forms of scientific reasoning; we have also studied the authority and relations of the laws of nature, as well as the warrant and use of scientific systems; and in order to complete my survey of the general methods of science, I propose lastly to consider very briefly certain general principles by which students of nature have been greatly guided, and which, therefore, have exerted a marked influence on the progress of knowledge. As I have already said, the mental process of induction is subject to no known laws that can be accurately defined. It is a product of genius whose antecedents we can rarely trace, and whose conditions we can seldom analyze. Nevertheless, even genius is guided by experience; and there are two dictates of experience so wide in their application, and so generally trustworthy, that they claim our notice in this connection. I refer to the principles of analogy and of continuity, which although often found deceitful guides, yet when followed with caution and judgment very seldom lead astray. Other suggestions of experience, like the principles of least action, of least waste, of the sufficient reason, of successive approach, of adaptation, and of intelligent plan, have been found at times of great value in the study of science ; but they are not principles so generally accepted as those first named, and are more restricted in their application.

There can be no question that the suggestions of analogy have led to more discoveries in science than all other influences combined.

If the force of the earth's gravitation is not sensibly diminished at the summits of the highest mountains, why may it not reach to the moon? Since the phenomena of light resemble in so many respects those of sound, why may they not be, like these, the effects of wave-motion? If there be in masses of matter an internal molecular motion which produces thermal changes, why should not these motions obey the well-known laws which govern the motions of the masses themselves? If, as Malthus has shown, the struggle for existence has exerted such a marked influence on the history of the human race, why should it not produce far deeper and more lasting effects among the lower animals, where the struggle is vastly more intense? Thus it is through analogy that men have been led to each of the great systems of science now dominant in the intellectual world. So also in unnumbered other instances analogy has given the suggestion which observation or experiment has verified.

The astronomer noticed through the telescope

patches of dazzling whiteness around the poles of Mars; and since this planet moves around the sun under relations similar to those of the earth, he inferred that the greater brilliancy was caused by the reflection of light from snow-caps like those which render the earth's poles so inaccessible; and when on watching the planet's disk from year to year, he observed that these patches alternately increased and diminished with the changing Martial seasons, he felt assured that this suggestion of analogy was correct.

Down to the beginning of this century the so-called earths and alkalies, such as alumina, magnesia, lime, soda, and potash, had been regarded as elementary substances; but towards the close of the last century Lavoisier had shown that several materials closely resembling the earths, such as iron-rust, litharge, and tinstone, were compounds of metals with the then newly discovered oxygen gas. Analogy at once suggested that the earths and alkalies must also contain metals united to oxygen; but although the analogy inspired a confident belief in this inference, the chemists at the time did not succeed in decomposing the compounds, because the means at their command were inadequate. But the discoveries of Galvani and Volta gave the world a new agent in voltaic electricity, which by the decomposition of water proved to be a reducing force of wonderful power; and the first moment he could command a voltaic battery of sufficient strength Sir Humphry Davy applied the new force to the alkalies, when out at once the metals flowed.

In 1812 iodine was discovered by Courtois in the

crude soda-salt called kelp, which is prepared by burning wrack, and is simply the ashes of this seaweed. For a long time previously burnt sponge had been used as a remedy in cases of goitre, which in the mountainous regions of Switzerland produces such wide-spread and distressing results. As sponge in its habitat and relations resembles sea-weed, analogy suggested that the burnt sponge might contain a minute amount of iodine, and that its efficacy might be due to this new elementary substance; and in 1820 Dr. Coindet, a physician of Geneva, aided by the young chemist Dumas, succeeded not only in proving the presence of iodine in the sponge, but in replacing a nauseous dose by preparations of iodine which have proved almost a specific for the terrible disease.

Such examples might be multiplied indefinitely; but we have only time for one other, which is, however, very striking. As we have before said, the elementary rays of a beam of light must be regarded as moving in a definite plane; and a beam all whose rays are moving in the same plane is said to be polarized. By optical means we can readily determine the position of this plane, which we call "the plane of vibration," sometimes also "the plane of polarization." When a polarized beam of light passes through a plate of quartz in the direction of the axis of the well-known hexagonal crystals of this mineral the plane of polarization suffers a rotation, to an extent depending on the thickness of the plate. Now on some of the hexagonal crystals in which quartz crystallizes there are to be found certain small planes, called "plagihedral," which are distributed after a helioidal, or spiral-like, type of symmetry; and according as the spiral ascends to the right or to the left, the plane of polarization is rotated to one side or to the other. Remember also that the effects of crystals on light are referred by the undulatory theory to their unequal elasticity in different directions, and that similar effects can be obtained with homogeneous glass by subjecting this transparent material to unequal strains, and thus developing unequal elasticity in different directions; add to all this the further fact that when a current of electricity flows through a spiral of copper wire wound round a bar of iron, and renders it magnetic, a screw-like strain is developed in the bar,—and you will then have the basis from which Sir John Herschel, to whom these facts and theories were very familiar, inferred by analogy that if glass or other transparent material could be subjected to a similar magnetic strain, we might obtain under such conditions the same effect of rotating the plane of polarization which is so markedly exhibited by quartz; and further, that possibly such a strain might be developed by a powerful electro-magnet. Herschel himself never verified this suggestion of analogy; but the effect was subsequently realized in a most striking manner by Faraday.

The validity of analogical reasoning unquestionably depends on the harmonies of nature. Since the universe has been made throughout on one plan, and, however varied the details, the same general patterns reappear in all its parts, both great and small, we can safely infer from our very limited experience in a narrow field what are the conditions and relations in remote and inaccessible provinces which we can never directly explore with our senses. Hence it is that we can infer that molecules and atoms obey the same laws of motion as suns and planets. It is wholly conceivable that the microcosmos should have been planned on a system entirely different from that of the macrocosmos; but apparently the very reverse is the truth; and a theory, which assumes that within the masses of material bodies the motions of suns and systems are reproduced on a scale so minute as to task our power of imagination to grasp the conception, is found to be in complete accordance with all the facts which can be observed. Moreover, whenever we have been able to obtain evidence we have found our reliance on the unity of nature fully justified.

Within a comparatively few years our confidence in this regard has been very greatly strengthened by the revelations of the spectroscope. If our globe was once thrown off from the sun we might expect that it would be a chip of the old block; but we can conceive of no necessity which requires that the materials of the fixed stars should be like that of our earth. Still, the spectroscope tells us that in those immensely distant bodies the same elementary substances are glowing with which we are so familiar in our laboratories. And if anywhere in the depths of space there revolves around one of those centres of energy a globe which has been reduced to the climatic conditions of our earth, we can infer with a confidence which approaches certainty that its rocks contain the same minerals, and that its plants and animals are fashioned after the same patterns with which we are so familiar; and, if it has also become the abode of intelligent beings, that they have been discussing the same great problems which have perplexed man.

It is solely the unity and harmony of nature which renders analogical reasoning valid. To this harmony our own being answers, and it is only because we are in unison with nature that we are able to interpret her methods. Were our minds not in harmony with our surroundings, or those surroundings not in harmony with the rest of creation, our intelligences would have been confounded, and all nature would have been to us a sealed book.

Man cannot conceive in a concrete form of anything he has not previously received through the senses. No hypothesis can be so much as framed in the mind which has not some semblance in previous experience; and as through our senses we have direct cognizance only of material things, we cannot picture to ourselves any existences without associating with them some of the qualities of matter. The most we can do is to alter the combinations of our experience, or to change in degree the qualities we have actually observed. This is all we have done in forming the most subtle conception man has ever grasped, — that of the luminiferous ether. We are familiar with elasticity, and we can predicate an elasticity a million or a billion times greater than any that is known to us. We know what density

FAILURES OF ANALOGY. 267

is, and we can at least in words describe a material less dense than any known substance in a similar extreme degree, and then in imagination combine these extravagances. But what we reach is a condition of matter, and all our calculations in regard to it are based on its likeness to matter. We can, in imagination, vary the known qualities of matter to an unlimited degree. We can combine these qualities in other than the accustomed relations. But, however much we may think or talk about other states of existence, we cannot actually picture to ourselves any existence or mode of action of which experience has not given us some semblance. Thus all our science — that is, our knowledge of things — rests on experience, and never could have been built up had not the unknown been of a piece with the known.

But while analogy is thus the guiding rule of scientific thought, it is a rule which cannot be blindly followed. The suggestions of analogy have often proved delusive, — either because the resemblances on which we counted were superficial and not real, or because our scientific methods and appliances were inadequate to establish the relations we suspected. The history of science is full of examples of misdirected efforts whose failure is to be attributed to one or the other of these causes. Two marked instances will serve as illustrations.

After the elder Herschel with his large telescope had distinguished in several of the nebulæ points of light, and later Lord Rosse with a much larger reflector had resolved still more of these distant star-clusters, it was inferred by astronomers that all the nebulæ were groups of stars, whose resolution was only a question of telescopic power. But since the application of the spectroscope to the problem it has been found that there is a very large class of these objects which are masses of luminous vapors; and it is evident that the astronomers were at first deceived by a superficial resemblance.

Faraday, after he had investigated with such consummate skill the relations of electricity to magnetism, conceived that similar relations must exist between these modes of energy and gravitation; and devoted a great deal of labor and thought to the investigation of the subject. He made several series of laborious experiments in the clock-tower of the Houses of Parliament and elsewhere, but with absolutely no results. To use his own words, "The experiments were well made, but the results are negative;" but he adds, "I cannot accept them as conclusive." So the question remains to the present day; and it is possible, as Faraday evidently believed, that the failure arose from the want of appliances sufficiently delicate to show the expected effects; although, if the opinion previously expressed in these lectures in regard to the nature of gravity be correct, it was the seeming analogy which was at fault, as Faraday himself at times suspected.

In his failures not less than in his successes, the example of Faraday may teach us most important lessons. A mind so subtile as his is apt to be captivated by fanciful resemblances; but he never followed vaguely the suggestions of analogy, inquiring diligently at every step whither they were leading, and always submitting desire to the control of experience. As thus curbed, analogy may be always safely followed; and as Bishop Butler so tersely wrote, "Analogy is the very guide of life." She leads us when we are least aware of her guidance. She colors all our language. She determines half our thoughts. In submitting ourselves, as we must, to her control, let us consider well the situation; and while we acknowledge our dependence, never part with our more precious birthright. Our guide is moulded of the same clay as ourselves; and there may be things in earth, as well as in heaven, not dreamt of in her philosophy. And, moreover, if harmony with nature be a test of reality, then harmony with the spiritual life, then adaptation to the needs of the soul, is also a mark of certitude, an equally overpowering evidence of truth.

Generalization in science is only a form of analogical reasoning. We are said to generalize when we ascribe to a class of objects qualities or relations which have been shown to be true of certain characteristic members of the class. Thus a certain number of substances having a brilliant lustre, and to a greater or less degree ductile or malleable, and at the same time good conductors of heat and electricity, which we class under the general name of metals, have been found after repeated trials to resist every attempt to decompose them, and are therefore regarded as elementary substances. Hence we conclude that all metals are elementary substances; and when a new one is discovered, as is not unfrequently the case, we never think of attempting to analyze it, because experience with similar bodies assures us that all such attempts would be fruitless.

Again, it has been shown by Davy, Wöhler, and others, that alumina, magnesia, and several of the similar earths are metallic oxides, and the metals of which they consist have been extracted and studied; indeed aluminum and magnesium are now articles of commerce and familiar to every one. Hence we conclude that all amorphous powders resembling alumina and magnesia, and having like chemical properties are also metalliferous; so that when, within a few years, a large number of new earths were distinguished the chemist accepted them at once as metallic oxides, although in most cases the metal has not actually been isolated.

Obviously, our assurance in all these cases rests on our confidence in the unity of nature's plan and method; and the argument which convinces us differs from the ordinary argument from analogy only in the extent of the ground covered. When Davy inferred from analogy that potash must contain a metal, and successfully followed out the suggestion, he reasoned from a comparatively superficial resemblance between a few things to a deeper relationship. When we conclude that the new earths are metallic oxides, we reason from a wide knowledge of a class of bodies that a new substance, which has been shown to have the other qualities and relations of this class, also has an additional character, — though as yet unobserved, — which is common to all the other members therein grouped. The reasoning in the last case is far more conclusive than in the first; but evidently it rests on the same assurance, the uniformity of nature. Prior to experiment Davy's inference was only probable; our conclusion is as certain as that the sun will rise to-morrow. In either case, however, the argument is based on resemblances more or less remote, and the difference is one of degree and not of kind; and so we may have every degree between the certitude of a far-reaching generalization and the mere suggestion of a feeble analogy. In science the merest hint may be of value; for when in an investigation bewildered by complex conditions we are hesitating which way to turn, or what to try first, the faintest suggestion of analogy may decide us. On the other hand, in the relations of the spiritual life we must remember that even in our grandest generalizations we cannot escape from the material clogs of our mortal experience; that all our knowledge is necessarily relative to our environment; and that though its material forms are doubtless symbols of higher realities, yet these earth-born fancies can never be an exact picture of things spiritual, or a precise measure of things divine.

Man lives in time, and he cannot release his thoughts from the fetters which this condition imposes. Continuous time and a corresponding continuous change or growth are so inseparable from human experience that existence in time, with progressive change, is the only mode of being of which the mind can form a concrete idea. We can reason and talk about a Being who is the same yesterday, to-day, and forever, and to whom a thousand years are as one day and one day as a thousand years, — we firmly believe in the reality of such a Being; but we cannot picture the existence to our minds, as the very imagery plainly shows. As we cannot escape from the limitations of matter, so we cannot escape from the limitations of time. As regards every event, the mind demands an antecedent and a consequent. The common axiom that "every event must have a cause" is another phase of the necessity which the conditions of our environment impose on our being. The necessity is so interwoven in the complex web of material existence that we cannot dissociate it if we would. It is not a necessity of thought; for that Being who is from eternity to eternity the same had no antecedent and no cause. But it is a necessity of the imagination, and therefore a necessity of scientific knowledge.

In science we call this lesson of experience "the principle of continuity," and it is a belief which exerts a profound influence on all our reasoning about material relations. It is this principle which alone gives strength to the doctrine of evolution; but it is equally a controlling power in almost every department of scientific inquiry; indeed it controls the very process of thought itself.

Examples of continuity of action are all around us, and illustrations of the successful application of the principle in scientific reasoning might readily be cited. The science of geology is especially rich in examples of this class; and our knowledge of the relative ages of strata, and of the succession of life on the earth, is in very large measure the result of tracing out the evidences of continuous changes; and in physics we often reason from what we can see to what we cannot see, through a chain of sequences which connects the parts of a continuous series, and thus exhibits relations which would be otherwise obscure. The same principle underlies all classification in natural history, and, as has been already said, is the warrant of the theory of evolution. Evolution is simply a wider growth, and is implied in the only conception of being of which the mind can frame a definite image. For our purpose, however, it is not necessary to multiply illustrations; and we turn next to some examples of the break of continuity which have a much more important bearing on our subject; for they indicate that beneath the obvious material relations there may be other influences at work in determining the course of events.

While we can usually safely follow the indications of continuity, yet, as in the case of analogy, we are frequently deceived, and even more frequently than in the application of the cognate principle; and examples of break of continuity present a striking feature of nature which cannot be overlooked. Often the break is only apparent, resulting from the inability of our senses to follow changes succeeding each other with more than a certain limited rapidity. When a ball is fired from a rifled cannon it gains in the two hundredth part of a second its full and fearful velocity, and yet we know that while in the gun it passed through every stage of motion from indefinite slowness onwards. So also with molecular motions, which may last only some thousand millionths of a second; between successive collisions all the phases of the recoil, the free path, and the rebound, must follow each other in due order.

We do however find in nature phenomena which, after making every allowance for the imperfection of our senses, appear to be absolute breaks of continuity. One of the most striking of these is to be seen in the process of crystallization. I confess that I never witness the process without amazement. That out of a perfectly homogeneous and structureless liquid there should suddenly separate a perfect geometrical solid, with all its sparkling facets grouped with mathematical exactness, is to me one of the greatest wonders in this world of beauty. The structure of a crystal is of course not so complex as that of a plant or an animal; but then it has no gradual genesis; it has no antecedents; it appears as a sudden break of continuity; its formation approaches as near to a sudden creation as anything we ever behold. This may seem to you inconsistent with what you have heard of the slow growth of crystals. But such statements apply only to the large, massive crystals, such as you may see in our museums, — some of which have doubtless been centuries in forming. I refer, on the contrary, to the sudden production of the minute crystals of which the larger crystals are gradually formed aggregates. These small crystals, when examined with a microscope, are seen to be as perfect as the larger specimens; indeed, they are often far more perfect; and they seem to drop out of the solution instantaneously, — the creation of each one, if I may dare to use the term, being in some cases attended with a flash of light as if to attest its mysterious origin.

Another circumstance which sometimes attends on crystallization is even more indicative of a break of continuity than the facts I have mentioned. In the liquid menstruum, as it is called, the constituents of the future crystal are often mixed in variable proportions; but the crystals which form unite these ingredients in absolutely definite proportions, conforming to the great law of combining proportions of chemistry. This law in itself is probably the most general and striking break of continuity in nature. You may mix two substances, by solution or otherwise, in any proportions whatever, and there appears to be a perfect interpenetration of the masses. Then when an electric spark, or some other cause, determines chemical union, these substances unite in certain constant, definite, and calculable, proportions, excluding the excess of one or the other ingredient; and this is what takes place in the example of crystallization just referred to. In order to reconcile this striking phenomenon with the principle of continuity, several chemists have endeavored to show that these definite proportions were merely a maximum effect of such restricted range that we failed to recognize the gradations; and I have myself sought to test this suggestion by experimenting, — thinking that the range must be greater in proportion as the combining force was feebler, and that possibly in cases of weak chemical affinity it might be detected. But although at first I thought I discovered an indication of such an effect, my later experiments have proved that the proportions are just as definite in weak compounds as in strong. I see therefore no escape from the conclusion that this apparent break of continuity is a reality; and should not such results teach us that the preconceptions of our experience are not infallible? Thus may even the study of science prepare us to recognize other possibilities of being than those of known material relations.

That mode of being not directly cognizable by our senses we call the supernatural; and we often reason as if it were something apart from and above nature. But is it not the more consistent theory that the supernatural and the natural are simply different phases of one system; and that while with our bodily senses we apprehend only the material relations of this system, we can with our spiritual sympathies and aspirations reach out towards those higher associations for which this life is a preparation? Or may we not rather say that the supernatural embraces the natural, modifying in numberless ways the more obvious material relations, and thus constantly apprising us of its omnipresence; and do not such indications as we have been studying ever remind us that the material is not all of knowledge or all of life, and give us a confident expectation of more life and ampler knowledge behind the vail?

When we fully comprehend that the fundamental conceptions comprised under the doctrine of continuity are simply a product of experience, and dependent on material relations, we shall be able to think and reason more justly about spiritual relations in which the limitations of the material do not exist;

and although difficulties of conception may by no means be removed, yet a way is opened by which the seeming contradictions of theological doctrines with our experience may possibly be reconciled.

As has already been intimated, we have no experience, and therefore no actual knowledge, of any state of existence, except of that in which continuous change and growth constitute the invariable order of being. Our idea of time is simply a conception based on the succession of events. The fundamental conception of duration arises unquestionably from the succession of thoughts in our own minds. It is thus that we reach an idea of short duration, as of the swing of a pendulum; and it is only of such durations that we can be said to have any direct consciousness. Longer durations are to us simply the multiples of such short intervals as we can directly perceive and appreciate; or else have known relations to the periods of events which we assume as the standards of measure. The day is the period of the rotation of the earth on its axis; the hour is one twenty-fourth part of a day, the minute the one sixtieth part of an hour; the second the one sixtieth part of a minute, and at any given place is the duration of the swing of a pendulum (about one meter long), whose exact length is easily adjusted. It is only this smallest unit of which we can be said to have any direct perception. Our knowledge of much larger periods, however exact, is purely formal. When a boy learns that a year is the period of the revolution of the earth around the sun, the most he gains is the idea that this, to him already familiar period in human relations, during which the succession of seasons is completed, is the duration of a continually recurring astronomical event. Nor does his knowledge become any more real when he is further informed that the year comprehends three hundred and sixty-five days, five hours, forty-eight minutes, forty-seven and seven tenths seconds. But he can be thus impressed with the fact that the durations of the events by which time is measured bear a constant relation to each other, and hence, be led to the conclusion that the quantity measured is a real attribute of material relations, and hence, also of material life.

A very few considerations, however, will show that time is solely an attribute of material relations, and no adequate measure, even of that phase of our spiritual life which terminates with the death of the mortal body. Conventionally, we measure man's life in years; but who does not recognize that Descartes, dying at fifty-four, or Raphael, dying at thirty-seven, lived not only a richer, but a really longer life than most of the Methuselahs and Nestors of history. He lives longest who is able most fully —

> "To crowd the narrow span of life,
> With wise designs and glorious deeds."

Life should be measured not by years, but by thoughts, events, and deeds. The succession of thoughts in the mind is a far more accurate measure of conscious duration than the beats of a pendulum; although as compared with the standard of time, the flow of thoughts is so variable, not only in the minds of different men, but also in our own minds under varying conditions. After some critical experience, how often do we say that we have lived longer during the past day or week than during months or years before; and these words are no mere figure of speech, but on the contrary express an important truth.

During our mortal lives, the rapidity of thought is limited by our physical organization; but we can easily conceive that it might be indefinitely increased; and such conceptions appear in part to be realized both in the phenomena of dreams, and in the experience of drowning men; who, when subsequently resuscitated, often have said that, during the brief interval before they became unconscious, the whole course of their lives flashed through the mind.

Could we increase the rapidity of thought, we should increase the conscious duration of life during a given time; and it is a perfectly rational conception, that with a finer organization the life of a century might be crowded into a day. Obviously, we can apply magnifying power to time as we can to extension. As under our microscopes, an area barely perceptible to the eye becomes spread out into a broad plane, teeming, it may be, with life, so we can conceive that a duration barely perceptible to our senses may be to a more delicate organism a period of vast activities.

" Alike in God's all-seeing eye,
The infant's day, the patriarch's age."

Magnify, now, duration indefinitely, not by extending time, but by crowding activities into the present, and you annihilate time,—or rather, you eliminate the element of time from the spiritual life; and such considerations will lead the mind to recognize the truth that eternity consists not in limitless time, which would be unendurable, not in passionless contemplation, which would be weariness, but in the removal of the limitations of time from our mental activities. Time, like space, is an attribute of material relations; and although in this life even our mental processes are controlled by the limitations which these relations impose, and although the imagination can form no distinct image of a state of being freed from the limitations of time and space, yet we are able by such considerations as we have here imperfectly presented so far to dissociate in our thoughts these conditions from our spiritual life as to recognize the aptness of the imagery by which such a state is prefigured in the Scriptures, and also to admit the possibility of spiritual relations which to our material vision seem to be contradictory. We cannot be said to have actual knowledge of any state of being unconditioned by time and space; but the circumstance that we are able to recognize some of the attributes of such a state is in itself weighty evidence of its reality.

To a being freed from the limitations of time there are no beginnings and no ends; or rather, those transitions which to us appear as the beginnings or the ends of events, are simply phases of the ever present and the ever actual. God's prescience is not foreknowledge, but actual knowledge. He seeth the end from the beginning, because both are ever present;

and His knowledge is not inconsistent with man's free will, because that will is limited in its exercise by the very conditions of time and space which the Creator has imposed on the material universe.

In all material relations man's free will is a definite factor, as much so as any other form of energy; and the final attitude of man's mind towards his Maker is equally within his own power of determination; but here man's prerogative stops. Man as a living creature has a subordinate power in the material creation. Man as a living soul may regulate the attitude of his mind to other living souls; but however completely he may control actions, he cannot force the wills even of those nearest and dearest to himself. In a word, his will has control only over material relations and over himself; and to one who does not wait on results, but who sees at once every stage of our material processes and of our mental conflicts, the foreknowledge of events may be perfectly consistent with the freedom of His subordinate actors in the drama of human life. The architect, who in his imagination sees his building completed in all its details, may be said to have a foreknowledge which is compatible with a large degree of freedom among the workmen in their respective spheres; and although this illustration fails in essential details, it may serve to prefigure that fuller prescience when the limitations which here exist are removed.

Such illustrations do not of course remove the difficulty we have in conceiving of a being freed from the limitations of time; and, by dwelling on the thought that it is impossible that we should be free if God foresees all our actions, we can easily make the incompatibility appear as marked as ever. All that we can hope is to recognize the possibility of conditions which may make such relations intelligible, without expecting to comprehend them. Free will is a fact of consciousness, and such considerations as we have advanced make God's foreknowledge a clear inference of our intelligence from facts of consciousness; and here as elsewhere we must be content to accept our limitations, and wait for the clearer day when we shall know even as we are known.

It is not solely in spiritual relations that our reason leads us to inferences which lie beyond the powers of conception. This is equally the case in the higher forms of mathematics, where, as we have before said, we often deal with relations, like the higher dimensions of multiple algebra, of which it is impossible for the mind to form any distinct idea; and no mathematician questions that these relations are realities, yet he can only describe them by inadequate and figurative language which deals with types and symbols.

This power of the human mind of reaching out in various directions beyond its own experience, to relations of which it can form no concrete and material images, is to my own mind one of the strongest evidences of the reality of a higher life in which these dim visions shall be realized.

We do not, however, care to deal with theological subtleties; but the overlooking of the distinction between the material and the immaterial, which we have attempted to emphasize, has led to a fallacy in much of the reasoning about the genesis of nature which it is important to expose.

We can form no clear conception of any act except as taking place at a given time. The battle of Waterloo was fought June 18, 1815. America was discovered on the 12th of October, 1492. Julius Cæsar was assassinated in the ides of March, 44 B.C. The battle of Marathon was fought September 28 or 29 (according to somewhat uncertain computations), 490 B.C.; and the popular belief is that the world was created at an equally definite date in the remote past, which could be stated in equally precise chronology if we only had the knowledge. At the basis of this belief is a tacit assumption that all intelligence, the Creator as well as the creature, must act under the limitations of time. "God spake and it was done;" and we assume that the word of the Creator, like the word of man, was spoken at a definite moment in the succession of events which measure time. But science shows that the genesis of the world was a process of gradual growth; and the inconsistency of this conclusion in a great variety of phases with man's preconception of the mode of creation, has always been a hindrance to faith.

It is by no means perfectly clear how such a general preconception arose. It certainly did not come from the study of nature; for, as has been said, the whole scheme of nature, so far as we understand it, is wholly at variance with such an idea. Growth is the order of nature; and although as yet no man has been able to discover any distinct and unquestionable traces of the first introduction of a new species into the world, yet it cannot be seriously questioned that the theory of the gradual development of organic types is in harmony with all that we know of biology.

Nor does it appear probable that the preconception came from the Hebrew Scriptures; for although in Genesis it is distinctly declared that all things were created by Jehovah, the great "I Am," the mode of creation is described in such obviously figurative language that no difficulty has been found in reconciling it with any result of science when once clearly established. Nevertheless, it is very generally assumed that a creation "ex nihilo" at a definite moment of time is expressly declared in the Bible, and on this basis it is constantly urged, in answer to the apparently irreconcilable evidence of science, that the Almighty could instantly call a universe into being out of nothing if He chose. Granting a clear revelation, such a plea might be relevant. But there is no such clear revelation; for admitting whatever authority the most extreme literalist may claim for the Pentateuch, it must be conceded that the language of these early books admits of the most diverse interpretations; and the mode of creation still remains an open question for scientific investigation. The question is not how to reconcile observation and revelation, but to find out as far as possible what the facts really were.

If, then, the preconception cannot be traced either to a distinct revelation, or to the observation of nature, must it not result from the normal action of the human mind under its limitations? In all human relations creation, whether in art, in literature, or in science, implies effort, often long-continued effort, which taxes all the strength and all the perseverance that the most gifted men can command. There are obstacles to be overcome, and there is a consciousness of weakness and inefficiency, which ever reminds us of our limited powers. Moreover, at most our creation consists in transforming old materials into new shapes. The potter moulds the clay; the sculptor chisels the marble, and both clothe with beauty the rude materials on which they work; but all the while they are painfully conscious of the limitations which the material imposes on their art. It is natural, therefore, to think of the Almighty as a power before which all obstacles yield without effort, and which can call order and beauty not only out of chaos but out of nothing. There is, however, an illusion which vitiates this inference; and the old aphorism "Ex nihilo nihil fit" is much nearer the truth. The error consists in overlooking the limitations of time by which we are circumscribed, but which cannot bound the Creator. Our times are in His hands; but God himself does not work in time. "God worketh hitherto and I work," said the Saviour; but He worketh not as man worketh. "He seeth the end from the beginning, and looketh under the whole heavens;" and what to us appear as consecutive and consequent are to Him parts of a plan whose purposes will be fully revealed only when time shall be no more.

The view, therefore, that a theory of creation by slow development derogates from the attributes of the Almighty is a pure illusion resulting from our limitations. To Him who inhabiteth eternity purposes are valued, not as they seem to ripen fast or slowly to us, but according to their beneficent design. God, who is ever present throughout all time both to will and to do of His good pleasure, comprehends our temporal relations in His all-embracing Providence, and adopts methods in view of the universal, and not solely of a temporal good.

In all material relations we have every reason to believe that the knowledge we have acquired is accurate and trustworthy; but in speculating about spiritual relations, we must always remember that we are liable to be deceived by the aberrations of our material vision; and we cannot safely build a theory of the universe on such treacherous foundations as our preconceptions of the methods of the Divine government can alone furnish.

The conception of the creative power as acting through an indefinite time, or rather as independent of time, was familiar to Origen and the other Nicene fathers, and was embodied by them in the famous doctrine of the "Eternal Generation," which, although usually limited to the second person of the Trinity, was by Origen, at least, extended to the material creation.

The recognition of this doctrine as applicable in some limited measure to the genesis of nature would tend very greatly to reconcile the systems of theology with the systems of science. For if the theologian accepts the eternal generation of the Son as one of the most fundamental of his tenets, how can he consistently find fault with the analogous doctrine of science which involves a similar idea?

We do not advance the doctrine of the eternal generation of matter as positive knowledge, or even as a legitimate inference of science; but we do claim that it is a possible inference from the observed facts of nature, and that it is in entire harmony with the most profound dogmas of theology.

Such speculations may have little value towards establishing truth; but they at least show how foolish it is to set theological dogmas in opposition to systems of science. All real knowledge must eventually be found to be in harmony, and the only way to find truth is to seek it with untiring effort, and to keep the mind unbiassed by any theories during the search. The path is difficult, the labor exhausting, and without faith in eternal verities the investigator will soon lose heart, and abandon the search. If, however, with singleness of purpose the student keeps the one great aim in view, and not only has faith in truth but the courage to face it in whatsoever guise it may appear, he will gather strength as he proceeds; and, although his vision in this life may be restricted, and he may not rid himself of earthly clogs, yet in the end he will at least be satisfied that throughout the universe of being One Mind ruleth over all.

Moreover, such speculations may have this positive result in so far as they show that time is not the measure of spiritual being. There are often periods in life when crowding opportunities demand more time than we have to give. But taking life as a whole there is time enough for all we are able to accomplish, and it is more energy, and not more time, that we really need: —

> "'T is life of which our nerves are scant;
> . . . . .
> More life and fuller, that I want."

LECTURE X.

THE SYSTEMS COMPARED,—RELIGION AND SCIENCE.

IN the necessarily imperfect sketch of scientific methods which has been given in the previous lectures, my main purpose has doubtless been obvious from the first; and I think it must have clearly appeared that the speculative objections to Christian belief which are so confidently set forth are no greater than must be encountered in every department of abstract thought, and are inseparable from our material relations. The close resemblance in this particular between the systems of science and the systems of religion presents, as it seems to me, by far the most cogent of the evidences of natural theology; and after examining the features of the scientific systems it remains for me to bring together the separate threads of the discussion and present the opposite side of this very striking analogy.

I enter, however, on this part of the task I have undertaken with great diffidence. Thus far I have been, for the most part, on my own ground; now I pass over on to yours. And at the same time I feel I ought to change positions, and in this distinguished school of theological learning to seek instruction, and not attempt to teach. I feel, moreover, that my education in great measure unfits me for the office which I temporarily fill; and as it is impossible that I should see the subject from your point of view, I fear that I may weaken the force of my argument by overlooking features which you deem important; or even involuntarily offend by ignoring doctrines which you deem essential. While I feel the firmest assurance of the underlying truths of Christianity, and the deepest respect for every honest conviction, still I must confess that my whole education has made it impossible for me to attach the same importance to details of doctrine, or forms of ceremonial, as do those who have been trained in a different school, though I would not by any hint of mine wound the sensitive realist, or the conscientious ceremonialist. I say this without the least assumption of greater freedom, or suspicion of complacency,—freely acknowledging that the judgment of those who minister to spiritual needs is much better established, and not questioning that their spiritual insight is far deeper than mine.

In my own province of thought I know so well how an exact knowledge of relations will often set aside judgments which a superficial knowledge might seem to justify, that I am fully sensible that the same principle must hold in other departments of learning as well; and I therefore offer the argument I have to make simply as a suggestion,—feeling sure that it will receive your thoughtful consideration, and be accepted for all it is worth. Nevertheless, I have thought — for otherwise I should not be here — that a certain advantage might arise in presenting the subject from a point of view other than that in which a theological student is accustomed to regard it; and that the opinions of a student of science, who had given much thought to such questions, however crude his theology, might help you to meet similar questions which sooner or later in your ministry will be forced by thoughtful men on your attention. I may overestimate the strength of my argument, — for the force of an analogical argument depends very greatly on the previous experience of those to whom it appeals, — but it has come home with overpowering force to my own mind; and I find it difficult to conceive how any one who has felt the bewilderment of scientific uncertainty, as well as of religious doubt, can resist its cogency. Take out the elements of feeling, affection, and faith, and the last is to me no more oppressive than the first.

The argument itself may be stated in a few words. As there are systems of science, so there are systems of religion; and among these, one both intellectually and morally so far in advance of the others that it alone claims the consideration of educated men. Regard now the Christian religion simply as an external fact, as an existing spiritual, moral, or intellectual force, independently of all supernatural sanctions, or superhuman obligations, and all must admit that it is the greatest power in the world. However originating, or however appointed, there is no power over men's minds and hearts which can for one moment be compared with it. Throughout Christian lands this power is everywhere pervasive, and even in lands not recognized as Christian its indirect influence has softened the asperities of barbarism, and mitigated the cruelties of savage life.

Compare, in its mere external or intellectual aspects, Christianity as a system with gravitation.

As the way was prepared for Newton, so was the way prepared, and in a most remarkable manner, for the Founder of Christianity. For centuries before His coming all that was purest and noblest in the world's thought was leading up to the expected Messiah. Then as the greatest advance ever made in the knowledge of material things came by one man, who greatly raised the level of scientific thought, so Christianity came like a great induction of spiritual truth, which so greatly raised the level of spiritual thought that after nearly two thousand years the Christian world does not yet appreciate the elevation that was reached.

As modern science dates from Newton, so all that is noblest and best in man, all that is pure and lovely in life, all unselfish morality, all heroic chivalry, all holy charity, is dated Anno Domini.

The Founder of Christianity was no mythological hero; but, whatever views we may entertain of his nature, he was in form and likeness a man, living at one of the best known epochs of the world's history; and every account of his character is in perfect harmony with his elevated doctrines and momentous declarations.

That doctrine and those declarations present difficulties of conception. We cannot reconcile them with our experience of natural relations; and in the same way we cannot reconcile the system of gravitation with our knowledge of the mode of action of the other forces of nature.

While, however, there are these difficulties of conception, the practical application of Christian doctrine as a rule of life, like the use of the principle of universal gravitation in astronomical computations, is perfectly simple and definite. Indeed, Christianity was revealed as a life, and has been handed down to us pure and undefiled in the lives of its disciples.

Like systems of science, Christianity deals with symbols, which are obviously the signs of realities in their essence incomprehensible by man; and even if — as does at times happen in both cases — the sign is mistaken for the substance, still such symbols are of the very greatest value in aiding the imagination and guiding the thought.

Newton so greatly raised the level of astronomical conceptions that since his time astronomers have been fully occupied in deducing the consequences of his great induction; and so, since the Christian ages began, apostles, saints, and fathers, with lowly and learned men of every name and calling, have been diligently unfolding the beauties, the marvels, and the glories of the truth that was then revealed. No wonder that the interpretations did not always agree, that bitter controversies arose, and that men professing the faith used power and influence as instruments of oppression and persecution; for the same sad features have disgraced the history of science, without the excuse of intense feeling to inflame passion or of blind fanaticism to obscure reason. But as in spite of follies and quarrels astronomy has grown to be a noble science, worthy of the most gifted human intelligence, so in an immeasurably greater degree the Christian Church through weakness has been made strong, and has become a holy temple in which the loftiest aspiration finds satisfaction, the purest affection repose, and unsullied charity its full reward.

Lastly, as the system of gravitation has been tested and ratified by the complete accordance of natural phenomena with the deductions that it involved, so has a most commanding seal been set on Christianity by the entire harmony of the system with the spiritual needs of man. It is in that harmony that all its strength lies. It has been tested by the most varied experience. The blood of the martyrs has been the seed of the Church; and the attestation of the great army of its confessors rolls down the Christian centuries with ever louder shouts of rejoicing and songs of thanksgiving and praise.

This test of experience, so clearly recognized in science, is also accepted in theology; and even Roman Catholic doctors admit that the decrees of Councils must be accepted by the public mind of the Church before they can be declared the voice of God.

While thus wonderfully adapted to man's spiritual needs, so just in proportion as our knowledge becomes enlarged, and our insight deepened, is Christianity found to be in harmony with all truth. The most gifted minds and profoundest scholars the world has known have not only confessed Christ before men, and acknowledged Him to be the Lord, but have also testified that increasing acquirements and widening vision brought an ever deeper conviction of His truth.

If, then, man can in any case rely on his experience as a test of truth; if harmony with nature is any evidence of participation in the scheme of nature; if this world is not wholly a phantom and a deceit; if all knowledge is not equally delusive, — then the essentials of Christianity must be true. Such is the argument. You must have anticipated it as I traced out the features of scientific systems; and I have only to add, before concluding this course of lectures, some connected thoughts which may serve to enforce or illustrate special points of this strikingly close analogy.

Remember, in the first place, that we are here treating Christianity as a fact of nature, as an existing system of religious truth, on the same plane as any other system of knowledge; and from this point of view only do we compare it with systems of science, like the system of gravitation. We all believe that Christianity has other sanctions and attestations; but in a question of Natural Theology we leave all this evidence on one side, and deal with Christianity only as an external fact of nature, as an historical phase in the development of humanity, as a system of morals, as a system of philosophy, or as a guiding and directing motive which controls large masses of mankind. I trust that I am not misunderstood; although there is an obvious rhetorical difficulty in dealing with the subject in this way. My language might very easily be misconstrued, although I have earnestly endeavored to avoid the occasion. No one who has deep religious feeling can associate even in the most indirect way Christianity with a system of science; or the Founder of Christianity with the originator of such a system, however great and worthy, without feeling the incongruity which the comparison involves; and it is difficult to find language which shall convey my meaning without a suggestion of irreverence. You will, I am sure, appreciate the difficulty and pardon any infelicity.

We are dealing solely with the evidence of nature, and we must treat Christianity as a part of nature, just as gravitation is a part of nature, if we would estimate the value of the evidence which nature alone can give apart from all other sanctions. Of course other evidences have their due place, and to most minds have such a paramount authority as to wholly hush the feeble voice of nature. But I am here to show you, as far as I am able, how forcible the testimony of nature is by itself, apart from any supernatural credentials; and I affirm that Christianity as an external fact is a part of this evidence. Christianity is a definite force in the world, and is as essential a factor in the development of humanity, as steam-power, electricity, or natural selection. The supernatural evidence of Christianity is wholly additional to the sanctions we urge; and the former is rendered vastly more credible and persuasive by the evidence of nature. If you can remove the antecedent presumption against the miraculous, you place at once the overwhelming historical evidences of Christianity on the same basis as all other historical testimony; and how can you accomplish this so effectually as by showing that the resulting system is in entire harmony with what are always regarded as earth-born systems?

I must, however, myself protest against the last term, while using it to point a distinction. I believe most firmly that all truth is one and inseparable, and that there is no real distinction between heaven-born truth and earth-born truth. I believe that in the strict sense of the term, gravitation was as much a revelation to man as Christianity. I cannot, therefore, call one human and the other divine. Grant the widest difference between the modes by which the revelations were communicated. Grant that the very diverse nature of the revelations required this difference; yet in either case the truth is God's truth; and in the last analysis, the ultimate test of all truth must be its universal and perfect harmony. To me the most weighty evidence of Christianity is its supreme naturalness; that intensely human life in the past, that Holy Church ever since, in perfect harmony with all my purest affections and loftiest aspirations, is the strongest assurance of truth,— and truth is always and everywhere divine.

Again, Christianity as a fact of nature involves all prior questions as to the personality of the Godhead, or the attributes of Deity. We have no occasion to go back to questions of design, or plan in nature. We deal with the most conspicuous design, the most wonderful plan; and if these are shown to be of a piece with the rest of nature, why need we further testimony? In the first lecture of this course, we endeavored to show that all arguments from adaptation or from general plan were inductions based on analogy; and that like other inductions their force depended on the fulness with which they harmonized the facts of nature. We claim for our present argument the same validity; and if the claim is allowed, the argument has a far greater range than any previous argument of natural theology; for it secures all that Christianity, as an external fact of nature, can be justly claimed to include. And looking at the question in its simplest aspect, why is not the adaptation of Christianity to man's spiritual wants as direct an evidence of design as the adaptation of the eye to seeing, or the lungs to breathing? — and regarding the plan of redemption simply as it was first exhibited by the life and death of Christ, and as it has been exemplified in the lives and deaths of saints and martyrs ever since, as conclusive an evidence of intelligence as the plan of the vertebrate skeleton, or the spiral distribution of leaves on the stems of plants?

We have in the most positive manner affirmed that inductions based on analogy or otherwise are not, and from the nature of the case cannot be, demonstrations; and have shown that they may offer every degree of conclusiveness depending on their agreement with the phenomena of nature. We could have no more perfect accordance than Christianity offers. But however conclusive such evidence, there is always room for speculative doubt; and we freely admit that our argument is not a proof, but it affords all the certainty we can have in natural theology.

As I have before said, it is a striking fact in regard

to all scientific inductions that they never come to
fruition until the time is ripe. If premature, they
fall on barren soil, and the numberless anticipations
of genius are well-known illustrations of this truth.
And when we consider the obvious law of progression which the development of knowledge obeys, we
are forced to recognize that individual men, however
great their genius, are not essential to the result.
Like the prophets of old, they are interpreters of a
preordained purpose. No one can question that the
law of gravitation would have been discovered within
half a century, if Newton had not lived; and, great as
his influence has been, and greatly as he hastened
the progress at the time, astronomy would certainly
have been as far advanced to-day if the work had
been left for other hands. Since the time of Hipparchus the way had been preparing for the great induction; and Isaac Newton was the name given to
the faithful and gifted servant who was born into
the world when the time was ripe.

Again, how striking the analogy with the coming of
Christianity! Here also the way was prepared. "But
when the fulness of the time was come God sent forth
his Son, made of a woman, made under the law;"
and although the messenger was the Divine Son, and
the message was the redemption of man, yet the gospel came in the same simple naturalness with which
every great truth has come to the world. Before
John came crying in the wilderness, how long, how
tedious, and how devious, had been the way, how
halting the progress; yet from time to time seer and
prophet had caught glimpses of the coming truth as

they diligently toiled in the vineyard, and sought to make ready for the vintage of the Lord.

As I ponder this sublime history I cannot resist the impression that this conformity to natural methods is an irresistible evidence of genuineness which we cannot afford to overlook. God introduced Christianity into the world by the same methods by which He has opened to us all knowledge, — in order that He should not confuse the understanding, or confound the intelligence, of His creatures; and thus it is that our expanding science becomes to us on a lower scale a type and similitude of the methods of Divine revelation; and the certitude of the one gives us a confident assurance of the certitude of the other.

It was because I wished to set forth this analogy in a strong light that I dwelt at some length on the prelude to the discoveries of Newton, — in order that you might see that his way was prepared by methods not always direct, and by servants not always worthy, and yet that all conspired to ensure the final result; and that thus you yourselves might draw out the analogy with a power which I am unable to command.

In entire harmony with the perfect naturalness of the whole dispensation was the coming itself. It was not in an obscure period of human history, or in a remote corner of the earth; but in the midst of the Roman Empire, and during the Augustan age of the ancient civilization. The coming was not heralded by signs and portents which inspired awe and commanded attention; but in all the simplicity of childhood, and in all the naturalness of growth. What a lesson is there in the simple statement that " the child grew, and waxed strong in spirit." And so unobtrusive and unobserved was this growth, except by a few humble peasants, that when the glory of His mature powers broke upon the Jewish world it excited the wondering remark, " Whence hath this man letters, having never learned?"

In respect only to this natural growth, but as a further incidental illustration of the fact that the most glorious of all advents came to the world with entire conformity to natural methods, allow me in all reverence again to call your attention to the striking circumstance in the life of Newton, which I have before dwelt upon, — that we find him, while still a college-student, in possession of mathematical power, and of a new calculus, not only far in advance of his teachers but also of his age. The advent of new truth has always been by the same gradual unfolding ; and is there not the strongest antecedent presumption that He of whose fulness we all partake should in His mediatorial office conform to the same methods He had Himself ordained? And is not the harmony of the result with this antecedent presumption the strongest possible evidence of genuineness? Would man's invention in a pre-Christian age ever have conceived of such a method or pictured such a likeness?

The feature which above all things else is most striking in a great induction is that such an advent raises the level of human thought. Therefore such inductions mark epochs in science. Astronomy points back to Newton; and no one can question that for years to come natural history will point back to Darwin. How is it with religious thought? The comparison may seem almost irreverent; and yet it is highly instructive. Looking at Christian institutions simply as outward facts, without regard to sanctions, dogmas, doctrine, or creeds of any kind, what do we see? No less than this: that everything in the world which is loftiest and profoundest in thought, which is most ennobling and heroic in character, which is bravest and most unselfish in action, which is purest and loveliest in art, which is most consoling or hopeful in philosophy, and above all this, every form of beneficent charity, every movement for the amelioration of mankind, every influence which sanctifies family ties, dates from one conspicuous and definite epoch of the world's history from which civilized men began to count anew the revolving years.

I certainly need not in this place attempt to draw a parallel between the ancient and the modern civilization, to show how great a change was wrought, and how great an elevation was reached in one short life. But if in the interest of natural theology I can induce you to look at the subject from my point of view, and for the sake of argument to consider the claims of Christianity as simply an external feature in human society, I hope I may render a real service by giving you the command of a very powerful argument which can be pressed, not only without compromising or invalidating any supernatural evidences, but on the contrary, which will furnish a secure basis on which such claims can be established. It must be that a system which is so obviously a part of nature has the same authenticity as the rest of nature; and then comes home with redoubled force the old argument that men unaided could not have raised themselves by one leap to such an elevation.

Even in relation to scientific discoveries it inspires confidence to know that the investigator was in full relations with his subject, and in all respects equal to his work; and we have shown how conspicuously this was true in the case of Newton. But who can "speak the matchless worth" of the Founder of Christianity? Certainly not a layman in this place. It is to be your great privilege to rehearse this story; and, as told by your lips, in simplicity and power, may it bring consolation, comfort, and conviction to many a weary and troubled soul. In seeking to make evident that "Nature and the Supernatural," are "The one System of God," a most gifted and spiritually minded American clergyman, the late Horace Bushnell, has sounded forth the glories of that wondrous tale "in notes almost divine;" and in following his chaste, beautiful, and effective presentation of the character of Christ, the one feature that most impresses the reader is its supreme naturalness. The consciousness of power is all there; the mystery of personality is all there; the terror of justice is all there; the awfulness of sacrifice is all there. But it is the sweetness of affection, the tenderness of compassion, the earnestness of pity, the fervor of charity, the ardor of zeal, the devotion to duty, the submission to authority, the perfection of manhood, which rivets our attention, which engages our sympathies, which commands our reason.

All systems of science, as we have seen, present

insuperable difficulties of conception, because material relations are the measure of our experience and therefore the measure of our positive knowledge. Can we expect that the philosophy of religion will be more intelligible? And the more we study, the more plainly it will appear that in this respect also the two orders of truth present a most striking analogy; and that in either case the difficulties arise from the impossibility on our part of picturing to the mind any relations not realized in our own experience or in that of our fellow-men. Even in regard to material relations there is a great difference among educated men in the power of realizing unseen conditions; and to rude, unimaginative folk nothing exists beyond the range of their immediate perceptions. With those whose imaginative faculties have been most cultivated, the limit of power is soon reached; and however much the philosopher may speculate about transmundane realities, and however firmly he may believe in them, he can form no mental images of such beings that are not painted in colors of clay. Hence it is that I have dwelt so fully on the difficulties of conception which the fundamental concepts of physical science present,— in order that you might appreciate how very close the analogy is which I am endeavoring to enforce.

The incongruities and apparent inconsistencies which the systems of science involve do not invalidate their essential truth, but they do most conclusively indicate that we are dealing with relations beyond the range of our experience; and our attempts to represent these relations to our minds by means of ethereal media or assumed attractions resemble the play of children with their dolls and toys.

In like manner it is no objection to a theological system that it involves much that is incomprehensible and seemingly contradictory. The question simply should be, Does it give a faithful representation of known facts and relations? and if so, the inconsistencies indicate no more than this, that it deals with forms of being beyond the range of human experience.

It is to me a striking evidence of the truth, as well as of the naturalness of the gospel narrative, that throughout there should be such an accommodation to the necessary limitations of human intelligence. On all occasions the truth is presented in the simplest material imagery, and the most tender regard is paid to the Marthas and Thomases of every age, to whom seeing could give to belief the only adequate certitude ; and when it was necessary to certify to eternal realities and to arouse men from their material lethargy, how unaffectedly it is done with a few simple but grand sentences. How differently it would have been, how differently it has been, with every human teacher to whom has been opened a vision of things eternal. How irresistible has always been the tendency of the human mind, however enlightened, to dwell on all that is anomalous, incongruous, or awe-inspiring, in the situation described. We find this most markedly in the elder dispensation. We find it even in the vision of the Apocalypse. And is there not a lesson in such facts which we may well ponder?

In teaching physical science it would be very unwise to give prominence to the difficulties of conception on which for a special purpose we have dwelt in these lectures. These are real difficulties, and must be met by every thoughtful student sooner or later; but they have no practical significance, and are wholly ignored in the every-day work of the laboratory. Of course no feeling is here involved, as in religious questions; but with all this difference is it wise, in an age which is so much engrossed with material interests, to give prominence to similar difficulties of theological doctrine that have as little bearing on Christian living? Is it not better that they should be ignored than become hindrances to faith? and does not all experience teach that a faith well-grounded on personal experience and active benevolence will accept any doctrine once delivered to the saints whose holy lives it seeks to imitate?

Our Puritan forefathers delighted in theological dialectics, and sought to exaggerate rather than to reconcile the paradoxes and contradictions of dogmas. They were thoughtful men of speculative dispositions, whom both political circumstances and sensitive consciences had debarred from the intellectual life of the world, and who found the chief exercise of their intelligence in the discussion of theological dogmas. But it may be doubted whether this at times morbid exercise of their faculties induced any more humble and loving lives than those of many a devoted saint who never so much as heard of Foreknowledge or Predestination.

In connection with the difficulties of conception

which the Christian system involves, the question of the Christian miracles at once suggests itself; but this is too large a subject to be discussed here. Two principles, however, which we have sought to establish, have a bearing upon the matter. The first is that, with certain obvious limitations, there can be no prodigy in nature so wonderful that it may not be accepted on adequate evidence; and the second is that so far as our knowledge extends there is ample room for the appearance of new forces in the chain of causation. Obviously these principles, if established, remove in very great measure the antecedent presumption against miracles, and leave their authenticity to be established in every case by the evidence alone. In weighing evidence men will be guided by the self-evident truth that it is more probable that a witness should be deceived than that the usual order of nature should be altered; and if the evidence is in question, the counter presumption thus created is overwhelming. But in the presence of well-attested fact all questions of probability scatter to the winds; and what better attestation of an historical fact can you have than continuity of life? and I question if any one who has fully partaken of that life ever questioned the validity of the evidence.

Thus the continuous life of the Church from the beginning becomes the most convincing evidence of the Resurrection, that of all Christ's miracles the most vital to the authority and influence of His Church; for "if Christ be not risen then is our preaching vain, and your faith is also vain." Just as the religion of Mahomet, as a power in history, dates from the

Hegira, and, however surprising the effects ultimately produced by such gross materialism, presents a perfect continuity from the first, each step of the progress being natural and intelligible, — so Christianity, as a force in society, dates from the Resurrection, and shows an unbroken line of sequences from that event. Granted, if you demand it, that the Resurrection was a condescension to the conditions of our material existence. Explain the outward aspects of the event as you please. Still there remains the fact of history that something occurred at that time which produced conviction on the minds of the beholders, and to which the origin of the Christian Church must be traced.

The high morality of Christ's teaching cannot account for the founding of such a church. The Crucifixion destroyed all hope even in the small band of followers who were faithful to the last; and without some remarkable attestation, Christ's teaching would have produced no more effect on the world than that of Socrates, or of Plato, even if the records had been preserved. Something must have occurred which changed despondency to hope, and which inspired the disciples with courage and enthusiasm. The gospel narrative gives an explanation which accounts for the result. The wonderful event which had been predicted took place. Man could have no conviction except through experience, and the experience was furnished.

We cannot suspect the founders of Christianity of deliberate falsehood, any more than we can believe that an event from which such great consequences immediately flowed was a myth. The witnesses must have believed that they saw what they described. Explain away the facts as you please. Regard the phenomena observed as purely subjective to the minds of those present, and the outward appearances as delusive, it still must be admitted that something occurred, either outwardly or inwardly, which produced such a profound impression on the minds of the beholders as to arouse the highest enthusiasm, and the most unselfish devotion, the world has ever known; and from which a chain of consequences has been forged link by link until all that is best and noblest of the human race has been enchained in its bonds of love.

Herein lies the great wonder. The miracle was not wrought for us. Thank God! we cannot investigate the circumstances now, or analyze all the material imagery that was accessory to that solemn scene. But of this at least we may be sure: at that time a new motive came into operation which changed the whole order of society, and to this time history points continuously back, as it does to Cæsar crossing the Rubicon, or to Luther nailing his theses to the door of the Schlosskirche at Wittenberg. If there be such a thing as order in the evolution of nature this event was a part of that order. If there be an intelligent Ruler of the world this event was ordained by Him; and whether He worked through methods intelligible to us, or by means past our finding out, and which with our limited knowledge and experience we call supernatural, the event was no less miraculous in its occurrence, no less wonderful in its result.

Turning now to the practical working of the Christian system, how simple are the principles of action, how plain the duties; and what Christian mother watching over her sick child, what aged saint nearing his rest, or what soldier of Christ in the midst of the conflict were ever troubled by difficulties of conception? Our analogy here again is perfect.

I hope further that the analogy of the symbolism of science may aid us to a better understanding of the purport of the symbolism of Christianity. We have endeavored to show that the symbols in chemistry were something more than mere conventionalism; that although absurd and grotesque if regarded as the exact patterns of realities, they were obviously the signs of an underlying truth as yet only dimly apprehended. How characteristic this is also of all the legitimate symbols of Christianity, including under this term much of the imagery both of the Old and of the New Testaments. These are professedly types, not likenesses of spiritual being; but like the symbols of science, they are aids to the imagination, they give definiteness to thought, they give substance to things unseen. Such types, however, must resemble in certain features their original, inasmuch as they form a safe basis of inference, and, like the symbols of science, guide the mind to the discovery of truth. Like the ladder seen in vision by the patriarch at Bethel, they rest on earth, but they lead upwards to where the material blends with the spiritual in the effulgence of Divine glory. On the other hand, as the conventional forms of science often acquire an undue prominence, and become invested with an imaginary concreteness in the thoughts of those who are constantly occupied therewith, so the symbolism of Christianity is also too frequently materialized, and the spirit that giveth life completely hidden by the letter that killeth.

In all great scientific inductions which have permanently raised the level of human knowledge, the advantage gained has never been appreciated at the time, and it has been the work of years to develop the consequences of a single lofty intellectual conception. Here again the parallelism is most striking with the Christian revelation. How faintly did the earlier disciples comprehend the work of their Master; and, as century after century has passed since, how slowly has the world come to a realization of the truth; and in proportion as man has become enlightened, how steadily has the scope of the grand scheme widened before his enraptured vision. So also if we consider solely the intellectual aspects of the Christian system, where in literature shall we find a power of deductive reasoning comparable with that of the great apostle to the Gentiles, whose boast was " Not as though I had already attained, either were already perfect, but I follow after." Pressing this analogy still further, we may not inaptly compare theological systems with the deductions of science, and like the last those also must abide the test of experience, and be judged by the united voice of that great multitude who have been redeemed to God " out of every kindred and tongue and people and nation."

I have quite failed in one of my chief aims in these lectures if I have not succeeded in impressing you with the strong sense which I feel of the uncertainties and limitations which encompass the student of nature on every side. I am well aware that such feelings as I have expressed are in part a matter of temperament, and that some men are more susceptible to such impressions than others. Still, your own knowledge of literature will sustain me in the assertion that in all that I have said I am in sympathy with the noblest thinkers the world has known. Unnumbered scholars, of whose attainments the world has been proud, and of whose contributions to knowledge the human race will be ever grateful,— men like Plato, Marcus Aurelius, Copernicus, Descartes, Newton, Faraday, — have left written evidence of a more or less deep conviction that the intellectual life has a nobler destiny than the life of the body; that there may be modes of existence of which the senses take no cognizance; and that, while the things which are seen are temporal, the things that are unseen are eternal. There has always been with such minds a "reaching forth unto those things which are before," and although they may not have recognized the goal, a pressing "toward the mark for the prize of the high calling of God in Christ Jesus, . . . who shall change our vile body, that it may be fashioned like unto His glorious body, according to the working whereby He is able to subdue all things unto Himself."

How true it is now of our systems of theology as of our systems of science that "we know in part, and we prophesy in part. But when that which is perfect is come, then that which is in part shall be done away." And how obviously the recognition of such limitations in our present life points beyond the veil. The consciousness of limitation is an evidence of things unseen, and thus our material hindrances become educators of faith. They are a law in our members "which is our schoolmaster to bring us unto Christ."

The harmony of the Christian system with the methods of nature, and the force of the argument which rests on this analogy, nowhere appear more conspicuously than when studied in relation to the most recent of the great systems of science. Man as an animal is weak as compared with many of the higher vertebrates, and unfitted to cope with them in the fight for existence. Place man naked, but in the full command of his physical powers, in a jungle with tigers, or even in a forest with wildcats, and he would have no chance in the inevitable struggle that must ensue. The element of intelligence, and that alone, makes his superiority; and this mental endowment has made a comparatively weak animal the lord of creation. According to the new school of naturalists, man's development must have begun ages back, when intelligence became an important factor in the struggle for life. Remember, however, that, as I have before shown, this factor may have been a preordained condition then appearing for the first time in the chain of causation; and that as yet certainly we have no knowledge whatever which would render such an interference (if the preordained can be called an interference) either impossible or improbable; and further, recall the opinion then expressed that geological evidence indicates a marked break at the advent of man. You may then without prejudice accept the necessary inference from the theory that man after the flesh was descended, not from any species now existing, but from some species far less fitted to cope with its surroundings than the monkey, the ourang, or the gorilla have become. These anthropoids are not regarded as the ancestors of man; but both they and man are, according to the modern hypothesis, descendants of a common ancestor. Man has remained comparatively feeble in his physical powers, but has gained supremacy through his intelligence. The animals most like him in outward form and structure, not partaking of his intelligence, have been developed in one or another direction to a far higher degree; because they have had to wage the fight for existence with physical powers alone.

In considering the influence of intelligence in the struggle for existence, remember that it has led men to combine in societies, and establish governments so as to protect the weak. Under such conditions, while man's collective power to cope with brute forces has been greatly increased, his individual power has been weakened; and circumstances constantly remind us what a weak, miserable animal man is when left to his own resources. When you consider what a delicate, helpless creature the human infant is, it will require no aid of poetry or art to show how soon the race would be extinguished if the human mother were left to defend her offspring with her own strength. The tales of the wilderness chiefly owe their interest, as it seems to me, to the vividness with which they picture the features of that fierce and terrible warfare from which civilized men are so greatly protected through their institutions and their inheritances; and they show us that even in the savage state the protection, such as it is, arising from association and combination, is equally essential to the continued life of the race; thus plainly indicating that even the feeble intelligence of the savage gives him an immense advantage over the brute in the struggle for existence.

As intelligence has been the chief factor which has given the race of man its pre-eminence, so it has been that gift in a special degree which has given to individual men the power of advancing their race. The great men who have marked special epochs in history, or to whom great movements may be traced, have been men of great mental power in some phase or other, or else men endowed with unusually clear spiritual insight. Recall the great names of history, the great conquerors, the great rulers, the great lawgivers, the great in literature, the great in art, the great in science, the great in philosophy, the great in theology, the founders of states, the founders of religions, the heroes, the saints, and the prophets of every age. Who of all these men whose names are household words, remembered and cherished when all other records of the past are forgotten, who, I say, has exerted the greatest influence, and produced the most lasting effect on the progress of mankind? There can be but one answer. Theorize about the matter as you please, explain the influence as you may, by far the greatest effects ever produced in history can be traced directly to the teaching of the one Man who was born of Mary in the manger at Bethlehem. Frame what theories you please about His nature, He is, on the lowest view of His nature, the greatest leader of humanity. It is the reasonable course to accept His own theory of Himself, and to act upon it; and men by acting upon it have raised themselves and their fellows immeasurably in the scale of being.

Let us not fail to remember also in this connection that development, or slow growth, is plainly the method of creation. Nothing is more distinctly taught by nature than this. Every advance in knowledge only makes this truth more plain. Before Darwin published his now famous work on "The Origin of Species," an English poet wrote: —

"The solid earth whereon we tread

"In tracts of fluent heat began,
   And grew to seeming random forms,
   The seeming prey to cyclic storms,
Till at the last arose the man;"

and this plain teaching of geology can be supported by overwhelming facts from almost every department of knowledge. If the Bible in some passages may seem to imply otherwise, these passages must be interpreted by the spirit of the writing, which throughout enforces the reverse idea, and nowhere more impressively than in the teaching of Christ Himself. It is not, as some seem to think, a question of power to create, but solely a question of method. One of the most striking features in the life of Christ is His submission to the slow, halting, and apparently cruel methods of nature; while all the time there is an evident consciousness of power to secure the end and avoid the pain. When we are impatient with these methods, and think that they derogate from the majesty of the Almighty, let us remember that scene under the olives of Gethsemane, the impatience of the disciple, the calmness of the Master, and the memorable words, " Thinkest thou that I cannot now pray to my Father, and He shall presently give me more than twelve legions of angels?"

But although we may not without exaggeration push our analogy further, yet we can catch glimpses of a meaning still deeper than any we have as yet grasped; and I hope I shall be pardoned if with deepest reverence I allude to this obscure and terrible significance. We recognize the struggle for existence as an agency in nature, and the naturalists discuss its effects as they would those of heat or electricity. But do they, do we, realize what is implied by these words? They cannot; for they would be staggered by the thought, and overwhelmed by the horror, and could not write or speak so coolly if they did. "For we know the whole creation groaneth and travaileth in pain together until now." Those who minister in the slums of your cities know how true this is; and they will tell you that these impassioned words of St. Paul convey no adequate conception of the reality. Even fiction does not dare to depict faithfully the terrible death struggle, and art is powerless before it. When we turn pale at the bare recital of the horrors of the siege of Jerusalem, of the plague at Florence, of the hecatombs at Comassie, or of the battle-fields recorded on every page of history, and also of the visitations of earthquake, shipwreck, tornado, and pestilence, which at times come near our own homes, and are stirred from the inner depths of our souls by the distant roar of the conflict, what must have been the ordeal through which our race has passed, what the sorrow and anguish through which every advance has been won! And do we ourselves realize that our civilization, our education, our well-being, and all that constitutes our birthright has been purchased with all this blood?

If this be true of man, the most favored of creatures, and through his intelligence the most capable of protecting himself, we can readily believe the declaration of naturalists that the destructiveness of the internecine warfare among the lower animals is wholly beyond the power of imagination to conceive. Swift destruction is the rule, — life, however short, the great exception; and one is astonished by the enormous productiveness of nature which can people the earth in spite of such a drain. All naturalists are agreed that it is this wholesale destructiveness which alone gives efficacy to what is called natural selection. As the animal is higher in the scale of being, the destructiveness is less; but in the same proportion the suffering is greater; and among men the capability of suffering is almost a measure of intellectual and spiritual growth. As then in the struggle for existence perfection is reached through suffering, so in the spiritual world men rise to higher things through sorrow ; and though as they rise their power of suffering is increased, yet in the beauty of holiness their sorrow is at last turned into joy. " Blessed are they that mourn, for they shall be comforted." Thus the Cross becomes the type of perfect character, as well as the type of deepest sorrow; and as we pass beneath its shadow, nature will help to teach us the deep significance of those solemn words, " And if I be lifted up I shall draw all men unto me."

On the quai which lines the banks of the Loire at Tours stands a noble statue, erected in honor of the greatest philosopher France has ever known; who, although he thought and wrought elsewhere, and died in a foreign land, was born in Touraine. On the pedestal is engraved simply

"RENÉ DESCARTES ; "

but at the foot of the statue we read, as from the great man's lips,

" COGITO, ERGO SUM."

Most beautifully has this famous aphorism been paraphrased by the great English poet whose verses I have several times quoted because nowhere else do I find so forcible an expression of the overpowering force of natural phenomena which weighs on my own soul, but which my feeble words are powerless to reproduce : —

" The baby new to earth and sky,
What time his tender palm is pressed

Against the circle of the breast,
Has never thought that ' This is I.'

" But as he grows he gathers much,
And learns the use of 'I' and 'me';
And finds 'I am not what I see,
And other than the things I touch.'"

The mystery of evil and the mystery of suffering have their counterpart in the mystery of personality. Science has not shed one single ray to lighten the darkness of either mystery. We have faith "that somehow good will be the final goal of ill." We trust that Omniscience and Free Will, Omnipotence and Sin, Beneficence and Suffering, will one day be reconciled to our intelligences; and we look for the explanation to those awful necessities which an alliance of the spiritual with the material implies. Still, amidst all this darkness our analogy does not wholly fail us, and we have clear indications that the provisions of Grace are of a piece with the provisions of material nature.

If there is one attribute of our being which more than any other marks our individual existence, it is the consciousness of personality; and yet that entity which thinks and wills is so blended with our material nature that we cannot, except in thought, dissociate the two. The conclusion of the profoundest analysis which philosophy can make is still expressed in the three words " COGITO, ERGO SUM." Nevertheless, this personality is the most conspicuous fact in all human history, and every attempt of false science or of poetry to resolve or obscure it, has been wholly

SPIRITUAL LIFE. 321

vain. Personality, with its free will, is, then, an elementary principle of nature; and how wonderfully is Christianity throughout in harmony with this fundamental principle. The great object of the Gospel is to purify and sanctify the sources from which it proceeds, but the personal will is always left free and inviolate. The recorded miracles all dealt with material nature. Christ never constrained a human will. When He knew that it was to betray Him, and a single word would arrest the action, He allowed it free course; and in the final passion — " then said Jesus, 'Father forgive them, for they know not what they do.'"

We have time for only one further thought. Man knows nature because he is in harmony with it; man knows spiritual truth in the same way; and certitude in either case rests on similar evidence. Such are the general propositions which I have sought to maintain in these lectures. We have to thank the evolutionists for a plausible explanation of the first of the propositions, and they will not object if we apply the same principles to the second. A simple cell, at first only slightly sensitive to light, has developed into that organ of wonderful adaptations, the eye. By the survival of the fittest, each advantage gained has been held and handed down; and thus the organ has been gradually adjusted to the environment, and fitted to give to the mind of man truthful information about external objects and accurate impressions of the beauties of the outer world. So another cell, specially sensitive to the vibrations of the atmosphere, by associating with itself other sensitive cells and bequeathing every small gain by which the resulting structure became more responsive to the tremors of sound, has grown into that other organ, not less wonderful, through which the mind receives equally faithful impressions of harmony, melody, and articulate speech. The method by which these results have been worked out is, however, a question of no importance to our argument, so long as we all admit — as all do, evolutionists with the rest — that the capacity of these organs to give accurate information about the external world is wholly due to their adaptation to the environment.

But if man's harmony with his environment physically is an evidence of truth, then his harmony with his environment spiritually must be equally so. If a sensitive nerve can be trusted, a sensitive conscience is not less trustworthy; otherwise man's mind must have grown into harmony with its environment in one relation, and not in the other. If when man longs for beauty and harmony the impressions which flow in through the eye and ear are to be trusted, then it must be that when in his higher moods he yearns for purity and righteousness and holiness, the assurances which come to him on his bended knees are equally well-founded.

Finally, if there be any knowledge, if there be any truth, if there be any certainty in this mortal state of being, if there be any consolation in the past, any satisfaction in the present, any hope in the future of this world, it is only to be found in the spiritual life of man. That alone is permanent amid ceaseless change; that alone is satisfying amid constant satiety; that alone is comforting amid constant disappointments; that alone is sustaining amid constant suffering; that alone is consoling amid constant bereavement; that alone is assuring in the presence of death; that alone is triumphant in the confident hope of immortality. And if I have been able, in however imperfect a way, to make more evident to your understanding that our power of apprehending spiritual things, our discernment of righteousness, our thirst for affection, our aspiration after purity, our communion with holiness, are as truly evidences of external realities as any impressions of our senses; and further, if it has appeared that the inductions based on the experiences of our spiritual life are just as authentic, and just as valid, as those drawn from material phenomena, — then I have accomplished the object at which alone I have aimed in these lectures.

I am well aware that I have not sounded the keynote of theology; but this was not my office. I was intrusted with the very subordinate task of sustaining the harmony of the refrain in which alone nature can join in the heavenly song; and I even fear that I have made my part too prominent.

You will receive commission to preach the glad tidings of a risen Lord, and no more noble service can man render on earth. If I have in any measure helped to prepare your way, it is all that I could hope to accomplish. You are intrusted with a message before which all the learning of the world must bow. Proclaim it confidently and fearlessly, not in "oppositions of science falsely so-called," but in the name of Him who alone is "the Way, the Truth, and the Life."

March, 1887

BOOKS

PUBLISHED BY

ROBERT CARTER & BROTHERS,

530 BROADWAY, NEW YORK.

THE CRISIS OF MISSIONS; or, The Voice out of the Cloud. By the Rev. ARTHUR T. PIERSON, D.D. 16mo $1.25

"It is as fascinating as a novel, and yet overflowing with facts that make one wonder how it can be possible that such great progress has been made in missions, even during the recent years, and he not have known more of it. This book can but stimulate the followers of Christ to greater love for, and more earnest efforts in, missions." — *Christian Work.*

"This is a book for every Christian to read with prayer and a sincere desire to know his personal duty in this great and glorious work." — *New York Observer.*

"In the little volume before us, the history of missions is unrolled as a scroll, the marvellous providences of God are traced in letters which glow with the intensity of the writer's convictions, the trumpet-call of God's providences to the Christian world is sounded so loud and clear as to reach, one would think, the dullest ear." — *Baptist Herald.*

"One of the most important books to the cause of Foreign Missions — and through them to Home Missions also — which ever has been written. It should be in every library and every household. It should be read, studied, taken to heart, and prayed over." — *Congregationalist.*

*A. L. O. E. LIBRARY.

50 vols., 16mo, in a neat wooden case, *net* 28.00

"All these stories have the charm and pure Christian character which have made the name of A. L. O. E. dear to thousands of homes." — *Lutheran.*

ARNOT, Rev. William.

On the Parables. 12mo 1.75
Church in the House; or, Lessons on the Acts of the Apostles. 12mo 1.50

(1)

BERNARD, T. D.
    The Progress of Doctrine in the New Testament. 12mo $1.25
    "The style is absolutely perfect. A broad, deep stream of fresh thought, in language as clear as crystal, flows through the whole devout, instructive, quickening, and inspiring work. Simply as a model of style, every preacher might profitably study it. . . . This volume makes the New Testament a new book to me." — *Rev. T. L. Cuyler, D.D.*

BICKERSTETH, Rev. E. H.
    Yesterday, To-day, and Forever. A Poem. Pocket edition, $0.50; 16mo, $1.00; 12mo 1.50
    "If any poem is destined to endure in the companionship of Milton's hitherto matchless epic, we believe it will be 'Yesterday, To-day, and Forever.'" — *London Globe.*

BLUNT'S Coincidences and Paley's Horæ Paulinæ. 12mo 1.50

BONAR, Horatius, D.D.
    Hymns of Faith and Hope. 3 vols. 16mo 2.25
    Bible Thoughts and Themes. 6 vols. 12mo 12.00
    Way of Peace 0.50
    Way of Holiness 0.60
    Night of Weeping 0.50
    Morning of Joy 0.60
    Follow the Lamb 0.40
    How shall I go to God? 0.40

BOWES, Rev. G. S.
    Scripture its own Illustrator. 12mo 1.50
    Information and Illustration. 12mo 1.50

BRODIE, Emily.
    Jean Lindsay, The Vicar's Daughter 1.25
    Dora Hamilton's Choice. 12mo 1.25
    Elsie Gordon. 12mo 1.25
    Uncle Fred's Shilling. 12mo 1.25
    Lonely Jack. 12mo 1.25
    Ruth's Rescue. 16mo 0.50
    Nora Clinton. 12mo 1.25
    The Sea Gull's Nest. 16mo 0.60
    Norman and Elsie. 12mo 1.25
    Five Minutes too Late 1.25
    East and West 0.60
    His Guardian Angel 1.25

CHARLESWORTH, Miss M. L.
    Ministering Children. 12mo 1.50
        "   "   16mo 1.00
    Sequel to Ministering Children. 12mo 1.50
        "   "   "   16mo 1.00

CHARLESWORTH, Miss M. L., *continued.*
Oliver of the Mill. 12mo $1.00
Dorothy Cope, containing "The Old Looking-Glass " and
"Broken Looking-Glass." 12mo 1.50

CUYLER, Rev. T. L.
Pointed Papers. 12mo 1.50
Thought Hives. 12mo 1.50
From Nile to Norway 1.50
Empty Crib. 24mo 1.00
Cedar Christian. 18mo 0.75
Stray Arrows. 18mo 0.60
God's Light on Dark Clouds. Flexible, red edges . . . 0.75

"In this beautiful little volume the author presents a grateful offering to the ' desponding and bereaved.' . . . He offers to others what he has tested for himself. The book is written out of a full heart and a vivid experience." — *Presbyterian Review.*

*D'AUBIGNÉ, Dr. Merle.
*History of the Reformation in the Sixteenth Century.
5 vols., 12mo, cloth, in a box 4.50
*History of the Reformation in the Time of Calvin. 8 vols.,
12mo, cloth, in a box 8.00

"The work is now complete; and these later volumes, together with the original five, form a library relating to the Reformation of incalculable value and of intense interest. The pen of this master of history gave a charm to everything that he touched." — *New York Observer.*

**A very cheap edition of* Reformation in the Sixteenth
Century. 5 vols. in one, 890 pages, cloth 1.00

DICKSON, Rev. Alexander, D.D.
All about Jesus. 12mo 2.00
Beauty for Ashes. 12mo 2.00

" His book is a 'bundle of myrrh,' and will be specially enjoyed by those who are in trouble." — *Rev. Dr. W. M. Taylor.*

" Luscious as a honeycomb, with sweetness drawn from God's Word." — *Rev. Dr. Cuyler.*

DRINKWATER, Jennie M.
Only Ned. 12mo 1.25
Not Bread Alone. 12mo 1.25
Fred and Jeanie. 12mo 1.25
Tessa Wadsworth's Discipline. 12mo 1.50
Rue's Helps. 12mo 1.50
Electa ; A Story. 12mo 1.50
Fifteen. 12mo 1.50
Bek's First Corner. 12mo 1.50
Miss Prudence. 12mo 1.50
The Story of Hannah. 12mo 1.50
That Quisset House 1.50
Isobel's Between-Times 1.50

EDWARDS, Jonathan.
*Works. In 4 vols. 8vo $6.00

"I consider Jonathan Edwards the greatest of the sons of men."
— *Robert Hall.*

FRASER, Dr. D.
Synoptical Lectures on the Books of Holy Scripture. New
and revised edition. 2 vols. 12mo 4.50

"The plan is to give a general view of the scope and contents of each book in the Bible. It is designed not for professional students alone, but for all educated Christians. The careful reader will gain from its pages clear ideas of the arrangement, subject-matter, and salient features of the Sacred Scriptures." — *New York Observer.*

GIBERNE, Agnes.
Aimee. A Tale of James II. 12mo 1.50
The Curate's Home. 16mo 1.25
Floss Silverthorn. 16mo 1.25
Coulyng Castle. 16mo 1.50
Muriel Bertram. 12mo 1.50
The Sun, Moon, and Stars. 12mo 1.50
The World's Foundations; or, Geology for Beginners.
12mo 1.50
Through the Linn. 16mo 1.25
Sweetbriar. 12mo 1.50
Duties and Duties. 16mo 1.25
Jacob Witherby. 16mo 0.60
Decima's Promise. 12mo 1.25
Twilight Talks. 16mo 0.75
Kathleen. 12mo 1.50
Daily Evening Rest. 18mo 1.00
Beryl and Pearl. 12mo 1.50
Old Umbrellas. 12mo 0.90
Among the Stars; or, Wonders in the Sky. 12mo . . . 1.50
Madge Hardwicke 1.00
Father Aldur: a Water Story 1.50

GREEN, Prof. Wm. Henry, D.D.
The Argument of the Book of Job Unfolded. 12mo . . 1.75

"That ancient composition, so marvellous in beauty and so rich in philosophy, is here treated in a thoroughly analytical manner, and new depths and grander proportions of the divine original portrayed. It is a book to stimulate research." — *Methodist Recorder.*

Moses and the Prophets. 12mo, cloth 1.00

"It has impressed me as one of the most thorough and conclusive pieces of apologetics that has been composed for a long time. The critic confines himself to the positions laid down by Smith, and, without being diverted by any side issues or bringing in any other views of other theorists, replies to those positions in a style that carries conviction." — *Professor W. G. T. Shedd, D.D.*

The Hebrew Feasts. 12mo 1.50

GUTHRIE, Thomas, D.D.
Life and Works of Thomas Guthrie, D.D. New, neat, and cheap edition in 11 vols. 12mo $10.00

Life, 2 vols. ; Gospel in Ezekiel ; Inheritance of the Saints ; Parables ; Speaking to the Heart ; Man and the Gospel ; Way to Life ; Studies of Character ; The City and Ragged Schools ; Out of Harness. (The volumes sold separately at $1.00 each.)

" His style is a model of Anglo-Saxon, strong, plain, rhythmical, and earnest. It is music to read his rich and ringing sentences, all on fire of the Gospel. His sermons are more terse and educating than Spurgeon's, broader and deeper than Beecher's, and vivid, keen, convincing, and uplifting as only Guthrie's own can be." — *Methodist Protestant.*

HAMILTON, Edward J., D.D.
The Human Mind. 8vo 3.00
Mental Science. 12mo 2.00

HAMLIN, Cyrus, D.D.
Among the Turks. 12mo 1.50

HANNA, William, D.D.
Life of Christ. 3 vols. 12mo 3.00

HAUSSER, Ludwig.
Period of the Reformation. New edition 2.50

This admirable résumé of the History of the Reformation in Germany, Switzerland, France, Denmark, Sweden, and England, by the late eminent German historian, Professor Hausser, offers in compact form information which has otherwise to be sought for over a wide field of literature.

*HENRY'S Commentary on the Bible.
3 vols. 4to, cloth 10.00
*Another edition, in large type, 5 vols., 4to, cloth . . . 15.00
*Still another edition, 9 vols., 8vo, cloth 20.00

Persons desiring to purchase this Commentary can have a circular sent them without charge giving a specimen page from each of these editions, by sending us their address.

" King of Bible explorers yet." — *Cuyler.*

" First among the mighty, for general usefulness, we are bound to mention Matthew Henry." — *Spurgeon.*

" Sparkles with jewels of wisdom and incisive humor." — *Rev. Dr. W. M. Taylor.*

" Taking it as a whole, and as adapted to every class of readers, this Commentary may be said to combine more excellence than any work of the kind that was ever written in any language." — *Dr. Archibald Alexander.*

" There is nothing to be compared with old Matthew Henry's Commentary for pungent and practical applications of the teachings of the text." — *Sunday-School Times.*

HODGE, A. A., D.D.
  Outlines of Theology. Revised and enlarged edition. 8vo $3.00
  "At its first publication in 1860, this work attracted much attention, and ever since it has had a large sale, and been carefully studied both in this country and in Great Britain. It has been translated into Welsh and modern Greek, and has been used as a text-book in several theological schools." — *Presbyterian Banner.*

HODGE, Charles, D.D.
  On Romans. 8vo 3.00
  On Romans. Abridged. 12mo 1.75
  On Ephesians. 12mo 1.75
  On Corinthians. 2 vols. 12mo 3.50
  "Most valuable. With no writer do we more fully agree. The more we use Hodge, the more we value him. This applies to all his Commentaries." — *Rev. C. H. Spurgeon.*

HOLT, Emily Sarah.
  ### HISTORICAL TALES.
  Isoult Barry. 12mo 1.50
  Robin Tremayne. 12mo 1.50
  The Well in the Desert 1.25
  Ashcliffe Hall. 12mo 1.50
  Verena. A Tale. 12mo 1.50
  The White Rose of Langley. 12mo 1.50
  Imogen. 12mo 1.50
  Clare Avery. 12mo 1.50
  Lettice Eden. 12mo 1.50
  For the Master's Sake 1.00
  Margery's Son. 12mo 1.50
  Lady Sybil's Choice. 12mo 1.50
  The Maiden's Lodge. 12mo 1.25
  Earl Hubert's Daughter 1.50
  Joyce Morrell's Harvest. 12mo 1.50
  At ye Grene Griffin. 12mo 1.00
  Red and White. 12mo 1.50
  Not for Him. 12mo 1.25
  Wearyholme. 12mo 1.50
  John De Wicliffe. 12mo 1.25
  The Lord Mayor of London 1.50
  The Lord of the Marches 1.25
  A Tangled Web 1.50
  In All Time of our Tribulation 1.50

JACOBUS, Melancthon W., D.D.
  ### NOTES, CRITICAL AND EXPLANATORY.
  Genesis. 12mo 1.50
  Matthew and Mark 1.50
  Luke and John. 12mo 1.50
  Acts. 12mo 1.50

KITTO, John.
Bible Illustrations. 8 vols. 12mo $7.00

"They are not exactly commentaries, but what marvellous expositions you have there! You have reading more interesting than any novel that was ever written, and as instructive as the heaviest theology. The matter is quite attractive and fascinating, and yet so weighty that the man who shall study those volumes thoroughly will not fail to read his Bible intelligently and with growing interest." — *Spurgeon.*

LEE, William.
The Inspiration of the Holy Scriptures: Its Nature and Proof. 8vo 2.50

"We consider 'Lee on Inspiration' as beyond all comparison superior to any work on the subject yet issued in our language." — *Church Journal.*

LEIGHTON, Bishop.
Complete Works. 8vo 3.00

LEWIS, Prof. Tayler.
The Six Days of Creation. 12mo 1.50

LORD, Willis, D.D.
Christian Theology for the People. 8vo 2.50

"I do not hesitate in expressing the opinion that this work is, so far as I know, the best book in existence for the purpose of popular instruction in theology." — *Dr. E. P. Humphrey.*

LOWRIE, Samuel T., D.D.
The Epistles to the Hebrews Explained. 8vo 3.00

"It gives evidence not only of diligent and thorough study, but of a high degree of scholarship and acquaintance with the Scriptures. . . . We think we hazard nothing in saying that this exposition of this important portion of Scripture is at least equal to any that has been produced in this country." — *Herald and Presbyter.*

MATHEWS, Joanna H.
Bessie Books. 6 vols., in a box 7.50
Flowerets. 6 vols., 18mo, in a box 3.60
Little Sunbeams. 6 vols., in a box 6.00
Kitty and Lulu Books. 6 vols., 18mo, in a box 3.60
Miss Ashton's Girls. 6 vols. 7.50
Haps and Mishaps. 6 vols., 16mo 7.50

MATHEWS, Julia A.
Dare to Do Right. 5 vols. 16mo 5.50
Drayton Hall Series. 6 vols. 4.50
Golden Ladder Series. 3 vols. 3.00

McCOSH, Dr.

*Works. New and neat edition. 5 vols., 8vo, uniform . $10.00
Comprising:—

1. Divine Government.
2. Typical Forms.
3. The Intuitions of the Mind.
4. Defence of Fundamental Truth.
5. The Scottish Philosophy.

Any volume sold separately at 2.00

"Thousands of earnest, thoughtful men have found treasures of argument, illustration, and learning in these pages, with which their minds and hearts have been enriched and fortified for better work and wider influences." — *New York Observer*.

Dr. McCosh's Logic. 12mo 1.50
Christianity and Positivism. 12mo 1.75

MACDUFF, J. R., D.D.

Morning and Night Watches. 32mo 0.50
Mind and Words of Jesus, and Faithful Promiser . . . 0.50
Footsteps of St. Paul 1.50
Family Prayers. 16mo 1.00
Morning Prayers for a Year 2.00
The Bow in the Cloud 0.50
Wells of Baca 0.50
Gates of Prayer 0.75

MILLER, Hugh.

Life and Works. 12 vols. 12mo 9.00

Comprising "Life and Letters," "Testimony of the Rocks," "Old Red Sandstone," "Footprints of the Creator," "First Impressions of England," "Schools and Schoolmasters," "Tales and Sketches," "Popular Geology," "Cruise of the Betsey," "Essays," and "Headship of Christ."

These are sold only in sets; but the separate works can be still got at the former prices, as follows:—

Footprints of the Creator 1.50
Old Red Sandstone 1.50
Schools and Schoolmasters 1.50
Testimony of the Rocks 1.50
Cruise of the Betsey 1.50
Popular Geology 1.50
First Impressions of England 1.50
Tales and Sketches 1.50
Essays 1.50
Headship of Christ 1.50
Life of Miller. By Bayne. 2 vols. 3.00

"Was there ever a more delightful style than that in which his works are written? Smooth and easy in its flow, yet sparkling ever more, like the river as it reflects the sunbeam, and now and then raging with torrent-like impetuosity, as it bears all opposition before it." — *Rev. Dr. W. M. Taylor*.

NEWTON, Richard, D.D.
  THE JEWEL CASE. 6 vols. 16mo $7.50
    The Best Things 1.25
    The King's Highway 1.25
    The Safe Compass 1.25
    Bible Blessings 1.25
    The Great Pilot 1.25
    Bible Jewels 1.25
  THE WONDER CASE. 6 vols. 16mo 7.50
    Bible Wonders 1.25
    Nature's Wonders 1.25
    Leaves from the Tree 1.25
    Rills from the Fountain 1.25
    The Jewish Tabernacle 1.25
    Giants, and Wonderful Things 1.25

    Rays from the Sun of Righteousness 1.25
    The King in His Beauty. 12mo 1.25
    Pebbles from the Brook 1.25
    Bible Promises. 16mo 1.25
    Bible Warnings. 12mo 1.25
    Covenant Names. 12mo 1.50

"His books for children have never been excelled in their aptitude to the young, and the pleasing form in which they convey religious truth. While they are called sermons, and each passage is expository of some passage of Scripture, they are so simple, so full of striking and apposite illustrations, that a child will read them with as much curiosity as he would a narrative of travel or adventure, and certainly with far more profit." — *Episcopal Methodist.*

NEWTON, Rev. W. W.
  Little and Wise. 16mo 1.25
  The Wicket Gate. 16mo 1.25
  The Interpreter's House. 16mo 1.25
  The Palace Beautiful. 16mo 1.25
  Great Heart. 16mo 1.25
  THE PILGRIM SERIES, comprising the above five volumes
    in a box 6.00

*OLIVE LIBRARY.
  40 large 16mo volumes, containing 15,340 pages, in a neat
    wooden case, *net* 25.00

PALEY, Wm.
  Evidences of Christianity. Edited by Professor Nairne.
    12mo 1.50

PEEP OF DAY LIBRARY.
  8 vols., 18mo 4.50
  Line upon Line. 18mo 0.50
  Precept upon Precept. 18mo 0.50

PEEP OF DAY LIBRARY, *continued.*

The Kings of Israel. 18mo	$0.60
The Kings of Judah. 18mo	0.60
Captivity of Judah. 18mo	0.60
Peep of Day. 18mo	0.50
Sequel to Peep of Day. 18mo	0.60
Story of the Apostles. 18mo	0.60

*POOL'S ANNOTATIONS.

3 vols. Royal 8vo. 3,077 pages. In cloth. (Half the former price) 7.50

"Pool's Annotations are sound, clear, and sensible; and, taking for all in all, I place him at the head of English commentators on the whole Bible." — *Rev. J. C. Ryle.*

PRIME, E. D. G., D.D.

Forty Years in the Turkish Empire. A Memoir of Rev. W. Goodell, D.D. 12mo 1.50

"The genial spirit, the humor and wit, the shrewd sense, the sincere and cheerful piety of Dr. Goodell made him one of the most interesting companions, and now make his Memoir one of the most agreeable books." — *Bibliotheca Sacra.*

"We know not what to say of 'Forty Years in the Turkish Empire,' except to advise our readers to get the book at once and devote their first spare time to its perusal." — *Presbyterian.*

RYLE, J. C.

NOTES ON THE GOSPELS. 7 vols. 12mo	10.50
Matthew	1.50
Mark	1.50
Luke. 2 vols.	3.00
John. 3 vols.	4.50

"It is the kernels without the shells, expressed in language adapted to the quick comprehension of all readers." — *Christian Union.*

"The 'Expository Thoughts' are excellent and useful aids to Bible study and devotion, and many souls will be comforted, blessed, and instructed by so clear, practical, and evangelical a work." — *New York Observer.*

SHAW, Catharine.

The Gabled Farm. 12mo	1.25
Nellie Arundel. 12mo	1.25
In the Sunlight. 12mo	1.25
Hilda. 12mo	1.25
Only a Cousin. 12mo	1.25
Out in the Storm. 18mo	0.50
Alick's Hero. 12mo	1.25
Left to Ourselves. 12mo	1.00
Fathoms Deep. 12mo	1.25
On the Cliffs	1.25
Dickie's Attic	1.25

SPURGEON'S WORKS.
NEW SERMONS.

1. Storm Signals. 12mo	$1.00
2. Hands full of Honey. 1883	1.00
3. Return, O Shulamite! 1884	1.00
4. Healing and Service. 1885	1.00
5. Pleading for Prayer. 1886	1.00
6. Present Truth. 12mo	1.00
7. Types and Emblems. 12mo	1.00

SPURGEON'S SERMONS.

Comprising nearly Two Hundred and Fifty Discourses, with complete Indexes of both Texts and Subjects. 10 vols. 12mo 10.00
None of the previous named volumes is in this set.

SPURGEON'S SERMON NOTES.

I. From Genesis to Proverbs	1.00
II. From Ecclesiastes to Malachi	1.00
III. From Matthew to Acts. Just ready	1.00
IV. From Romans to Revelation. (Shortly)	1.00
All of Grace. An Earnest Word with those who are seeking Salvation by the Lord Jesus Christ. (New.) 16mo	0.50
Feathers for Arrows	1.00
Morning by Morning; or, Daily Readings	1.00
Evening by Evening	1.00
Lectures to my Students. 12mo	1.00
John Ploughman's Talk. 16mo	0.75
John Ploughman's Pictures. 16mo	0.75
John Ploughman's Talk and Pictures. In 1 vol. 12mo	1.00

WALTON, Mrs. O. F.

Christie's Old Organ. 18mo	0.40
Saved at Sea. 18mo	0.40
Little Faith. 18mo	0.40
Christie's Organ, Saved at Sea, and Little Faith. In one vol. 16mo	1.00
A Peep behind the Scenes. 16mo	1.00
Was I Right? 16mo	1.00
Olive's Story. 16mo	0.75
Nobody Loves Me. 18mo	0.50
Nobody Loves Me, and Olive's Story. In one vol. 16mo	1.00
Shadows: Scenes and Incidents in the Life of an Old Arm-Chair. 16mo	1.00
Taken or Left. 18mo	0.40
Poppy's Presents	0.40

WARNER, Anna B.
  Blue Flag and Cloth of Gold. 12mo $1.25
  Stories of Vinegar Hill. 3 vols. 16mo 3.00
  Ellen Montgomery's Bookshelf. 5 vols. 5.00
  Little Jack's Four Lessons. 18mo 0.50
  A Bag of Stories. 16mo 0.75
  The Shoes of Peace 0.75
  Tired Church-Members 0.50

WARNER, Susan.
  The Old Helmet. 12mo 1.50
  Melbourne House. 12mo 1.50
  Pine Needles. A Tale 1.25
  My Desire. 12mo 1.50
  The End of a Coil 1.50
  The Letter of Credit 1.50
  Nobody. 12mo 1.50
  Stephen, M.D. 12mo 1.50
  The Red Wallflower. 12mo 1.50
  Daisy Plains 1.50
  Small Beginnings. 4 vols 5.00
  Say and Do Series. 6 vols. 7.50
  The King's People. 5 vols. 7.00

  "There is a charm about Miss Warner's books that insures each new volume of a welcome from a wide circle of readers."—*Herald and Presbyter.*

WIN AND WEAR SERIES.
  6 vols. 7.50

  By the Same Author.

  Green Mountain Series. 5 vols., in a box 6.00
  Ledgeside Series. 6 vols., in a box 7.50
  Butterfly's Flights. 3 vols., in a box 2.25
  The Highland Series. 6 vols., in a box 7.50
  Hester Trueworthy's Royalty 1.25
  Mabel's Step-mother 1.25
  Faith Thurston's Work 1.25
  Robert Graham's Promise 1.25
  The Gillettes. 6 vols. 4.50

YOUNG, John.
  The Christ of History. 12mo 1.25

  "The work belongs to the highest class of the productions of modern disciplined genius. . . . We commend it heartily to all earnest thinkers, for such alone know the worth of a helpful book."—*London Morning Advertiser.*

www.ingramcontent.com/pod-product-compliance
Lightning Source LLC
Chambersburg PA
CBHW030320240426
43673CB00040B/1226